9.04

God's Fool

The Life and Times of Francis of Assisi

JULIEN GREEN

Translated by Peter Heinegg

HODDER AND STOUGHTON
LONDON SYDNEY AUCKLAND TORONTO

British Library Cataloguing in Publication Data
Green, Julien
   God's fool: the life and times of Francis of
Assisi.
   1. Francis of Assisi, *Saint*   2. Christian saints
   —Italy—Assisi—Biography   3. Assisi (Italy)
   —Biography
   I. Title   II. Frère François. *English*
   271'.3'024   BX4700.F6

   ISBN 0–340–39078–6
   ISBN 0–340–39077–8 Pbk

Contents

Part One

IDLE YOUTH

Elle est retrouvée
Quoi?—L'Eternité

ARTHUR RIMBAUD
Fêtes de la patience.

Giovanni

At certain moments in history destiny seems to hesitate between weal and woe, as if awaiting the arrival of someone—who usually doesn't come. But toward the end of the twelveth century a child appeared who almost managed to turn the Christian ideal into a triumphant fact.

Was it September 1181 or early 1182? He was born sometime between those dates in Assisi, a town in Umbria whose roots are lost in antiquity, a Christian town to be sure, but a place where immemorial pagan traditions seemed to spring forth from the Etruscan soil. This little city in the heart of Italy followed the calendar of either Pisa or Florence, but so far the archives have told us nothing about the name chosen for a newborn whose family was not illustrious. Which explains the uncertainty over his birth.

Historians are still trying to locate the house where he came into the world. Various sites have been pointed to, the latest research claiming, provisionally, that he was born, not in a stable between an ox and an ass, as some enthusiasts would have it, but in a solid, handsome residence near the Piazza del Commune.

His father was away when his mother gave birth. Her name was Giovanna, but they called her Pica, no doubt because she came from Picardy. She was still confined to her bed when a man knocked on the door of the house, asking for alms. At the time of a birth, as at Christmas, pilgrims were never turned away. The family thought they could get rid of this one by giving him a wing from the chicken prepared for the recuperating mother. But the old man wasn't satisfied with the wing and asked to be shown the new baby. Lady Pica protested a little, but she had a stubborn customer to deal with and when he pressed his mysterious demand, she sensed some kind of supernatural influence and finally agreed. She let him come in and even take the child in his arms. He began at once to prophesy, declaring that on that day two boys had been born in Assisi, one of whom would be among the best of men, while the other would be among the worst.

Here I can't help thinking of those allegorical characters in Haw-
thorne's stories whose veiled words become clear only long after they
have been uttered. Two boys, the best and the worst. Perhaps they
were one and the same boy, the carnal and spiritual man of Saint Paul.
Doesn't each one of us have the makings of both a saint and a hardened
sinner? Every serious Christian has experienced that cruel war between
those two irreconcilable enemies.

Back then, of course, this explanation never crossed anyone's mind.
People already knew who the best one was, and they wondered who
the worst could be. Years later they found him in the shape of a wretch
who had been born on the same date and had died on the gallows.

In any case, after she had been churched his mother brought him
to the cathedral of San Rufino. He had barely crossed the threshold
when he entered the kingdom of legends where he was destined to
remain. He had already fallen prey to God.

We don't know a great deal about Lady Pica, except that she was
very pious. The name she gave her child was not a random choice:
Baptismal names were indelible and left their mark on one's entire life.
The water flowed down his forehead, and he was called Giovanni, not
the Evangelist, but the Baptist, the man who had plunged Jesus into the
waters of the Jordan. *That* Giovanni had announced the coming of the
Messiah and preached repentance as the way to salvation. And Jesus
had said of him that he was the greatest of men. For this reason Pica
felt sure about her son's future, now that he had been put under the
protection of the most honored saint of all.

Pica's neighbors believed she had the gift of clairvoyance. She
would readily prophesy, after the fashion of the time. "You'll see that
his merits will make of him a son of God," she would say some years
later. So little Giovanni was brought back home in the arms of his
mother who loved him as much as she was proud of him. He was a
pretty, bright-eyed boy with a tiny, slightly pale face; but he seemed
sickly and he had to be carefully nursed all through childhood.

Time passed, and his father returned. Then the troubles began,
troubles that proved to be never-ending.

Pietro di Bernardone looked at his son. When he learned that in his
absence the child had been baptized Giovanni, he flew into a violent
rage. A cloth merchant by trade, he was just back from Champagne,
where he had bought finer quality fabrics than those made in Italy; and,
as if infatuated with France and all things French, he got the idea of

calling his son Francesco, that is, "Frenchman." Though not as bad as occasionally portrayed, Pietro di Bernardone was every bit as tyrannical as parvenus often are; and his word was law within the four walls of his house. The baby would be called Francis. Naturally he couldn't be baptized all over again, but Pica's objections were overruled, and she had no choice but to give in.

So Francis it would be, an unusual name, a little bizarre, something like a surname. But then his mother had one herself. Still, no French boy would be burdened with the name "English" or "Italian." Perhaps not, but a close inspection of the archives turned up two obscure Francescos, neither of them canonized. That was enough.

Bernardone's anger shows that, like his wife, he believed in the crucial role a name could play in the destiny of the baptized child. This notion, which has largely faded today, can be traced all the way to Scripture, where a person's name was part of his being and identity. How curious that our banal passports and IDs are connected to the Hebraic *shem*, but we go back further than we suspect. At all events one could hear in Francis's vocation an echo of the vocation of Saint John the Baptist, which was precisely what Bernardone would have none of.

If, like Pica, the cloth merchant had been capable of seeing visions, his would have been altogether different. Already he saw his son behind the counter of his store, selling his fine fabrics to a select clientele and fattening the family's money bag. For Bernardone was notoriously greedy and, though he considered himself a good Christian, a zealous servant of Mammon. The house nowadays thought to be his could have passed for an aristocratic mansion—quite apart from all the land he owned in the surrounding countryside. But there was nothing of the feudal lord about Bernardone. Thanks to his great wealth he belonged to the very important class of the big bourgeoisie. Pica, as far as we know, came from France. She was said to have made a pilgrimage to the Holy Land, and possibly met her husband on the way back, in Provence. That's as far as our information goes. On the other hand, if she was a native of Umbria, then her name would come from her loquacity (taking *Pica* to mean magpie, rather than Picard). But that runs counter to our intuitive sense of what she was like.

Anyhow, very early in life the boy would have heard his father speaking French to him. Was it northern or southern French? Probably both, because if Pica set her sights high, Bernardone took the long view, thinking especially of the advantages this fluency would give Francis on future business trips across the Alps, in Provence and Champagne. Besides, the *langue d'oïl* was the language of tourneys and princely courts. The beauty of the Gallic tongue was admired all over Europe and was beginning to become an international language.

Hence, from Bernardone's standpoint, speaking French would put Francis on the level of the nobility. For her part, Pica saw things quite differently. Like all mothers, she sang her favorite songs to the infant. She must have known the villanelles of the Provençal troubadours, and bits and pieces of the *chansons de geste* dinned into Picard ears by wandering minstrels. Then, of course, there would have been the spinning songs and the love poems sung by the trouvères in the misty woodlands, the forest of Ardennes and Flanders. One such song was "Fair Doette":

> Fair Doette at the window sits,
> Reads in a book, but her thoughts, they stray
> She thinks of her friend, Doon the beloved,
> He has gone off a-jousting far, far away.
> And I weep . . .

Pica remains a fairly dim figure, but from what we know for certain about her, a lovable one. At a painful juncture in Francis's life we shall see her giving proof of her courage and love.

But what sort of upbringing did she give him? Presumably she lavished on him all the care that a woman gives to a child she believes predestined to greatness. If her name really was Giovanna and "Pica" was only a nickname, then she must have wanted a bond between herself and her son forged from their baptismal names. And when, as it chanced, Giovanna had her Christian name taken away, little Giovanni did too. Who was responsible for that—the father, as biographers have always claimed, or the lad's friends, because of the French songs forever on his lips? It's of little consequence. His mother too would have sung him tender lullabies in French. And soon she would gently teach him his prayers in the peace and quiet of home. Two other sons would be born there, but Giovanni would always be the favorite.

The First Witness

Readers will object that I'm taking a very rosy view, and that a thousand maybes don't make a single certainty. Well, perhaps things weren't as simple as I have described them. Call the witnesses. The first is Thomas of Celano.

He was a friar, and a poet of genius, the best writer who could be found to carry out a commission for Pope Gregory IX, a friend of Francis and the man who had just canonized him. The year was 1228, and the pope wanted to give the new saint something like an official stamp of approval. Thomas of Celano knew the value of words and didn't use them lightly. He would show this in the *"Dies Irae,"* one of the greatest religious poems ever written. Translators have attempted to render it in a style worthy of the original, but their efforts have gone for naught. The rigorous structure of the Latin has defied some of the finest writers, such as Sir Walter Scott, who gave up after two stanzas. Celano's Latin is hard, powerful, restrained, but it has an immense sweep to it. The man who wrote that song of death gathered together all the terrors of his age before the judgment seat of God. He knew better than anyone the burden of fear that every syllable of those dismaying verses might contain.

What did he think of the young Francis of Assisi? He would paint a portrait of his character and provide a detailed catalog of his virtues, but he had to begin with the young man in the world, and here he willy-nilly became the devil's advocate, which was, frankly, a dirty job.

Celano worked on the project in Rome. Why not somewhere else, at Assisi, for example? No, Rome it had to be, because there he had access to all the depositions, pro and con; and there he could take counsel, when necessary, with any number of shrewd clerics.

The good Franciscan was distinctly at a loss, for he had known the saint ever since joining his order in 1215. Then, after returning from a mission in Germany, he met Francis again in his last years. He admired Francis wholeheartedly, but he knew about some embarrassing matters he would have preferred not knowing, truths in need of extenuation. At the least he would have to mention Francis's youthful errors, without elaborating on them, but he had neither the desire nor the right to suppress them; and he would never have forgiven himself if he had. Besides, everyone in Assisi was aware of the wild, joyous years of the recently canonized saint.

One can say anything at all in skillfully veiled phrases, that is, by muddying the waters. There was no law, for example, against sharply reducing the responsibility of the eighteen-year-old boy by accusing the downright scandalous childrearing methods then in vogue, which were more than likely applied to Francis. Thus the era itself was to blame. This approach gives rise to passages like the following: "The baneful custom took root everywhere, even among those reputed to be Christians, and the pernicious theory was laid down as imperiously as a public edict, namely that children were to be raised, from the cradle onwards, in an atmosphere of permissiveness and sensuality. Infants were scarcely born and beginning to stammer and speak, when by signs and words they were taught truly shameful and abominable things. Once weaned, they were led not only to say indecent things, but to do them."

Celano is careful not to say that Pica followed this custom, because the father begets the child but the mother shapes it. But then we wonder why he talks about all this if not to insinuate that she behaved just like all the others. Something in us revolts at that idea. We seem to hear a woman's voice rising above the tumult of the Revolution— the voice of Marie Antoinette, queen of France, accused of the same vile acts with her son: "I appeal," she said, "to all mothers everywhere."

With these preliminaries deftly attended to, the story can come to more or less all the right conclusions. Friar Thomas can now relax a lot more, and his conscience will feel much easier in speaking about what he calls the "follies" committed by Francis in his youth. Yet, twenty-two years later, when it came time to write his *Vita Secunda,* he would forget his earlier assertions about Francis's mother and paint an ideal portrait of her. Such as it was, however, with its disturbing opening pages, the *Vita Prima* was presented to the pope, who read it and pronounced his satisfaction with it. Let us take a closer look.

Saint George and the Dragon

Francis's parents sent him to Saint George's, a school right next to the town walls and rather far from home. The school belonged to a church of the same name, whose canons taught the children rhetoric, or the art of self-expression, and the dismal rules of grammar. But the boy had his head full of dreams and doesn't seem to have learned very much. He would always remain, to use his own word, an *idiota*, that is, an ignoramus; and this ignorance would even help him, as if he had wished to leave a void in his memory so that later on there would be room for nothing but the Gospel. In any case, he grew much more attentive when an old canon named Guido told the story of Saint George and the dragon.

That immortal episode was depicted in a fresco on the church walls, inspiring the narrator as he went along. Everyone knew the tale by heart because Guido kept coming back to it, embellishing it with new details each time. It was the ancient legend of the Minotaur adapted to Christian tastes. Day after day this horrible monster terrorizing the kingdom needed fresh victims to devour. In vain the king dispatched his most valiant knights to destroy the wicked beast, but sooner or later they all took to their heels. All the young people had fallen prey to it, now only the king's daughter was left. With tears in his eyes, he sent her off, wearing her crown and moaning as she drew near the spot where the beast awaited her. Suddenly—and here the children's ears perked up—there appeared a magnificent knight, young, handsome, resplendent in his armor. After reassuring the princess and begging her to be patient, he snatched up his lance and flung himself upon his adversary, whose thick, scaly skin made him a sort of infernal knight.

For young Francis there were so many reasons to stare in excitement. First of all, the gorgeous warrior prancing on his mighty horse around the monster. All noblemen were ipso facto knights. Otherwise the only way to nobility was to wear armor and fight well: Then one moved up from knight to nobleman. The dragon who gasped out his life after a thousand convulsions stood for evil; and the beautiful princess waiting with folded hands for her marvelous defender to set her free—what to call her? Francis didn't know, but for him, as for all the lads in the Middle Ages, knighthood was an ideal he scarcely dared to dream of. But any man could become a knight. Even the son of a clothier, like Francis? That seemed impossible, and yet . . .

It was enough to have a suit of armor and above all a fearless soul. That much at least could make a ten-year-old boy's head spin. Caught up in all that, Francis would never spell properly till the day he died, but his dreams would enjoy a strange triumph.

The old canon may have repeated himself, but that didn't dampen the spirits of the little Italian boy whose eyes burned with intelligence. The edifying twaddle went on and on, feeding who knows what fantastic visions of future glory. All at once the child becomes a knight. He fights the devil, landing tremendous blows. The narrator, his Italian blood up, mimes the combat with great sweeping gestures. But even in the heat of battle Francis never loses sight of the princess, who prays without budging from the spot. She is lovely—who can she be? He must deserve her. What a strange tumult in the still innocent soul of the boy listening as if his life depended on it. His heart beat wildly, and once outside the classroom the schoolboy with an "F" in grammar but drunk with an unknown joy, began to sing. He always sang when he was happy.

At Home

Putting aside Celano's exaggerations in the opening lines of his *Vita Prima*, we have to note the elements of truth that have slipped in there. There seems to be no doubt that in his parents' home Francis enjoyed the easy life lived by the rich in those days. His father steadily added to his fortune by acquiring parcels of land from noblemen in need of cash. And, although he was not himself a noble lord, or anything like it, his residence might be described as above his condition: luxurious, hung with delicately colored fabrics in the style of the period (*secundum saeculi vanitatem,* as Friar Thomas puts it), not to mention the choice fare and the many servants, as benefitted one of the most notable men of the town.

What sort of figure did Francis cut amidst this circle of parvenus? All the evidence we have depicts him as the most likable lad in the world. *Amiable* is the adjective that keeps recurring. And people noticed his constant gaiety, his laughter, everything about his person that won them over at first glance. As time passed he must have become aware of that mysterious power and the temptation to abuse it, but nothing in his childhood pointed to the budding libertine that Celano presents. Something in him fought against that. His family might have turned him into a demon; instead he became just a spoiled child whose good disposition and, in particular, whose generosity remained intact. Young as he was, he gave to the poor.

He admired everything that struck him as beautiful: the precious objects his father brought back from the northern countries, enamels, miniatures, tapestries. He sometimes turned down some of the best food he was served, because it wasn't to his taste. His whims were overlooked because of the courteous way he said no, which revealed good bloodlines—his mother's. His father may have been irritated, but his self-esteem was nonetheless secretly flattered: He found anything with a noble flavor impressive.

In any event, what was there to criticize about Francis? He was respectful and obedient and never gave anyone reason to worry, except for his health, which called for some attention. He had to be treated with kid gloves. For his mother especially he was what the Germans call a trembling joy.

Winter in Umbria can be glacial. So great logs blazed away in the huge fireplaces, and the boy fell into daydreams as he watched the flames do their joyful dance. The fire had a fascinating power that was at once fearful, yet like a friend and brother.

When summer came, it was deliciously pleasant to seek out the cool spots beneath the trees deep inside his father's garden where a stream babbled along. All the sweetness of life conspired to steal the young man's sensitive heart. How good it felt to breathe beneath the clear skies occasionally echoing with birdsong. Everything on earth was beautiful.

At Saint George's and in the street the meditative boy unexpectedly proved to be a fierce competitor in war games. The children mimicked the conflicts that broke out every year between the upper town and the

lower town. Whatever side he took, Francis was the leader. He wanted
to be first at all cost, and since the others instinctively followed him,
he knew how to make them obey without effort or violence, simply
because he was himself.

Religion and Mischief

He received his early religious education at San Nicolò, which was
right next to home and therefore his parish church. In what would later
be called catechism class the children were taught the Our Father and
the Creed. Naturally the lives of the saints and the miracles of Christ
were retold with all the appropriate marvels, as in a golden legend. Up
to this point there was nothing out of the ordinary, but on December
6 the townsfolk celebrated the feast of the church's patron, the great
wonder-worker Saint Nicholas.

This was also the day chosen for the exaltation of the virtue of
humility, a strange festivity whose roots went back to immemorial
pagan times. All the schoolchildren of Assisi were invited to the church
to pay honor to that privileged parish. The youngest ones then elected
one of their number to be *l'episcopello,* the boy bishop. This lad made his
entrance into the church wearing bishop's vestments and followed by
a train of acolytes. With a miter on his head and crosier in hand, he
went up to the altar, entoned a hymn, and sat down in the episcopal
armchair. This burlesque ceremony drew a crowd, and the church filled
up. Then the whole thing began to take on the flavor of the Saturnalia,
as the feast gave way to what were bizarrely called the freedoms of
December, where in a sort of general subversion the masters became
the servants and the servants ordered the masters around. Very quickly
sex got the upper hand.

The debauchery went so far that it provoked indignant admonitions
from Rome. In 1207, for example, Innocent III, writing in a brutal Latin,
mentions "obscene songs, dances, and fornications." Men, women,
children, clergy, and laity abandoned themselves to their appetites, and
the fever spread from the church to the street. To the music of cymbals

and sistra, ancient instruments that ordinarily accompanied Bacchic processions, they danced, they gorged themselves, they got drunk. The orgy spilled out over the public square where half-naked women crowned with flowers and bound hand and foot were exhibited and sold on carts, while a peculiar song rang out: It was Adam's curse on woman, enemy and mistress, desired and detested, the scourge of the world who had driven man from paradise.

> From my fair dwelling in paradise
> I was driven for a girl
> Who shone like a star—
> Never trust a woman.

And the crowd all roared:

> Set yourselves free, set yourselves free,
> Never trust a woman.

The powers of the little bishop expired three weeks later on December 26, the feast of the Holy Innocents. On that day the boy, still dressed in his disguise, surrounded by his court of little boys, proudly made his way on horseback to the bishop's palace. To the refrain of *Sinite parvulos* ("let the little children come unto me"), the prelate received him at the door of his residence and incensed him. After that the whole mob came in. The little bishop subjected his grown-up counterpart to a close interrogation, demanding an account of his almsgiving and reprimanding him, while the bishop meekly went on with this absurd game, until wine was brought in for a general libation. Finally the real bishop reassumed his official rights, and the young usurper sped away.

I wonder how Francis was affected by those explosions of carnality and that challenge hurled at society. Did Pica keep him at home when the "mystery of iniquity" took place? To suppose so would be a bit naive, since we are in Italy, and medieval Italy at that. And if he did assist at the merrymaking, did he escape contamination? It's impossible to say precisely, but we know for sure that later on he treated sexual sins pitilessly and on one occasion he expelled a lascivious friar from the order.

Assisi, Black or White?

What a mysterious town Assisi was, a place where the phantoms of bygone eras lay sleeping. The oldest inhabitants remembered what their parents told them of the running of the bulls, an event still held at the beginning of the twelfth century in the Roman amphitheater. A hunger for battle and rebellion lodged within the heart of its people, who had to be continually won back to the Christian ideal. In vain the churches multiplied and rang their bells from dawn to dusk. There was faith, but there was also the irresistible hankering after pleasure, luxury, and profit.

It would be a mistake to view Assisi as a town steeped in devotion. It was forever being swept by swirling currents of violence and sensuality. It *was* pious, but ready to indulge in every kind of excess, as on December 6. In the days of Francis Bernardone it had twenty-three hundred homes, or twenty-two thousand inhabitants, in a city less than a third the size of modern Assisi. It was a populous town, especially if we add the monasteries and the German garrison, which were not included in the census.

Assisi was an enigmatic town. It seemed to have been thrust to the surface of the earth by the subterranean Roman city whose place it had usurped. Vestiges of the pagan community were everywhere, as if lying in wait for the moment to take their revenge. The churches were built on the ruins of temples where before the Romans the Etruscans had adored their gods. Santa Maria Maggiore, the first cathedral, arose on the site of the temple of Apollo. Minerva, having been willy-nilly Christianized, still kept the Corinthian columns that the young Goethe would fall in love with. San Rufino had come forth from the foundations of the shrine of the Good Mother, adored under the name of Gaia, the Earth. One monastery stood on the ghostly remains of Hercules, another on those of Mars. No doubt it was the same all over Italy, but in Assisi, which would later be seized by a frenzied love of the Gospel, the ferment of primitive beliefs was still strong enough to produce a sudden, violently paradoxical explosion.

One day every year at the hour of vespers the afternoon bells began to toll as the doors of the amphitheater swung open and a fierce bull burst forth, drunk with rage and freedom. A symbol of unleashed sexuality, he charged right into the street, greeted with cries of fright and secret pleasure. The thrill of fear could be so much fun! People fled into their houses and threw flowers down from the upper windows on the maddened beast who butted and charged amid loud cries till dusk. Then the young men attacked with their swords and put him to death as the sun went down before the doors of San Rufino: a magnificent image of the eternal struggle between the furious demands of sex and the no less violent urges of the soul. Francis must have known something about these things.

The citizens of Assisi had a deep streak of atavistic savagery. The white and pink town rising in tiers on the side of Mount Subasio could lie dreaming in the sun all it wished, it was nonetheless always ready to wage war. At each of its gates the soldiers of each district took turns watching the road to Perugia, its hated rival and subject to the pope while Assisi was an imperial city. On both sides a deadly hatred smoldered away. At any moment they might fling themselves on one another. And besides war was good for business.

From the broadest streets to the narrowest alleys, the houses of the city stood out, one above the other, as if craning their necks to see everything in the streets below and the fields beyond. The town was humming with life and toil: the dyers swarming around their vats, the clothiers in the stores, the armorers clanging deafeningly away, the blacksmiths hammering, and all this amidst a din of cries, laughs, melodious bursts of talk, and occasional disputes leading to brawls. The need to fight slept with one eye open. Every year the lower town went on a rampage against the upper town. The lower town came pouring in from the suburbs outside the walls where the serfs were sheltered from the elements in their mud huts. For this one day they had permission to settle their accounts with the people of the upper town, who were better housed though not necessarily prosperous. It was a rivalry between sections of the city, with wounded and sometimes dead combatants paying their debts on the spot. By next morning all vendettas were forbidden, thus allowing the hatred to build up for another year.

Father and Cloth Merchant

One is tempted to think that Pietro di Bernardone was first a clothier and then a father. After all, he left for Champagne when his wife
Pica was seven months pregnant. The family tried in vain to get him
to postpone his trip, but business is business. Famine was raging in
Italy. A hurricane had blasted the whole peninsula, destroying the
wheat in the blade and uprooting the fruit trees. France had been
spared and so remained the land of lucrative operations. There was gold
to be gotten at Troyes and Provins. The mere names of those two cities
fascinated Bernardone like a mirage. Pica could wait, and so could the
baby. Cloth came first. Once he had returned home, the man would
talk about nothing but France. There may have been famine in Italy,
but no one in Bernardone's house lacked for anything. He knew how
to manage his property, and that stay in Champagne looked to him like
a sign of approval from heaven. He would turn the child—a boy, thank
God—into a little Frenchman, and that name would bring him luck. He
would work in the store: The boy represented a conspicuous increase
of capital.

Character is formed quickly in the first years of adolescence. Slender
and graceful, Francis could already sing with that "sweet and powerful" voice that would make such a profound impression on the men
and women of his time. He was known for his invariable cheerfulness
and the *joie de vivre* that throbbed in the latest cantilena he had picked
up from the troubadours and minstrels who were forever passing
through the country. This mysterious exultation found expression
mostly in the French language he was so fond of. No one was surprised
by his gaiety, but that it never let up. Was there no sorrow in his
nature?

Nobody ever seemed happier or more at home in the world, in that
corner of Italy with its dreamlike beauty. If the heavens were telling
the glory of God in the depths of the sky at night, then by day the
meadows, woods, and rivers surely continued the song of praise filling
the young man's heart.

Were there no shadows hanging over that life? The troubles with his health scarcely affected him. In his parents' fine house someone was always available to take care of him. They spoiled him—and he was so warmhearted. His father probably took him along on his travels to France, because if Bernardone wanted to make a clothier out of him, he obviously would have to bring the boy to places where he could do his apprenticeship, where the father could get his son to handle cloth from all the different countries and familiarize him with the world of the merchants. On the other hand, the love Francis felt for France could not have simply grown out of the stories his father told him. One doesn't get so attached to a country one has never seen. He had become Frenchified on his travels.

Twice a year, at the time of the great fairs, travelers would assemble in caravans of ten or so—clothiers, wool and silk merchants, goldsmiths, etc.—and, together with an armed escort hired in town, they would journey through regions where they had to pay tolls, but where the serfs glowered at the armed, prosperous strangers. From Orvieto or Terni, by way of Cortona, Florence, and Lucca, they went along the shore to get to Provence, then up the Rhone Valley in the dust of highways and sunken roads all the way to the lands of fog and mist. The trip took weeks. Coming back, their coffers would be stuffed not only with precious fabrics, new colors, and cloth woven in different ways at Bruges or Ghent where the water had special qualities for use in fulling, but also with works of art, jewels, enamels, ivories, everything needed to captivate vain noblemen with immense wealth who would squander it on such things or at least, Bernardone thought, part with splendid tracts of land to cancel their debts. Nowadays merchants traveled without carrying much gold coin, because the first letters of credit were discreetly coming into use.

Francis would have been perhaps twelve years old around this time. I can imagine his intoxication upon discovering new landscapes and cities humming with the sound of French, whose inflections he would try to imitate. Stopping in the churches, he would have been especially struck by the elevation of the host at mass, the custom, peculiar to France, of showing the Body of the Lord to the faithful. It was first established at Paris by Bishop Eudes de Sully. This silent protest against the heretic Bérenger, who a century before had denied the Real Presence, also corresponded to the people's desire to *see* the mystery. And it led to one of those secret encounters between Jesus and Francis that would one day send Francis off in the footsteps of the Savior.

In Champagne and Provence he listened to troubadours, trouvères, and minstrels, whose songs astonished him. He never tired of hearing them, learning them by heart so he could sing them in his turn. Not all the songs, perhaps, but the ones where the ideal lady appeared, the eternal faraway beloved, like the princess saved by Saint George. Besides, he wanted to sing them to his mother. Our ideas about the troubadours have come down to us directly from romantic literature and neo-Gothic statues: We picture them as elegant, curly haired, swaggering. But the hippies could supply an image closer to the truth, for those vagabond musicians were a motley group. Some were good, some were bad, "seducers of ladies," as they were called. They didn't all sing well—far from it—but on the whole these young wanderers had the public on their side. It was poetry making its way through the banalities of everyday life; it was free and adventurous young men who sometimes found a warm reception in the homes of the rich and powerful in exchange for a ritornello or a love song. Francis may have admired their independence, their disdain for any form of servitude. At all events he would remember them later on when he adopted their name, the minstrels of God, for himself and his companions.

We don't know what Bernardone thought of the troubadours. Most likely he found them unbearable, with their guitars, their languid refrains, their melancholy airs. Then too he had other things on his mind, like teaching Francis his future trade, the difference in the quality and value of fabrics, and so on.

These lessons did not go in one ear and out the other. Francis was storing everything away in his intelligent little head, the stuff of the here and now and the stuff of dreams; and his imagination boiled over. Because one saw a bit of everything on the road. A new world was opening up, with discoveries that bordered on the prodigious. Windmills dated from the time of Francis's birth, and people were still gaping at those great wings of canvas turning in the sky like the arms of giants. Perhaps he noticed, without quite grasping its immense significance, the soaring Gothic arch, like the shoot of a new flower in the churches built since he was a baby. Who had any notion that this was the blossoming of a new spirituality?

Back home in Assisi he had to go with his father to the store to learn something about the rudiments of the trade. Knowing how to talk to clients was an art, as was reading their faces to intuit their choices, their preferences, their means. All that called for a certain finesse. Francis had the necessary instincts: He would have made a first-class business-man. Along with his ever-alert intelligence went the magic of his smile and courteous manner. On that point Bernardone could rest easy. When he died, he would be leaving his shop in good hands.

He hadn't noticed—and it might have alarmed him if he had—that his clever, charming, smooth-talking son combined his practical sense with a penchant for dreaming and—horror of horrors—visions. Here once more the situation got muddled because of that duality whose ultimate cause Francis himself was unaware of. Whatever he might do, he was God's prey. Faults, defects, even passions could do no more than delay the inevitable thunderstroke.

History in Motion

The travelers kept arriving with word of current events, like living newspapers. And in his frequent goings and comings from Italy to France, Bernardone brought back the latest reports of the struggles of the communes in Picardy and Flanders to win their freedom from the Church and the feudal aristocracy. In the shadow of the great hall where his father entertained his friends, the little boy must have listened eagerly to the echoes of those upheavals. The blood flowed copiously in such thrilling stories, and Francis grew up in an atmosphere of political unrest and rumors of war.

In Italy, six years before he was born, the Lombard League, after many setbacks and the leveling of Milan, united Genoa and the cities of the Po and on May 29, 1187, defeated the imperial troops at the battle of Legnano. It thereby won recognition from Frederick Barbarossa of its communal rights and left the emperor with nothing but his stamped image, that is, his title, his pomp, and all the useless appearances of power. In 1187 news that the sultan had captured Jerusalem shook all of Christendom. The princes of the West vowed to go on crusade against Saladin but only the emperor kept his promise. Unfortunately, just when Syria lay open before him, he drowned while bathing in the Cydnus, and the German forces soon dispersed. Since Barbarossa's corpse was never recovered, legend seized hold of it—in the Middle Ages anything might become the stuff of legend—and plunged him into the waters of a prophetic lethargy whose ripples we can see centuries later in the poems of Heinrich Heine. The world had changed, it was changing, as it always does, only in appearance, because in their hearts people felt the same anxieties.

Then Henry VI, son and successor of Frederick Barbarossa, swooped down on Italy as if to avenge his family and took back all the franchises his father had granted, installing his lieutenants wherever an uprising threatened. He was a big, tall, pale man, twenty-four years old, as prone to exhaust himself in work as in pleasure, with no code of justice but his own dictates. He carried out his policies with patience and guile, simply omitting the word *mercy* from his vocabulary. He had married Constance, heir to the kingdom of Sicily, and that tall blonde woman, who had been raised in Palermo by the nuns of the Holy Savior and later at the court of her brothers ("true baptized sultans," someone called them), won over her husband's Nordic heart.

As for love between the pair, there was none at all: This was a marriage for reasons of state. The wife was eleven years older than her husband, and he made up for that by a rigid authoritarian style. To take possession of his new fiefs, he went to Messina, crushing the most rebellious towns along the way.

In Assisi, Duke Conrad of Urslingen was charged with imposing the *pax Germanica*. He settled into Rocca Alta, the fortress overlooking the town, whence his troops maintained law and order. He was duke of Spoleto and lived from one castle to the next. There was a moment of forced but prosperous tranquillity. Francis was eight years old when Frederick Barbarossa died, and no one was talking about winning freedom, except in faraway France, his mother's homeland. In the South things were altogether different. There Henry VI laid down the law— *his* law.

At Palermo, in keeping with a thoroughly Byzantine custom, young William, son of the Tancred who had stirred Sicily to insurrection, personally had to carry the crown of the Two Kingdoms during mass and lay it at the feet of Henry VI at the end of the Credo. A few days later, the day after Christmas, this eight-year-old child had his eyes gouged out and was castrated. The bodies of Tancred and Roger of Sicily, who had been the soul of the Norman revolt, were ripped from their tombs and beheaded on the public square. As Henry VI came and went across southern Italy, terror marched in the van. Dreadful rumors were heard from Apulia. It was learned that Count Giordana, who had offered resistance, had been arrested and thrust into a red-hot iron chair. He had a crown of incandescent metal placed on his head and pounded in with a mallet, which sent a second crown of smoke billowing up from the tortured victim. Meanwhile, the empress, who was pregnant, had to stop at Jesi, where she gave birth in a tent hastily erected in the town square. It was a boy, the future Frederick II. Then she went on to the castle of Foligno, Conrad of Urslingen's favorite residence.

Little Frederick would be baptized several months later, early in 1195, at the same baptismal font of stone and porphyry as little Giovanni di Bernardone.

The Baptism of a King

The cathedral of San Rufino was the site of the grand ceremony that unfolded with all the splendor of the holy Roman Empire. For a day the crowd forgot its hatred of the occupying power and was lost in wonder at the magnificent display that impressed even the most hostile observers. Francis was there, his eyes as wide open as any other thirteen-year-old's, afraid to miss any of the glitter of all the gold and precious stones weighing down the copes, the gorgeous cloaks, and the tapestries. The throng of lords, the heralds bearing trumpets draped with flags, the thunder of the bells, the fanfares, and then, from within the choir ablaze with light, the incense, the hymns of triumph and joy, and the blood-red robes of the assembled cardinals—all this gave him a resplendent image of the Church. Totally unaware of the dangers it faced, he saw only its pomp and apparent power, and congratulated himself on being the son of such a glorious mother. What would he have thought, had he known that one day he would prevent it from collapsing? In fact he had some premonitions, but of an entirely different sort: He saw himself a prince, like the ones surrounding the little king, and he made no secret of it. How he longed for glory, human glory. "I give it to whomever I wish," a voice whispered to him.

Behind the Counter

The salvation of his soul would have been far from his thoughts when he walked around town or, still more, worked in his father's shop and watched the noblemen with the elegant manners that marked them off from the rest of the world. The secret desire to resemble them stole into Francis's heart. With his childhood now behind him, he became another person, not bad exactly—he was never bad—but different from the attentive little boy so taken with the marvels in the lives of the saints. Yet even now he fantasized about Saint George riding forth in his dazzling armor, as if there was room for chivalry even in paradise.

In order to be a knight one had to be a nobleman or else (Francis's imagination reeled at the thought) manage to buy a suit of armor, go off to war, and prove oneself. If ever a soul was tempted, it was Francis, but since his soul was noble, he would not be taken in by anything vulgar. He had to have a lofty ideal. God alone knows the hidden places of the heart. The devil may have sharp eyes, but he takes the short view. He succeeds only in the immediate present, not in the final say.

Francis was too intelligent not to have some sense of his morally dubious talent for seducing people. When he saw boys his own age who had been privileged since birth, how could he help thinking, "Why them and not me?"

But from the time he was fourteen, he had been forced to relinquish his dreams a little and come back to reality, to the store, where he worked in earnest beneath his father's pragmatic eye. For obvious commercial motives he wanted his son to dress with studied elegance —an order Francis obeyed enthusiastically. Fashion—the very latest fashion, more than that, the most extravagant, avant-garde fashion, the French kind—was the obsessive ideal. Francis willingly served as a model and kept trying to outdo himself. This was, after all, a period of one dress craze after another. Fine, multicolored cloth, delicate silks, velvet deftly spread out on the wide countertop by that young man with the gentle voice and nimble tongue, and the knack of saying just the right thing with inimitable tact. What a magician he was, without ever letting it show.

The young aristocrats, to whom he spoke with the proper nuance of respect, felt a bit gauche in the presence of this salesman who was so much more elegant than they were and who prodded them into spending money with an air of seeming innocence. One can tell a bird by its feathers. If the buyer had no cash on hand, the Bernardones would wait. The father approved with a glance, mentally adding up the acreage in woods and fields. *Their* fathers would pay the debts of their scapegrace sons with patches of ground. That iridescent silk came from Mosul and was preferred by the connoisseurs in Paris. To show it in broad daylight and point up its richness, the seller had the right to carry it out as far as the middle of the street, but no farther, except when fabrics of questionable size had to be measured by the ell. Then one went to the base of the town tower where the standard measures for silk, linen, and wool were inlaid in the stone.

What sort of professional game of temptation would the young Francis play? In this, as in other things, he would succeed, but wasn't he himself being played upon by some undetectable force? In any event his father, who was deaf to the voice of the supernatural, was delighted. His son had an evident gift for business, he was a born merchant, a *cautus negotiator.* What difference did it make that the townspeople murmured a little about the lordly style affected by the clothier's son? When her neighbors brought back such rumors, Pica gently replied that Francis would be "a son of God." In that belief she was immovable.

Idle Youth

So now he was an active member of the clothiers guild, a salesman. The family business was sound and, by a quirk in his miserly character, his father didn't haggle over the pocket money he gave his promising son. But their clientele wasn't made up exclusively of gentlemen's sons who were keen on fashion. There were also well-to-do bourgeois who wanted high-quality, long-lasting cloth. Everyone was well served: The young dandy tending the store learned quickly. Fourteen years seems very young, and a number of Francis's biographers have been misled on this point. The fact is that in those days it was the eve of one's majority. And in our time we have seen even younger boys intimidate a large crowd of people with submachine guns.

In Assisi around the end of the twelfth century adolescence was a hurried affair. Fifteen was the age when one became a man, and Francis must have felt he was flying toward his majority. If his father's shop was like a stage where he practiced the art of dazzling people, the town was his real theater, because Italians live in the street. There were no fewer than 150 religious holidays each year, which made for a lot of free time, and once the fair weather came, Francis had only to appear and play the troubadour with his Provençal songs for his friends to flock around him. They were incredibly numerous, as if he had cast a spell on the youth of the town. The reason was that with Francis they were never bored. Brief as his experience of life may have been, he knew how to organize festivities, how to order a table in a good inn, how to choose the best of everything. Just a beginning, perhaps, but a quite promising one—later on he would do better. He already had the manner down pat and then—that extremely convenient and useful detail—his pockets were always well lined. Where is that salesman from the house of Bernardone? He felt so naturally superior to his companions that with no ado he took charge of their joint operations, which were generally riotous and held at night. "You are our *dominus,*" cried the joyful band, who had all had far too much to drink, but so what, the little cloth merchant was treating. After the fine dinners they rushed off to dance. As the French saying goes, *"Après la panse, la danse."* The hour was late, dawn was about to break, shutters were opening, and sleepy townsfolk awakened by loud voices or serenades were protesting. It was that devil Francis again, leading the farandole through the heart of the town, which still lay buried in sleep. There were cries of scandal, but not very loud ones, because the guilty party happened to be liked by everyone, and so after grumbling a bit they let it pass and went back to sleep. The mad farandole whirled on its aimless way. None of the dancers knew where they were headed, least of all Francis.

The Earth Is So Beautiful

On the many religious holidays Francis rode out into the countryside from one of his father's properties to another. From his shoulders hung one of those wonderful light, flowing cloaks the upper class were so fond of, and the young Bernardone sat his horse so well that he might have been mistaken for a noble—a mistake he spent a lot of time encouraging. He was a little naive, but what of it? He was young, glad to be alive, and the landscapes of Umbria stirred him to rapture. He never tired of admiring the meadows, the woods, and the light, above all the light. Friends joined him in the pleasure of galloping through that intoxicatingly beautiful land.

Friends came his way from all over, ready to follow him anywhere. One wonders what they found so remarkable about this lad, this fifteen-year-old-man. If he dazzled so many people, what did he look like?—because after all that matters. Nearly middle-sized, slim and graceful, he was unforgettable without being handsome. A small, round head; a low forehead; a straight, well-formed nose; small ears that seemed to be pricked up; white, even, closely spaced teeth; fine hands, long fingers, smooth skin. And above all else, large, mercurial eyes. One senses something that eludes description: the radiance of his person, which was already leaving its mark on large numbers of people.

His secret undoubtedly lay in a joy that appeared to be inextinguishable, not just a joy in life, but another, much deeper joy whose nature he himself didn't properly understand any more than he grasped the immensity of the grace dwelling in him ever since birth. Someone loved him madly, and in some obscure way he must have felt it, but that feeling defied translation except in continual bursts of laughter and jokes that poured from his lips as if he were a giddy schoolboy. People enjoyed what they called his pranks, but what was in Francis's head, that he saw every day as a feast day? Had he never tasted sadness or boredom?

From his companions' viewpoint there was no mystery in any of this. He had everything he wanted—fifteen years old and his pockets bulging with money. One had to watch him tossing it to innkeepers with a patrician's careless ease or trotting around town in those surprisingly elegant clothes. His wealth might have prompted envy, except for the fact that he was also insanely generous. He gave to everyone who asked, and even the most jealous observers were disarmed by the way his gold or silver always flashed whenever a poor man stretched out his hand.

What did his father think about this—how seriously did he take it? He was, as the chroniclers put it, not simply *dives* (rich), but *praedives* (extremely rich), because his business instincts had a touch of genius. The style of life his son was leading offered stunning proof of this, because the deadly famine that had struck Italy was still raging. But there were no hard feelings toward the boy, even if he did scandalize some people by his luxurious habits. With his seductive charm Francesco was the king of youth, and all was forgiven him.

On the other hand, there was some not-so-friendly talk about old man Bernardone, the big speculator. His many properties, patiently acquired over the years, stretched hither and yon across the territory of Assisi. Woods, meadows, farms, shady gardens, bits of mountainside, trout streams, everything tumbled into his pockets. There was no end to the list of paradisiacal spots where Francis could bury himself in sweet solitude if he had a notion to. When that spoiled child went off by himself, did he think about the frightening contrast between his family's opulence and the country's affliction? One may well wonder, because the picture of his destiny was still a murky one. At that early age young people aren't much inclined to reflection yet. Francis would give alms, the vision of poverty would fade for a while, and then he would heed the call of pleasure.

His father's domains offered an opportunity for splendid outings. Bernardone had land everywhere, places to take refuge from the summer heat or from the threat of the plague, which could suddenly materialize in all its terror; and Francis, showing off ever so slightly, could gallop with his companions from one to another. To get to Rivo Torto, the site of his favorite pond, he had to go by way of la Fontanelle and the nearby building, whose very name evoked fear, *l'Ospedale,* the lazaretto where the lepers were confined. The youths held their noses, claiming they smelled the horrible stench, and unashamedly turned their horses back. And Francis? He was squeamish by nature, and he found bad odors incredibly disagreeable. Here human misery was breathing death right into his face. So the man who would become the greatest saint in Christendom held his nose and sped off like the other two. Francis himself confessed this moment of weakness in his *Testament.*

Wretches

What made those twelfth-century outcasts so frightening? For us in the twentieth century the word *beggar* conjures up a person dressed in a very humble fashion, but rags are not far from clothing that is dirty, threadbare, patched, and shapeless. This archetypal poor man (even if he is the real thing, for imitations abound, some of them flawless) bears very little relation to his medieval counterpart. The poor in the Middle Ages were often a bugbear that society never knew exactly what to do with, and so it made every effort to keep them at a distance, especially when it had caused their misery to begin with. Sometimes, in fact, as during the Crusades, it exterminated them.

In Francis's youth drought had devoured the standing crops, then wet years had come and rotted the wheat, and the number of poor wretches multiplied. They lay in agony at monastery gates, just as nowadays we see the poor dying in the streets of India. On top of the famine came wars. And then there were many different kinds of poor people.

Along with those who had been crippled in battle there were the humble folk ruined by war, who made just enough to survive. But disease lay in ambush for them, and they were destined to die the slow death of poverty. Then came the mobs of beggars—the downward slide into filth and foul odors. Finally, and quite apart from the others, cooped up in the lazarettos, came the lepers. Some of them still had a semblance of freedom and could walk about the country-side, almost entirely hidden beneath their gray rags, shaking their sinister rattles, as if to spread fear among those who were truly alive. Around the end of the twelfth century more than a third of the population was poor, and a good ten percent lived at the very bottom of the ladder of misery.

The poor no doubt went knocking on the doors of the monasteries, where they were given food, but when bread became scarce and times were very hard, they were reduced to eating ergot-contaminated wheat and rye. Such grains carried repulsive diseases, like Saint Anthony's fire, which burned the body from within, incurable shingles, oozing eczemas, whatever the skin could sprout. In the fields and even at the outskirts of the city it was a common occurrence to see these creatures with their putrifying limbs, their faces eaten away by ulcers, their skin blackened as if by coal. To avoid the disgust they inspired they sought asylum in the woods. There they protected themselves as best they could against the elements with a bloody, badly cut sheepskin, while they owned nothing more than a walking stick. The forests became a place of terror, and the man of the woods a hobgoblin who invaded children's tales and filled them with fright.

The corpses of lepers were often burnt in charnel houses to cleanse the air of those plague spreaders, because they smelled no better in death than they had in life. Fed on a diet of poisonous plants and small rodents that infected their blood with vile diseases, they could get nasty, especially when armed with a walking stick, and soldiers didn't hesitate to hunt down such squalid creatures.

In vain preachers appealed for pity from their listeners, whom they threatened with hell if they failed to give alms. The name of Lazarus, the poor man of the Gospel, was constantly invoked. The dogs had licked his sores, but when he died he went to paradise, while the rich man who had not deigned to notice him and had dined in splendor (epulebat splendide) burned after death in unquenchable fire. This parable never failed to work its magic, and terror untied the purse strings, all the more so because their horrible condition sometimes turned these victims of fate into dangerous adversaries. The Church was forever harping on the "loud cries of the poor," whose numbers were shooting up at an alarming rate. A sort of curse hung over them. The rich made donations to banish the specter of damnation, but love of neighbor would have to be invented all over again.

Yet it had not vanished. Ten years before Francis Bernardone was born, a rich man from Lyon, upon hearing someone sing the legend of Saint Alexis, suddenly realized that a true Christian must be another Christ.

Ideas, Those Tireless Travelers

Things were stirring in the twelfth century, and in all Italy no town was greedier for news than imperial Assisi. This unflagging curiosity could be satisfied by the merchants. They knew what was going on: Their long trips from one country to another made them peddlers of all the rumors of the day. For this reason their stores were seldom empty, least of all Bernardone's, where Francis worked. People would drop by for a moment, and not just to buy cloth or to keep an eye on the caprices of fashion. Owner and customers chatted away, asked questions, passed judgment on everything, while the salesclerks bustled about. The disturbances in Flanders, the struggle of the communes against the nobility, events in the East, where the silk was imported from, the pulse of History throbbed in this continual murmur of words. But there were other matters just as serious apart from political conflict.

Some of the religious opinions making the rounds were scarcely

believable. People talked a good deal about Pierre de Vaux, an otherwise reasonable man, who after he heard a minstrel sing the legend of
Saint Alexis, wished to imitate that holy man. On the morning of his
wedding day Alexis had fled away to live in wretched poverty. Later
he came home, after inflicting so many mortifications upon himself that
he was beyond recognition. He begged his father for hospitality and
was allowed to live in a corner beneath the stairs. He was fed with table
scraps, and as they passed by him the servants threw dirty water in his
face. When he finally died it was revealed that he was a saint. The
eccentric from Lyon decided that he too would live among the poor and
like one of them, as if there weren't enough paupers in the world
already. But the worst was that he found a following among the good
people who believed, as he did, that one day they would be just like
Christ. What were they dreaming of, wondered the crowd in the clothier's shop.

As if such bizarre notions were contagious, there was another group
called "Christ's Poor," who wanted to renounce everything and criti-
cized the princes of the Church for their sumptuous clothing, when
the "poor Lord Christ" had owned nothing. One ran into these people everywhere, in France, along the Rhine, even in Italy. Francis listened.

What madness was coming over the world? A monk from Calabria,
Joachim of Florida, outdid all those cranks in mystical delirium, because he dared to argue that the reign of the Father had ended, giving
way to the reign of the Son, which in turn would be replaced by the
reign of the Holy Spirit, that is, of Love. He wrote these fine things in
a book entitled *The Eternal Gospel,* which no one had seen much less read,
but from the pages of that phantom volume the most daring prophecies
took wing, and many people got carried away by them. Fortunately the
Church was keeping watch. Despite its best efforts, however, it could
not prevent error from spreading everywhere by the tongues of those
talkative characters with the blissful look on their faces. What right did
they have to read sacred Scripture in the vernacular when the Church
forbade it? What did they believe? Did they even know? They kept
repeating that Love would come to bring happiness to men, and the
world would be renewed.

"Pace e bene!" Peace, joy! One of those fanatics had been heard

uttering that cry in the streets of Assisi from morning to evening, in a terrifying voice. That was the year Francis was born.

And young Francis couldn't help lending an ear to these tales, though his own dreams were different. Still, he tried to understand. The Third Kingdom . . . What was that bugbear being raised to disturb the tranquillity of Christians? Wasn't fidelity to the Church's commandments enough? And how much did a suit of armor cost? Francis knew perfectly well: a fortune. But his father was rich. When the time came, the young man would know how to raise that enormous sum— because he would also need a horse and armor for the horse, a squire, and weapons. Without all that he would never make it to the nobility. Meanwhile, all around him people were talking about the continual procession of new believers down the roads of Europe.

The Cathars said that the world was evil, and that one had to free oneself from matter to ascend to God. They called themselves "Children of Light," but their faith was interlarded with obscurities. They went as far as Persia to nurture their beliefs at the source of nearly vanished sects. Even stranger were the Bogomils, who believed that the world was the work of Satan, that salvation came only through poverty and penance, and who formed a new counter-Church. And there were still others, isolated or organized in groups. There was no counting all the exalted souls who wanted to "imitate Christ" and to live in the manner described by the Gospel, as if that were possible. The only idea in their head was to be like Christ, and they were all forever preaching, preaching, preaching.

The "Brothers of the Free Spirit" called for nothing less than— horror of horrors—the sharing of all worldly goods, because once the Gospel got out of the Church's hands, people could find in it whatever they wanted. All these agitators used the Gospel to attack everything in sight. For the moment they could not be accused of violence: They wished to change the world with gentleness, to change their own lives. There lay the danger: You had to be crazy to live like Christ. Francis listened.

Love, love, love—the word came up at every turn. For years individuals had been known to try to follow that ideal: In Périgord there was a certain Pons who wound up as a Cathar; Robert d'Arbrissel, who in a more rational vein created a community of the poor, which struck some as revolutionary; and then Arnold of Brescia, the hope of the

Roman *popolo,* the humble folk who made him their leader before abandoning him to be strangled in a dungeon on orders from the pope.

These rebels, wherever they came from, seemed to be coming in to Bernardone's store, as if stopping along a highway and calling for help, in a mystical transport, from someone who had been lost. That is what Francis listened to, without saying a word.

The Troubled Years

Few centuries have come to a more confusing close. In twelve months, as if in sport, destiny knocked everything askew, as though to wipe the slate clean for the future. The unexpected death of Henry VI of Germany, who fell victim to malaria contracted while out hunting in the marshes of the Campagna, was greeted in Italy with cries of joy. It was in the late summer of 1197, it was hot, and he drank water from a spring. Perhaps it was poisoned, but in any case he was seized with fits of vomiting, and he wanted to return to his kingdom of Sicily. And as luck would have it, he died in early autumn, on September 28, at Favara, in an Arab castle on the road to Palermo, thereby prefiguring the destiny of his son, Frederick II, who would later cultivate ties with Islam.

The pope, Celestine III, was ninety-three years old. His gentleness, his desire for peace at all cost, together with his great wisdom, had earned him the nickname "the settler of disputes." This cautious, temporizing old man died three months after Henry VI. Thus the two thrones of the empire and the papacy fell vacant at the same time, and freedom rushed into the void. A period of feverish hope began that lasted for months. The Lombard League grew stronger, small cities set themselves up as free communes, and then, treading upon one another's heels, came two emperors and a pope.

The year 1198 was pivotal. The question of who was to succeed Henry VI seemed hopelessly tangled; the two-headed eagle was no longer just a heraldic device: The youngest brother of Henry VI, Philip of Swabia, an attractive young lad like all the Hohenstaufen, smiling, surrounded by poets and learned men, was elected at the Diet of Mainz, but two months later at Aachen an assembly dominated by the bishops passed him over in favor of Otto of Brunswick. Otto was a strange man, a schizophrenic, but intelligent and cunning, and he had the support of John Lackland. The story goes that once at a sort of Shakespearean royal dinner when the death of the emperor was announced, his uncle, Richard the Lionhearted, king of England, turned to him and said, "Gentle cousin, there's a place for you," whereupon the king of France brusquely took a seat on the opposite side. But now he did have a crown on his head, or rather half a crown.

In the meantime the conclave had elected a man only thirty-four years old, Giovanni Lotario de' Conti, who was from the great family of the counts of Segni and proud of it. He chose the name Innocent III. In the prime of his life he was coming after six old men who had succeeded one another for twenty years in the chair of Saint Peter. What would the new pope do? The two emperors were young, twenty-one and twenty-three respectively, and rumor had it that the pope, while still a cardinal, had promoted the second election, instinctively distrusting the idea of the Hohenstaufens' ruling the empire—as if he himself had his eye on the whole of Italy.

News travels fast. Upon hearing of the emperor's death Assisi rejoiced. But up at La Rocca the old governor, Conrad of Urslingen, duke of Spoleto, a creature of Henry VI, had to make a choice and, flying in the face of logic, he sided with Otto IV, in whose direction Innocent III was also leaning. The pope had many reasons to do so. Otto had held his stirrup for him, a sign of vassalage; and he thought he could rely more firmly on this act of submission than on that of a son of Barbarossa, who besides held the title of king of the Romans. The old duke's reasons were simple: He wanted to keep his duchy of Spoleto, and he thought that in this way he could better protect young Frederick, whose birth he had witnessed, who had been baptized at Assisi, and who that spring was still in the care of his wife in his castle at Foligno.

Conrad took massive action and began by offering two hundred armed men to His Holiness, a veritable army in those days. Innocent III at first accepted that royal gift, but when his entourage protested that it was a poisoned present, he changed his mind. It would have meant placing himself in the hands of two hundred Teutons. And he was only too aware of both his temporal and his spiritual power, so he summoned Conrad, duke of Spoleto, to Narni, to swear allegiance to him and at the same time to hand over the keys to the citadel of Assisi. This was not Canossa, but the pope was not unmindful of that episode.

The people of Assisi, who had learned to adjust to German lords, were not about to be downtrodden by a papal lord. Spring was in full flower, and men's minds were in a ferment.

As a culminating touch for that year, November would witness yet another death, an important one, that of the Empress Constance, who had become regent of Sicily in the name of little Frederick Roger. That old, gray-skinned mother (she had given birth at forty, an advanced age then) would practically be declared a saint. She had gently reestablished order in Sicily after her husband had crushed the revolts, and she had placed her son's crown under the protection of the pope, who would slowly push the four-year-old king like a common pawn across the chessboard of Italy.

But to return to the spring of 1198: The Germans were still in their citadel of Assisi; the pope and cardinals were taking the cure at Narni; everything was ready for a hot month of May.

Wounds and Bruises

There was no way for armed troops with their baggage in tow to steal away from a fortress. Too many people in Assisi had their eyes fixed on the beetling heights of Rocca Alta, which served as a continual reminder of foreign domination. Like a monstrous predatory beast it loomed over the town, which tumbled down the lower slopes of Mount Subasio like a joyous avalanche of sun-faded titles. Above the thick towers that made up Rocca Alta's grim skirts of stone arose the square turrets perched one on top of the other, as if to see farther in all directions. The people in the town below could not look up to it without cursing the proud, contemptuous stronghold. It was there to defend Assisi, but it threatened it day and night. Even today, anyone who climbs up there can peer straight down into the streets and see quite clearly what's going on in, say, the Piazza San Rufino.

The old duke of Spoleto was preparing for something very much like a camouflaged retreat. If anyone knew that this servant of the empire was about to put himself and part of his garrison at the pope's disposal . . . But the important thing was that he went off, and Assisi was boiling with excitement. It had been given an insane opportunity. They wondered how many soldiers the Teuton had left behind up there. Quite a few, but they had no leader. They could be taken care of.

Weapons were never lacking in an Italian town used to free-for-alls with neighboring communities. The common people were ready to go, but there was hesitation among the nobles, who had their doubts. Some of them were partisans of the German, and they stood aloof. You never know. But then, so what? They had to act quickly. At the first glimmer of dawn all the bells in town gave the signal to attack. It would be a hard struggle, and blood would flow. The crowd from Assisi had numbers and the wild taste of freedom on their side. In the dim morning light it wasn't easy to make out faces, but Francis was among the first to scale the fortress walls. The future knight would not have missed this chance to show his courage and cut a dashing figure. One hopes he didn't kill anyone, but we can't be sure. You don't charge a fortress empty-handed.

The garrison was helpless against the enraged multitude, and no quarter was given. The Germans were massacred, thrown out of the windows or over the walls. The common people had triumphed, and if Francis had fought alongside them for freedom, inclined toward the nobility though he was, he could take comfort from the presence of the aristocrats who embraced the popular cause and fought as he did.

Once the fortress had fallen, a commune was immediately set up by a man named Bombarone, who may have been the future Brother Elias, Francis's intimate, or perhaps his father. The duke of Spoleto was at Narni when he and Innocent III learned of the revolt of the

people of Assisi against the empire. The pope must have been delighted. What an opportunity to seize a town that Rome lusted after.
Legates were dispatched at once, accompanied by Conrad's repre-
sentatives, to request the keys to the city. The keys to the city? First
there had to be a lock to put them in: The pile of rubble where the
fortress had been made that point clear to the Holy Father's emissaries. One can imagine the kind of reception accorded those dignitaries:
impudent remarks flung at them in the best revolutionary style.
When one of the legates demanded the keys, he was asked what they
were good for since the gate was gone. And the demolition of the
fortress went merrily ahead right beneath their eyes while the ramparts around the town grew and grew. In the end they were told that
since Assisi had escaped the jaws of the wolf, it had no wish to fall
beneath the paw of the fox. Caught unprepared, the wolf's gentlemen
and the fox's legates watched pickaxes smash into the towers of La
Rocca, and then departed.

The demolition of the castle was carried out at top speed, and
everyone joined in. Francis was among the most active, and to cheer
the others on in the work he sang in French, as he would sing all his
life except at the end, when he composed his song of farewell to the
earth in Umbrian. And he kept on singing as he worked with all the
people at building solid walls to protect Assisi from counterattack, the
walls one still can see today. Its stones were taken from the dismantled
fortress.

And what was old Bernardone up to during that time? He bought
land from noblemen who wanted to leave town at any price. Peace had
not yet returned. If from the emperor's standpoint Assisi was tranquil,
since the terms of the Peace of Constance applied to all the communes
of central Italy, he still had to exterminate the rule of the petty lords
living in the shadow of the holy Roman Empire. It was less a civil war
than a reckless liberating assault on the images of power—the castles
and proud mansions. A certain number of noblemen surrendered and
went over to the commune. Others stubbornly resisted and holed up
in their castles. The furious rebels attacked them one after the another
and, once they had slaughtered the masters, put their stately houses to
the torch. Still others, wiser or less intrepid, took refuge in Perugia,
Assisi's perennial foe. Among these fugitives was the noble Offreduccio family, which got out just in time. A little longer, and the

insurgents would have put that aristocratic clan to the sword. Francis was with the hotheads who ransacked their house on the Piazza San Rufino, never imagining he was breaking into the home of Clare, his future spiritual daughter.

"At the Time When I Was Still in My Sins"

For the moment conversion was not on Francis Bernardone's mind. When Assisi refused to submit to Rome, the pope had slapped it with his interdict. The doors of the churches were nailed shut with planks in the shape of a cross. Inside, the crucifix was covered with a veil. The relics were locked up or taken down into the crypt. There were no church services nor were the sacraments administered, except under certain circumstances and without the usual pomp. For fear of the plague a prohibition had to be issued against leaving the coffins of the poor in front of the "portal of the dead." A man named Gherardo dei Ghilberti, a Cathar, had been elected podestà, or head of the commune. He was thrown out of office after a few months and replaced by a Catholic loyal to the Church but there was a long moment when general confusion reigned.

Nonetheless life went on amidst a typically Italian political turmoil where bloody reprisals alternated with banquets and festivals and all the inevitable excesses. People danced, sang, and celebrated love. Francis was caught up in a whirlwind of pleasures. And it is here that his biographers grope for the most respectable words to speak the truth without actually speaking it. Generations of prudent writers have handed down the term *farandoles:* Francis's misconduct was limited to dancing the farandole—and so the biographers dance around the truth. After which they move on with a quiet conscience to the various stages of his conversion. Celano, however, has left us some troublesome sentences: "He misspent his time, lamentably wasting it until around his twenty-fifth year. . . . More advanced in frivolity than all his comrades, he became the master of their revels, prompting them to do evil and vying with them in foolishness. . . . In other respects an exquisite youth, he attracted to himself a whole retinue of young people addicted to evil and accustomed to vice. He could be seen, flanked by his infamous band, striding forward, grandly, head held high, through the public squares of Babylon."

Later we shall see this delightful boy grappling with the angel in the most violent kind of struggle. He was sixteen years old, he had fought, he was a man. With the sons of the nobles who had stayed in Assisi and submitted to the new regime, the gay band of pleasure seekers got back together again. Francis took up once more his favorite role of master of the revels, the leader, the *dominus*. It was so easy. People liked him, they felt his charm, and then—a somewhat disagreeable fact— there was the magic of money. The clothier's son knew how to turn his father's cash into handsome presents. He had style, enough to pass (with a little indulgence) for someone to the manner born. The good-looking little plebeian was never vulgar, and his elegance became pro-verbial among his contemporaries, as did his inexhaustible high spirits and his jokes that unleashed hysterical laughter. Obviously it all went to his head, knowing how admired he was for his wit, for his silk capes that were always new and surprising, for his skill at ordering a dinner so fine a prince might envy it. He wanted to dazzle, and he also wanted everyone to enjoy themselves. On warm spring nights the tale was set in the open air. The guests ate ravenously, with the gluttony that marked the age, because however noble they might be, they had a monstrous appetite, all the more on account of the restrictions hard times had imposed on the aristocracy. They drank a lot and sang. The prettiest women in town were invited, despite the laws of the com-mune forbidding women to attend banquets held at night, which were an ideal setting for every kind of excess.

After leaving the table, the company sauntered through town, sing-ing. This was Francis's moment: He stood out by the quality of his voice, at once "strong and sweet, clear and resonant." He could imitate to perfection the language of the troubadours whose songs he had learned. We would like to know which ones, because there are all sorts of things in those poems, where sometimes love is gratified, sometimes mysteriously unfulfilled and unhappy.

At least we can discover what his songs sounded like, because learned societies in Germany and Italy have rescued from oblivion the tunes people heard at the dawn of the thirteenth century. The instruments of that era were descended from the lutes and harps of Sumer, the shepherd's pipes from the deserts of the Mideast, the organs of Byzantium. Listening to the *sirventes* of Peire Vidal, who sang during Francis's lifetime, one feels oneself suddenly transported to an unknown world still more unusual than the distant Middle Ages. One might almost be catching an echo from the heart of a dreamlike Orient. From the first notes the charm of this music puts a spell on the imagination. Though foreign to our sensibility it makes us pass from a state of bewitching melancholy to sudden wild gaiety, to a rhythm beaten out by tambourines, as if by the pounding heels of a furious dance. The falsetto voices arising from a sort of thicket of piping notes plunge down into the lower register. The Saracen guitar caterwauls, the Sumerian harp strums its languid sound. The chants, though marvelously enunciated, are hard to grasp, as they weave their way around the delicate complexity of the phrases. Then the psaltery will hum while a clear, pure voice bursts forth from that churchly murmur.

This art has everything in it: a few seconds of prayer, then a brief rush of hysteria. It could be barbaric, but it has a refinement whose secret we have lost. And, still more moving, we seem to hear in it the magical tone of Francis. A shepherd's pipe opens up a horizon where the muezzin's cry in an oasis sprung from the sands . . . no, we are in the gardens of love, and this is the unconsolably sad song of endless waiting. Strange words speak of lovers in love with love, of the lady one loves without ever failing—or ever touching her; and the young man's voice soars so high that the stars in the night sky appear to be listening to him . . . Francis had some extraordinary moments. His face glowed with pleasure, and he saw quite clearly that with the heat of delicious wine running through him it wouldn't take long to be all aflame. Hadn't he done everything to reach that state? Suddenly he became very serious when he heard some foul language and, as the *dominus*, he reduced the guilty man to silence with a look. Something had come over him, something incomprehensible was going on inside him. He insisted that the women had to be shown respect. Did they really want it, though?

After all, he was the one who had advised his companions to invite their sweethearts—would he now forgo looking at them? If he was so concerned about his virtue, why was he exposing it to such dangers? But then he always had prodigious mood shifts. No one could match him for fastidiousness. And how did the farandole end up? It wound interminably around the piazza, strung out into dark alleys, and dissolved in the muddle of casual copulation.

The *Tripudianti*

He had gotten the notion of founding a band of *tripudianti,* literally "stompers," but they weren't quite that. The *tripudium* was a dance with a strongly accented rhythm that went so far back in time its origins were almost forgotten. It was all the rage in Perugia, that city of scandals and debauchery. The *tripudium* was undoubtedly a vestige of the dance of the Fratres Arvales, a mysterious priestly confraternity that dated back to Romulus and each May celebrated a feast in honor of an agricultural goddess. The ceremonies lasted three days, with the second day devoted to games and, in particular, to dances accompanied by singing, about which a great deal has been written. By Horace's day the songs were no longer comprehensible; but as for the dance itself, the famous sacred *tripudium* is thought to have been in three-part time, the first beat strongly marked with the heel. Perhaps this was the source of the dactyls and spondees of Greek and Latin prosody. The claim has even been made that all Indo-European poetry has kept the cadence of the *tripudium,* which would make the dance far older than the founding of Rome. Its echo still lives on today in certain Greek or Latin verses when they are correctly scanned.

In any event, the *tripudianti* of Assisi enjoyed themselves to the limit, under the stirring leadership of their master of the revels, at the feast of San Ercolano; and naturally Francis danced at the head of the group, singing with his resonant voice. Where was all that headed—and how can we know? There was joy and panic in the pounding step. At Perugia the dance had been forbidden many times over because it served as a pretext for indescribable orgies, even in the churches when the general delirium led the young people there. A papal bull would later condemn those nights in Perugia with a blunt Latin that spoke the truth without disguise.

One wonders if that pagan feast had the same character when Francis was in charge of it. His aversion to any kind of vulgarity poses a problem here. The traditional picture we are given of him doesn't square with certain excesses. It seems more than likely that he fell into what are modestly called moments of weakness, but once again he was different. If he sang love songs, they sometimes had a mystical double meaning that only the initiated could perceive. The inevitable lady celebrated by the troubadours remained the inaccessible ideal of a soul in transport at the cost of a forcibly chaste body. Marriage would have tarnished the beautiful love that found fulfillment only in death. This was the voluntary chastity sung of by Chrétien de Troyes:

But I have so much pleasure in wishing it so
That I suffer agreeably,
And so much joy in my pain
That I am sick with delight . . .

What effect did such medieval intoxication of heart and brain have on Francis? More than once he had alluded to a mysterious beloved, but the people around him smiled. They suspected something less ethereal than the phantasmal lady, whose name he would not reveal. What sentimental game was he getting addicted to? Did he still dream of the princess delivered by Saint George? What was this troubadour's obsession, this chaste and patient love?

The Troubadours

We have to linger a moment over those enigmatic characters who were among the originators of European poetry in the twelfth century. Our knowledge of them raises questions that have never gotten definitive answers. These young lyric poets whom romantic tradition portrays in a generally flattering light could be violent and brutal, but they

were nonetheless delicate artists whose verse, even in modern translation, still has an astonishing freshness. The nobility enjoyed their cantilenas and opened its doors to them, especially the barons whose wives
they pretended to court right beneath their eyes but in keeping with
the forms of an amorous metaphysics that turned women into inaccessible creatures through whom God communicated with man. The eternally distant lady served as a pretext for all the erotic subtleties sanc-
tioned by so-called courtly poetry. Through its alternately clear and
obscure language ran a barely disguised current of Catharism. The
troubadours sang of unhappy love, excluding marriage and glorifying
chastity.

Traveling in pairs, they roamed the highways of Provence, Li-
mousin, and northern Italy. The Church had no illusions about them;
it took a dim view of their rakish guild and charged them with lewd-
ness. A few were even burned at the stake. It seems strange that as
joyous as they often were, they could peddle such serious and even
mystical ideas. But that, in turn, did not prevent them from plunging
into extravagant eulogies of carnal pleasure.

They may have been Cathars, but if so they belonged to the cate-
gory of simple believers, on whom few demands were made. And if by
chance they encountered a "pure" or "perfect" Cathar, they had to bow
three times to him: That sort were in deadly earnest. Saint Bernard
himself acknowledged the austerity of their way of life. They were the
pillars of the "Church of Love," which was tacitly defying the Church
of Rome

They were everywhere. Clothiers, merchants, anyone who traveled
from East to West was thought to belong to their number, Bernardone
among others. Pica was a good Catholic; he was not: That was common
knowledge. Francis lived between the traditional faith of his mother
and that strange religion (from Persia, no doubt) followed by his father.
What did the young man think of all that, of the curse laid on the body
as the instrument of the devil, of the secret revolt against the pope and
the clergy? Meanwhile, the faraway lady continued to wreak havoc on
the imagination of young and old alike. Esclarmonde de Foix, one of
the untouchable beauties, turned Cathar and foreswore all ties to the
Church at the time when Francis was on the eve of his conversion. He
may have halted just at the edge of an abyss. In his dreams he kept only
the fleeting image of the woman who waited for him somewhere in the

invisible world. Perhaps he was searching, in some dim sense, for the lady whom the Lord himself would have chosen, had that been thinkable, under similar circumstances. Was he already asking questions of this kind? Poverty stands at the head of the Beatitudes, but it was still too soon for him to see her.

Fair Appearances

Consciousness is a pure appearance in the sense that it exists only to the extent that it appears.

—Sartre (sic)

Who knew *la dolce vita* better than Francis? But there are times when the man of pleasure comes face to face with a totally different sort of person, and something like rays of light shoots across his uneasy youth. One day when he was working in the store and his father was away, a poor man showed up at the door and begged for an alms for the love of God. His timing was very bad.

The young clothier, attentive to his own interests, was conversing with some very important customers, and suddenly in the most elegant shop in town this awkward fellow—dirty, dressed in rags, and smelling bad—was mumbling about the love of God. Under different circumstances Francis would have given him something, as he always did, but not today. He was shamed by this intrusion of wretchedness into a group that was hard to please, that had to have the best, the latest fashions. He hesitated a moment, then with a word sent the importunate beggar away. The man disappeared, well schooled by the rich and their refusals. Now everything in the store was as it should be. It had almost been an aesthetic problem—Francis could not endure ugliness. Once again he unrolled the fine silks and spread them out on the counter with a purr of satisfaction.

All at once a voice began to cry out in the conscience of the young tradesman. No one else heard it, but to Francis it was deafening. "And

if that man had wanted something from you, not for the love of God,
but for a baron or count, what would you have done?" Leaving his
clients on the spot, a dumbfounded Francis raced out of the store and
caught up with the beggar. The one he had thrown out was, quite
simply, God. Appearances meant nothing. That is what our *tripudiante*
of the night before had just understood, and the beggar watched in
stupefaction as his hand filled up with silver pieces.

On a heartfelt impulse Francis promised never again to turn down
any request "for the love of God." Those words had knocked him for
a loop.

The Simpleton

And then there was the simpleminded man in Assisi. No one gave
him any grief. On the contrary, this sort of man was deemed to be
under God's protection; he went about wherever he pleased, surrounded by a kind of superstitious respect. He was obviously an innocent and inoffensive soul. He had only one crazy habit, which made
some smile and gave others pause, depending upon the mood of the
moment, because it bordered on veneration; and the object of that
veneration—oh, the ironies of life—was that rowdy, spendthrift, mad-
cap Francis. When the simpleton met Francis "by chance," he hastened
to remove his coat and spread it on the ground so that the "king of
youth" could walk over it. That was not enough. He announced that
one day "the young man will accomplish great things and will be given
magnificent honors by the faithful." We are not told how often he
made that surprising prophecy, nor whether it eventually came to
embarrass the young clothier whose behavior was not in the least
edifying, but everybody knew about it.

Francis must have fled from that prophet and his obsession with
beatifying him. While not wishing to exaggerate the peculiarity of this
situation, I feel confident that the future saint must have hurriedly
slipped away when he spotted his zealous admirer in the distance.

When did they meet for the first time, and how often did they meet later on? "By chance" allows us to suppose anything we like. We can in any event conceive the effect their first meeting must have had on an imagination as inflammable as Francis's. There was enough here to turn his head. "Given magnificent honors" was quite a surprise, not to mention an extremely satisfying boost to the vanity of a young man infatuated with glory and yet too intelligent not to sense the religious import of that dizzying prediction. But after all, it was only the utterance of a visionary. What did Francis think about it? We don't know, but if, as seems likely, chance arranged a second encounter with the same scenario and the same exclamation, that must have made Francis think hard. Living the sinful life he did, he found the man's insistance becoming a call. Still more, I believe—and the text supports me—that there was a third meeting, a fourth, and others after that. Instead of losing their force, such repeated reminders may have left Francis's soul distraught.

So we have no reason to be surprised that he should have moments of sudden seriousness in the middle of a feast. What did that mean? He wanted to be a knight, to take his place in the ranks of the nobility. What did all the "faithful," whom the simpleton spoke of, have to do with those ambitions?

Sisters and Enemies

In January 1200 war broke out with Perugia. Its pretext was the demolition of the castle of Sasso Rosso, at the gates of Assisi. The castle's owner, a great and powerful lord, had taken refuge in Perugia from the threatening townsfolk of Assisi, and there he rejoined the noblemen who had left earlier, when La Rocca was captured. His sons who stayed behind to defend the castle were killed, and his angry complaints were added to the exiles' cries for vengeance. They all demanded compensation for damages and the rebuilding of their houses. The commune of Perugia sent an ultimatum to the commune of Assisi, which haughtily rejected it, and hostilities began.

For two years this meant no more than skirmishes led by one side or the other, but on December 12, 1202, a decisive battle was fought. All the bells in Assisi began to toll, and the army was mustered in front of the cathedral. The infantry headed the parade, behind the banners of the various quarters of the town, San Rufino, Santa Maria Maggiore, San Lorenzo, then the cavalry encircling the *caroccio*, a large wagon drawn by white oxen and bearing an altar of lighted candles that framed a jewel-encrusted crucifix and relics. Priests continually celebrated mass there beneath the white and blue gonfalon of the commune, and the trumpets gave a gallant blast.

Our hero, of course, was with the knights. He had been splendidly outfitted by his father, who was anxious to see him among the noblemen. After the exciting descent into the plain, the army needed more than four hours to reach the banks of the Tiber, on the frontier of the two communes; then it took up a position of the hill of Collestrada, near the leprosarium. The long march had somewhat dulled its energy, if not its ardor, whereas Perugia's army had only to cross the river at Ponte San Giovanni to hurl themselves on their adversaries. No precise account has survived of this engagement, which quickly turned into a massacre. We do know that the exiled noblemen displayed an unparalleled ferocity toward the peasants who had despoiled them. The soldiers of Assisi scattered before the enemy, who pursued them into the valley and the woods above Collestrada till nightfall, and cut them to pieces. The Perugians set upon the fleeing troops with fury: Archers and infantrymen were butchered, but knights were taken prisoner. Owning a horse implied that one could pay a ransom, which was no minor matter. Contemporary writers say the river overflowed with blood—perhaps an exaggeration borrowed from Lucan. But there were heaps of corpses in the water.

By one of those shortcuts that destiny arranges, the battle was fought on land acquired by Francis's father, and more than likely the young man killed some people.

That night he and his companions in misfortune were led to the jails of Perugia. The Perugians did not press their advantage by seizing the enemy's town because the walls erected by their rivals made this a risky undertaking. Looking out from Assisi the townspeople saw only a few of its sons returning, and that evening there rose toward the sky a lamentation whose memory has never faded.

In Prison

Now Francis was a prisoner with many others, all noblemen except himself. He had been taken for one of the lords because he was on horseback and had the grand manner. Noble or not, the group was jeered by the crowd, loaded with chains, and then shoved into an underground dungeon. There they could make out one another's face by the gloomy light of a lantern. The aristocrats of Assisi in fetters! Life has its chilling ironies: He had wanted to be among the nobility, and now he was—for God knew how long.

In the evening darkness, echoes wafted down to him; they were feeble, no doubt, but cruel for the lost happiness they evoked. The youth of Perugia were known for their extravagant love of pleasure. They bustled noisily about in the streets of the victorious city. They gave not a moment's thought to the fellows their age who were chafing with despair in the basement of the Etruscan tower.

Nowadays walking around Perugia, which has preserved so many traces of its old magnificence, it is easy to imagine what Romanesque Perugia was like. From the immense piazza, surrounded by the cathedral, the House of the Commune, and ochre-colored palaces, a wide street runs down through the city, full of the deafening sound of Italian voices. How scornfully this patrician town must have looked down on provincial little Assisi with its tortuous back streets and its cramped houses. Brought to its senses by the Perugian army, Assisi could now rest quietly behind its thick walls and taste its humiliation in peace.

The first hours must have been awful for those fine gentlemen, thrown together like a gang of criminals, shivering from the cold after the heat of battle, within those sinister walls. Hardest of all was the intolerable blow to their pride. They had been beaten. One would expect to hear them shouting in protest and rage. Francis was the only one not to complain. They had been locked up in the depths of one of the towers that formed part of the city's defenses.

Days and nights went by in despair. None of these young people

were used to suffering: Life was made for nothing but joy, comfort, all
the delicate pleasures of the senses, and already the harsh Umbrian
winter was creeping down into the dungeons. With his frail constitu-
tion Francis must have suffered cruelly from the stinging cold, but
strangely enough his behavior remained the same, as if the king of
youth were as free and happy in prison as beneath a springtime sky,
at table during one of his famous banquets. He smiled, joked, and
sometimes even managed to get his companions to laugh, dejected as
they were. What wellspring of invisible happiness was he drinking
from to escape the tortures of neurasthenia? Some of the prisoners had
fallen sick; he helped them as best he could, but his perpetual good
cheer ended by becoming an irritant. There was in particular one surly,
arrogant knight who was shunned and never spoken to by the others.
Through some miracle of kindness and courtesy Francis overcame this
ostracism and obtained a reconciliation. But they couldn't know who
Francis was when he himself didn't know. In moments of exasperation
they asked him how he could rejoice with chains weighing down his
ankles and wrists. One day he gave a stupefying answer, which I
should like to dwell on because it has nonplussed his biographers.
According to Celano, he is supposed to have said, "I rejoice because
some day I shall be venerated as a saint all over the world." Was this
a reminiscence of the simpleton's prophecy? And not two months
before, Francis had been reveling with inexhaustible vigor in wine,
women, and farandoles.

He had already announced that the time would come when he
would be a prince, and now he saw himself a saint, an object of
veneration. No one could have held it against him because even under
those abominable circumstances they never stopped loving him, the
clothier's son gone astray among the nobles. I would imagine that this
apparently outrageous prophecy was met not by gales of laughter but
silent dismay: Francis had gone crazy, people who acted like that deserved to be locked up.

Modern writers translate differently the crucial phrase in this episode: "I shall be adored by the whole world" (Sabatier); "I shall be
adored" (Arvède Barine); "I shall be the idol of the world" (Englebert);
"The whole world will respect me" (various translators of the "Trois
Compagnons"); "The whole world will fall on its knees and pray to

me" (Jørgensen); "My body is imprisoned, but the mind is free" (Fortini).

It is worth noting that not one of them quotes Celano correctly, as if they felt uncomfortable in just the same way Francis's fellow captives felt. His comrades didn't believe their ears, and our authors don't believe their eyes. So they arrange the text to suit their own notions because they don't trust Celano. It's the word *saint* that bothers them. Perhaps they fancy that Celano wanted to provide an unretouched image before the official, immutable portrait that Saint Bonaventure would order of Francis once he had been canonized. I sympathize with their position, but I believe that the phrase is authentic. I think Francis said it in the grip of an unexpected divine inspiration. It clashes with the sort of life he had led up until that day. Of course, he had not lived like a saint, but a saint he would be, and he knew it, because the slow labor of his conversion was proceeding by sudden, inexplicable leaps. He was already an object of scandal: That was part of his strange vocation.

Predictably he fell sick. The cold, damp conditions overcame even the hardiest prisoners. Francis, whose health had always been frail, broke down; his lungs were affected. A year had already gone by since he was first imprisoned. His youth was passing, but the jails of Perugia stayed shut. At this point a charitable organization that looked after sick prisoners obtained Francis's release in exchange for a ransom. His father once again did what was necessary, and Francis got back to Assisi. He was twenty-two.

First Disillusionments

After the nightmare of prison, the return home must have seemed sweet to Francis, consoled by his mother's lavish affection. Most invigorating of all, he had his freedom, but what could he do with it? After those months of captivity he was sick, very sick indeed, with tuberculosis. And the memory of his comrades back in prison haunted him continually, like the thought of his friends massacred at Colles-trada. Peace negotiations were said to have begun, but they would not bring those absent ones back to life.

In the long run the care and attention he got restored his strength a little. Leaning on a cane, he was able to walk around the house and explore his old domain. Nothing had changed around him, to be sure, but he had. The man making his way from room to room was no longer the king of youth, and the change wasn't entirely physical. Francis, perhaps, felt aged and disillusioned by suffering.

But there were signs of spring with its irresistible call to joy. One could not imagine this season being more beautiful anywhere else than in Umbria, and once he was strong enough, Francis ventured a short stroll out into the countryside, which lay almost at his doorstep, at the end of the street. He was hoping for some kind of enchant-ment.

Having reached a spot from where he could view the whole plain as far as Perugia, the checkerboard of fields and orchards, the ponds glistening like silver and the meandering Teschio in the play of sun-light. Francis stopped and looked out over the landscape that had been so dear. But for all its beauty nature no longer moved him. Strangely enough, this man who was a lover of light, of the delicate shades of color in the meadows, of the woods just budding with green, felt the desolation of indifference. His inner self demanded something more than the visible world could give him that day. He was disappointed.

Once back in his room, he must have wondered why, but the work God does in us defies analysis. One simply doesn't know. The flavor goes out of things. One grows detached from the world and oneself. A sort of languor takes hold of the soul. His body's weakness may have played a part in this, as well as his obsession with the horrors of a lost, futile war.

As he recuperated, Francis still wanted the attention that was lav-ished on him—by his mother out of love, by his father for what were probably less noble motives. In Bernardone's calculating mind the fu-ture of his store depended on the health of his elder son. He had paid a lot of money to get him out of prison, so at all costs he wanted the good-for-nothing (as he still saw him) back on his feet. Angelo was still too young. With the way things were going, Francis began to look more and more interesting. He would be taking his place either in the world of business or the world of the nobility, where the father's dreams oddly coincided with his son's. But then too Bernardone cherished that strange bird he had brought into the world.

What was happening in Assisi? Having so many of its children to mourn, the town was recovering with difficulty from its wounds. Behind its imposing fortifications there remained only a handful of people to defend it, and so it had no choice but to submit to the demands of its victorious rival, the commune of Perugia—a commune, but controlled by the pope. As a matter of fact, the conditions for peace were not unreasonable. Assisi had to compensate the noblemen who had fled to Perugia and whose homes had been sacked and destroyed. Pay and rebuild was the plan. Assisi was rich and it complied, though not without grinding its teeth. In return, the noblemen, once they had been indemnified, would accept the government of the commune and promise not to seek help with any future disputes from its ancestral enemy.

Some echoes of all this got back to Francis. He learned that, little by little, Assisi's population was growing again. Like him, the town was recovering its health. He could think of himself as cured, and the time came when sickness, so apt to provoke spiritual musings, eventually loosened its grip, at least for a while. His weakened body, freed from all desire, had allowed the soul free rein, and the demands of the soul can be more urgent than the longing of the senses. But as he grew stronger each day, a world full of bewitching seductions was reborn. Lying in his sickbed, Francis had somehow forgotten the splendor of creation so that he failed to recognize it the first time he went outside. That was something akin to blasphemy. The obsession with beauty in all its forms regained its empire over this man so keenly attuned to both joy and pain.

Once more he plunged into the streets of Assisi, a little like a man taking possession of a recaptured citadel. Peace reigned, a precarious, humiliated peace, but happiness was possible again, and Francis could resume his singing. Friends who had escaped the massacre of Collestrada hastened to the side of the man they had given up for lost. Francis's old self made them forget the whole tragic year. As after every war, a burst of merriment swept over young men who were ready to sink their teeth into life the way they had in the best of

times. Once order had been more or less restored, the charming disorder of nights in Assisi could finally begin again, since the king of
youth was there with his songs, his peals of laughter, and his money.
He too was hungry for pleasure. His gauche remark about being a
future saint was fading from everyone's memory—even Francis's?
Would the party go on?

It did. In his emphatic style Celano tells us that Francis had "not yet
shaken off the yoke of his criminal slavery." He says not a word about
the war with Perugia and Francis's captivity. His sickness, according to
the chronicler, was the result of God's grace, designed to bring back to
the straight and narrow a young man who "strode forward, grandly,
head held high, through the public squares of Babylon." "Vice," he
adds soberly, "ends up being your second nature."

No fuzziness here. But listen to the voice of Bonaventure of Bag-
noregio, who never knew Francis and who assures us, thirty-five years
after his death, that "he never let himself be carried away by the
powerful tide of the passions." So burn all the earlier evidence to the
contrary. And the fact is that in 1263 a pile of troublesome documents
was committed to the flames. That's how plaster saints are made. We
might do better to pay heed to what the saint himself said when he was
shaken by incredible fits of weeping: "I lived in sin." And later with
that caustic touch he never lost: "Don't canonize me too soon. I'm
perfectly capable of fathering a child."

Dead at forty-six, he would not be converted until he was twenty-
five. He kept God waiting quite a while, but God loved him nonetheless. I'm not saying that we love him all the more for it, but his being
a sinner brings him closer to us. Unless he had sinned, how could he
convert? *"Etiam peccata . . . Felix culpa . . ."*

The wildest libertines fault pleasure for its monotony and, if they
happen to have read Lucretius, for that "bitter something" that arises
from the sources of sensual delight. With his almost morbid sensitivity,
Francis must have experienced the nausea that comes from satiety. It
takes time to reach this state of salutary disgust, and Francis was only
twenty-two.

What did he believe in? What did he want? He was perhaps the
greatest dreamer the world had ever seen. His faith, of course, was his
mother's, the most purely Catholic kind of faith, but naive and superstitious, at once deep and unenlightened. We know that he could not

endure blasphemy—a valuable clue. But was he disturbed to see how out of tune his carnal life was with his religion? Was a young Italian in that period aware of such problems? We may doubt it.

And yet the Cathars discussed these questions in their open-air sermons, and the troubadours sang of forever unsatisfied courtly love for the beloved. How could Francis not have picked up some of these ideas floating around him? That wouldn't quell the frantic prompting of the senses, but he himself never stopped singing out loud in his fine voice the Provençal cantilenas he was so smitten with. We may wonder what kind of response these songs, with their esoteric eroticism, evoked in a boy who was sensitive to everything, to the beauty of a flower or the force of an idea.

What did he want from life? Many, many things, but above all, glory. The thought of it haunted him, even after the defeat and humiliation of captivity. As he had when he was sixteen, he wanted to be the first, the most admired. "You'll see that I'll be adored" was a child's cry.

What strikes us about the young Francis is that he desired exactly what he would later despise. His faults were like a reversed mirror image of his future virtues. For the moment he was fascinated by the tinsel of chivalry. The idol of the day was an adventurer from Champagne, Gautier de Brienne.

Ideal Knight or Knight of the Ideal?

Gautier wanted the earldom of Lecce. His Norman wife had been deprived of it by the holy Roman Empire, and Gautier set off to conquer it in the name of the Hautevilles, but this reckless character had greater ambitions. In his heart he wished to seize all of Sicily, and the first step in that direction was to go through Apulia and to liberate all the villages subject to the German yoke. Innocent III could only encourage him, feeling sure he could use this hotheaded Frenchman, who was galloping across the peninsula to cries of *"Italia! Italia!"*, as a condottiere to recapture southern Italy in the name of Rome. Moreover the pope made him swear to limit himself to his hereditary fief, but Gautier would do just what he pleased. He besieged towns, took them by storm, and subdued the whole region of Naples.

After some spectacular successes, Brienne had the south of Italy in the palm of his hand. Then he began openly lusting after Sicily, and Innocent III could only look and wait, because to excommunicate him would mean reversing his earlier judgment. But the Germans in Sicily got frightened and sent out a call to the Pisan fleet, and the Pisans were happy as always to thwart the pope's plans. Then a storm at sea came into the picture, and as the thunder rolled, Gautier's ships were scattered. Sicily breather easier again, safe in German hands; and Gautier had to start over from scratch, because behind his back the towns he thought he had conquered rose up in rebellion, as any population will when it believes its conqueror vulnerable.

The Count d'Acerra, the best of the German captains, was cruel and rapacious, but an exceptional military mind; and he made good use of all the weapons destiny was offering him. On receiving news that Innocent III was ill, he spread a rumor that the pope was dead. Taranto revolted, and so Gautier had to lay siege against his own strongholds. But this time Brindisi, Otranto, and even Lecce were much harder to retake. Finally, when he thought his troubles were over, many of the knights who had helped him left for the Holy Land, because in the beginning they had enrolled beneath his banners for a Crusade. The pope, to be sure, had taken advantage of this: Becoming a Crusader meant fighting for the Church, didn't it? Innocent III had all the weaknesses of a politician even if, on the other hand, he had a sense of the greatness of his office. He exulted when one of his adversaries was struck down, and the letter that he wrote to Frederick II's advisers after the sudden death (following an operation for kidney stones) of the German seneschal Markwald, the very man who appealed to the Pisans for help, is a masterpiece of rancor, malice, and almost delirious joy—a bit thick for a pope. But now the affairs of the Brienne family were no longer the point; saving Jerusalem was.

The pope contented himself with issuing benedictions, waiting to see what would happen. And Gautier went back to winning victories. He thought he could lay hold of his enemy, when d'Acerra fled for refuge to the castle of Sarno, a robbers' den on the crest of Mount

Terranova near Vesuvius. This was a fortress with powerful walls along the edge of a cliff. Only famine could overcome it, and Brienne blocked all the ways out. But the Count d'Acerra had more than one trick in his repertoire. He decided to attack at night and had his men creep down the dizzying slope that separated his stronghold from the French camp, wrapping the horses' hooves in felt. In the deepest silence they came up to the camp, which was resting in complete tranquillity. Then just before dawn they surprised and massacred everyone they could. Gautier was captured beneath his tent: The ropes were cut, and as he thrashed around under the folds of the tent, they thrust at him with their lances as if at a netted beast. Covered with wounds, the prisoner was entrusted to the best doctors in Salerno, a town famous for that profession since antiquity (Arab surgeons practiced there too). Diepold d'Acerra wanted his man well again, relying on his own gifts of persuasion to wrench an oath from Gautier to stop fighting against him. Nothing doing. The one-eyed man—Gautier had lost an eye to an arrow at the siege of Terracina—refused to compromise, and rather than give in to the German, he ripped off the dressings protecting his wounds and died of septicemia.

This was the Don Quixote who, in 1204, wearing the dazzling carapace of medieval armor, set the youth of Italy on fire. He was the image of the knight that many young people dreamed of joining with. In Assisi a nobleman whose name has been lost proclaimed his desire of following the liberator. Francis, generous and impulsive, immediately did the same. He threw himself heart and soul into these sudden decisions, and the sight of the bales of cloth did nothing to bring him to his senses; quite the contrary. Bernardone's son on horseback, with a full suit of armor and lance in hand, would make the world see that he truly belonged to the race of great men.

The Suit of Armor

Every knight worthy of the name owed it to himself to set out to reconquer Jerusalem. Wasn't the honor of Christendom at stake here? Unfortunately, the Fourth Crusade preached by Innocent III had taken an unexpected turn, thanks to intrigue by the Venetians, who launched it against Constantinople in 1204. This was the "impious war" that resulted in the disastrous break between the Eastern and the Western Church. Byzantium was taken by storm and sacked by Christian warriors. The Crusade would prove to be a complete fiasco and a scandal. Nevertheless, a small number of Crusaders had refused to join in this brigandage and went off to the city of Christ to deliver it from the hands of Saladin's nephew, Malik al-Kamil, sultan of Egypt.

Francis's fondest dream of glory was about to come true. Perhaps he already saw himself battling over there for the Savior, but preparations for the departure were time-consuming. The young man was going to accompany a great lord. This anonymous nobleman—generally believed to be one of those Francis had known from the jails in Perugia—agreed to leave with the clothier's son to meet up with the troops of Gautier de Brienne in Apulia. Francis was so impatient he couldn't stand still. Luckily Pietro di Bernardone had no objection to the designs of Providence; in fact, he favored them. Since his son would be leaving with a nobleman, his armor had to be handsome, and the best craftsmen in Assisi set to work. We can scarcely imagine the amount of labor it took to make that steel garment with all its joints. Every possible movement of the body was taken into consideration, and since expense was not a factor, the steel surface was set off by artfully carved decorations in gold. It took weeks to finish.

How much money did the bill amount to—for the armor, the horse and all its trappings, not to mention the indispensable squire carrying his master's shield? The sums were fabulous—the price of a farm—but Bernardone went along with everything. Here we touch upon one of the most enigmatic features of that misunderstood character. He was greedy and brutal, but he felt some uncertainty about his son, seeing him now as a clothier, now as a nobleman, which explains the contradictory behavior of this perplexed and apparently narrow-minded man. He desired his son's success as keenly as Francis himself did, but Francis wanted money only as a means for climbing to the top of the social ladder and for lording it over others once he got there. How would he manage that? He didn't know. In Assisi they murmured more or less openly that he had lost his mind. When so many people were going hungry all over, that wild young man was squandering his father's fortune. And then he had all those whims. They made people smile when he was an adolescent, but now he was a grown man talking nonsense. Prison had failed to straighten out the ideas in that slightly frenzied brain. And yet they still loved crazy Francis.

At last the day came when, with pounding heart, he could ease his slender body into that metal suit. He must have felt its weight, but willpower provided all the strength he needed. The fitting session (what else can we call it?) went well. A magnificent cloak, generously cut and embroidered all over with gold, was flung across the shoulders of the young warrior. It was thought best that before the great departure he should walk along the road in this outfit. That way he could tell if everything was satisfactory.

Then an incident took place that struck with wonder the people who witnessed it. Francis must not have been far from the city when he came across a knight who had no doubt been ruined by war. He was dressed so shabbily that it made him lose caste and slip from the army of the lords into the numberless host of the poor. What a look of distress and envy he must have given that armed knight in all the glory of his golden youth. Instead of moving down the road Francis stopped. Did he speak to the unfortunate *déclassé?* We have no way of knowing. The only thing that remained in the chroniclers' memory is the gesture of the young knight: He unhooked his rich cloak and handed it, along with his weapons, to the penniless nobleman, who stood there thunderstruck.

That night Francis had a dream of the kind one could have only in the Middle Ages, a dream like one of those sumptuous, illuminated manuscripts glowing with gold and vivid colors. He was in a palace, or in his own house, but the family residence was prodigiously transformed. From ceiling to floor the walls were covered with valuable

arms, helmets, cuirasses, brassards, bucklers, lances, swords, all glittering and marked with a cross. There was enough to equip any number of young men from Assisi. But that wasn't all. In the middle of
that shining arsenal stood an utterly beautiful young girl. A voice
was heard that made Francis's heart beat faster. "These arms," she
said, "are for you and for all your companions." The girl herself
could only be the ideal lady whom every true knight had to serve—
and deserve.

Jolted from sleep, Francis felt beside himself with joy to see his
vocation confirmed. He would never sell cloth again, he would fight in
the ranks of the knights. He would be a prince.

On the morrow, the day of his departure, the clothier's son tasted
the first fruits of glory when he set off on his travels. He felt the
delicious pleasure of being marveled at in his darkly gleaming armor.
A more modest cloak hung from his shoulders, but he didn't regret
the one he had given away the day before. The town he had so often
scandalized with his high living was proud of him that morning and,
his heart was full of joy, he met his companion in arms, the patrician.

What did that individual think of Francis? All we know is that they
went along together down the road to Spoleto, their first day's ride. It
was springtime. Wending their way through that inviting landscape
they passed a succession of towns, big ones and little ones: some—
Spello, say, or Montefalco—perched on the hills like warriors keeping
watch over their lands; others—Foligno or Bevagna—down in the plain
like lookouts crouched behind their battlements. Isolated strongholds
rose up into the sky—Castel Ritaldi, Castel San Giovanni—crowning
the hilltops with their defiant towers. The immobile army repeated its
warning and its threats, as it stood defending vast expanses of vines,
meadows, olive orchards, and fields of wheat. There was no escaping
the silent call to arms that followed the travelers at long intervals like
an intermittent obsession. War, glory . . .

They arrived at Spoleto in the evening. Perhaps because of fatigue
from the journey, Francis fell sick that same night in the inn where he
took lodgings with his squire.

The Night in Spoleto

Much has been written about this moment, which may be the most mysterious episode in Francis's life. Once again he heard a voice speaking to him in the silence of the night. He himself vouched for it, and there is no doubting his sincerity. Nevertheless the celebrated dialogue has been dismissed as a feverish delusion. The voice, Celano tells us, asked Francis in an affectionate tone what he was going to do. Upon which the young man explained his plans:

"Who can give you more? The master or the servant?"

"The master!"

"Then why are you abandoning the master for the servant and the prince for the vassal?"

And Francis said, "What do you wish me to do, Lord?"

"Return to the land where you were born, and you will be told what you must do."

"Return home . . . " The words were harsh, but the voice was gentle, because it was the Lord's voice—that was how medieval commentators viewed the scene. Modern biographers have their own theories to offer. Reason demands precise explanations. In Assisi the Lord seems to have encouraged Francis to leave. In Spoleto he ordered him to stay. That strains logic, and the critics find it unacceptable. So this is what they imagine.

First hypothesis: Francis, who had never enjoyed vigorous health, arrived at Spoleto in a state of exhaustion. He wondered if he would have the strength to face up to battle in that heavy armor, not to mention the weight of the lance and the shield. The voice he heard was the voice of common sense but, with a little help from his fever, the supernatural dialogue was worked out in so edifying a fashion that he believed in it. The defeat at Collestrada had demoralized him.

Second hypothesis: In conversation with his brother in arms, who was a nobleman and the son of noblemen, Francis had been boastful, claiming once more that he would be a prince; and his companion's patience had worn thin. He put Francis firmly in his place: He was a burgher; let him remain a burgher. The idea of a puny clothier breaking lances with battle-hardened knights was unimaginable, ridiculous. He should go home.

Third and final hypothesis—a more humane one: Francis was evidently too weak to continue the journey. His companion left him behind, wishing him better health and agreeing to meet him at Lecce. Why Lecce? Because there in the heel of the boot of Italy lay the luxurious and refined court of old Queen Sibyl, one of whose daughters Gautier had married. Lecce was the new Troy. They would be reunited there to celebrate the victory, unless Francis was back on his feet before then.

No doubt Francis let his squire follow the young aristocrat, who thought he was bound for glory. We wonder what became of them, since Gautier de Brienne's adventure came to such a dismal end. And what would have become of Francis, if he had pressed on?

The Return

He stayed in Spoleto for a while, and it was during those very days when Gautier was captured and his men wiped out (though news of the disaster did not arrive till later) that Francis suffered a bout of the quartan ague. Was that the disease he had been suffering from ever since adolescence, or was it a case of malaria contracted the summer before in the humid basement of the tower that served as a prison in Perugia? When his strength was restored, he took the road back to Assisi. In what state of mind?

On his way through Foligno he stopped: Going back home wearing his armor was impossible. What a pathetic sight: the aspiring knight returning with all his equipment in perfect condition. One can imagine how his father and neighbors would have greeted him. Francis wisely sold his armor and horse and bought himself some simple clothes. It was the most intelligent solution. He would undoubtedly have to weather a domestic storm but, fortified by the voice of the Lord that he had heard in the night, he quietly presented himself at his father's house. We know nothing about the explanations that followed, but we may be sure that Bernardone raised his voice.

Down through the ages arguments over money have gone on and on with their monotonous vileness, and the one Francis had with his father was probably no different from the classical model. But in the end Francis had a rather vague view of the future, as he waited for the Lord to make his will known more precisely. God's language isn't always immediately clear. Francis had been ordered to return to Assisi, and there he was—but what was he going to do? Between the young man and his infuriated father—"My money! I want that money!"—an uneasy truce must have been reached (after a long and painful discussion), a settlement with more finances than feeling in it. Now that his grand chivalric daydreams had been so pathetically routed, Francis would go back and make his living as he had in the past. Back to the store.

Eight centuries afterward we can almost hear his outraged father. There was the enormous waste of money, the shameful retreat from combat, plus a number of more personal complaints. Pica must have cried very hard, but she understood; mothers understand everything. Her son would be a child of God. She had received that prophecy, and she believed it.

We have no documentary evidence for thinking that anyone laughed at Francis. He was smiling again, as usual. He had been touched by grace, but he was still uncertain about what he ought to do, so he waited. We don't know what his frame of mind was, and there's no point inventing scenes. The facts we have are eloquent enough. His old boon companions lost no time in flocking round him. Some of the group were missing, of course, but what was the use of disturbing the shadows of the past? Life was still as beautiful as ever, the earth just as much in love with the sky and the sun. The adolescent of old suddenly reawakened, Francis sang with that voice that carried so far yet kept its sweetness. How could he have resisted the charm of his own smile that brought back joy to the badly shaken troop of young people? Now that he was a man, he savored more than ever before the pleasure of dominating others. He had no illusions about their reasons for flattering him, but he could still feel, as they did, the surge of young blood toward gross fleshly happiness. His purse was still full of money, thanks to some makeshift arrangement with his father; and he could once again play the great lord when he got the urge.

His companions let him have his way in everything, "so they could fill their bellies," the pitiless Celano observes. Once again they crowned him the king of youth and put a rod in his hand by way of a scepter. Out of good humor, out of "courtesy," Francis ordered a sumptuous banquet that led to the usual disgraceful carryings on: "Stuffed to the point of vomiting," Celano continues, "the guests went off to defile the public squares of the town with their drunken songs." With their songs and all the rest. And who was that following them, with his fool's baton in hand, but the king of the feast? All of a sudden he stopped. The reeling farandole went on without him, and soon they noticed that he wasn't there.

Wounded with Love

Turning back, they found him standing motionless in the street. What was wrong with him? He had never had such a strange look before. He seemed to be sleeping with his eyes open. Had he seen an apparition?

"You've forgotten us," they cried. "What were you thinking about? You want to get married?"

That absurd question woke him up. His clear voice sounded in the dark like a murmur: "Yes, and I shall have to wife the noblest, the richest, and the fairest lady ever seen."

A storm of laughter exploded, and the word *pazzo* ran from one wine-soaked mouth to another. There was Francis raving again, having visions, the old megalomania. Nobility, fortune, beauty—nothing was missing. They came up to him but didn't dare to tease him. His expression was all different, this was not the man they had known, not even the man they seen a few minutes ago. It was somebody else.

What had happened? In the middle of that sorry feast Francesco, with that ridiculous fool's baton in his hand, had fallen in love. For years he had been fleeing someone or something, and suddenly that someone had caught up with him and blasted him with all the power of his tenderness. Francis was twenty-five years old. In the chess game of the absolute the knight had become the bishop (*le fou,* the madman), and God won.

Part Two

GOD'S FOOL

Alike and Different

Francis felt that mad joy of the convert who sees the world vanish before his eyes. Where was he? Had he been able to talk, he would not have found the words to say—human language no longer made sense. All notions of time and space faded away. He had no more awareness of his own identity. He was simply lost, swallowed up in indescribable happiness.

Later, if he tried to recreate with words the wonder of that minute, he would find himself toiling gloomily over lifeless adjectives. Once again he was the prisoner of a little universe whose unreality he had glimpsed in a lightning flash. Ambition, money, power, pleasure—all empty. Only one thing existed. The memory of it, which could not be communicated to anyone, made his heart flutter; and yet this was what he had to give to men.

And now what was he going to do? He was no longer the same man, and everything around the new Francis was different as well, as if he had become a stranger in an unknown country.

There was nothing wrong with him, but nothing was as it had been before in his daily life, though in appearance nothing had changed. He was simply not the same man doing the same things anymore. No doubt he went back to the store, and his father might have reason to think he was part of the household and the cloth trade once more, even though Bernardone hadn't been able to swallow the troublesome armor episode. Still he was relieved to see that his son had called a halt to those expensive banquets that did not bring him one step closer to high society. Francis would get there some other way. Business and money opened all doors, beginning with the doors to power.

All this seemed the furthest thing from Francis's mind. At home he sought solitude to pray, and, what surprised everyone the most, he was silent. They no longer heard him singing the way he used to. In the streets of Assisi he gave alms to every beggar he met, because the memory of the one he had chased away made his face burn with shame, and he promised God never to offend him that way again. If he happened to run out of money, he would give the beggar his cap, his belt, anything at all rather than let that outstretched hand remain empty. One day, with his mania for always going to extremes, he went off by himself, removed his shirt, and discreetly made a present of it to a poor wretch.

But whatever happened to his *Fortunatus*'s purse, that miraculous purse that seemed to be forever full? It was suspected that Francis's father had taken it upon himself to reorganize the finances of his son and heir. Francis was now nothing at all like the dandy of yore, and Bernardone began, or continued, to find it incomprehensible. Economizing was one thing, but wearing drab, simple clothes was another —and an irritating eccentricity when the wearer was the son of one of the richest bourgeois in Assisi. Soon he would be grumbling about it.

For her part, Pica could only marvel at the transformation of the man who was still her Giovanni, her favorite. Did he confide in his mother? At any rate, he had ideas that she found strangely beautiful. Once when he was dining with her and Bernardone was away, he covered the table with loaves of bread for the poor who would come knocking at the door, for the great famine was still raging. In earlier days he would be on the lookout for his friends to invite to a party; now he was looking for Jesus to come disguised in the rags of poverty. That was how the love of the poor grew and swelled within him.

The Cavern

Sometimes they asked him what was the matter. Nothing, he wanted to be alone, but how could he keep to himself the secret of a love that was devouring his soul? Who would be able to listen to him and understand him?

Only one person, whose name we shall never know. This was a

friend, a mysterious confidant who slipped like an angel into those first days of spiritual drunkenness. The scholars have tried in vain to identify him, but what's the use of grasping after something permanently beyond the reach of human curiosity? The unknown friend listened to Francis's revelation, interrupted now and then by tears of joy. Together with that soul still trembling beneath the touch of God's hand, the friend would leave the town, head into the countryside, and climb Mount Subasio, passing through the black firs to a cavern they both knew, far from the noise of the city. But this time Francis wanted to go alone into the shadows of their refuge. The other man would remain outside as if to ward off the world, safeguarding his prayer. The anonymous companion was truly quite patient and attentive. Did he realize that here was a rare soul on whom he might have some influence? History is silent on all this, but I suspect the stranger might have been someone whom we shall encounter later on.

And if . . . if the friend were only imaginary? I have almost been tempted to think that he existed only in Francis's mind, begotten by his new religious fervor, like the young man who went on a famous journey by coach from Rouen to Paris with a great seventeenth-century visionary, Father Surin . . .

Inside the cave the hours were passing, not in bliss, as before, but in the agony of repentance. Very few men have wept as Francis did. In a flood of tears he reviewed his past, which filled him with horror, and for the first time he became aware of the enormity of sin. Many saints have claimed to be the greatest sinners in the world—and without gaining any credence, even though in a way it was true. People like us cannot properly understand him, we have only a fleeting and faintly disturbing notion of our offenses; but the soul that sees itself as it is (by a terrible grace analogous to the flames of purgatory) will be forever disabused about itself. One would have to be a saint to understand a saint. Trials like those Francis underwent are beyond us and can't be described, but someone who has known suffering can at times conceive of them.

Francis left the cave broken with fatigue and disfigured by sorrow. Nevertheless, more visits followed. They were undoubtedly excruciating, but the day came when the young man reappeared, his face illumined by a smile that said it all: grace rediscovered, the heart surrendered to joy and love, especially love. The greatest sinner was becoming

the greatest lover in the world. And, being Italian, he gave free rein to
his old volubility. He began to talk once more about the princess, the
chosen damsel who was waiting for him. Was he raving as he had
before? Some people thought so.

The Talking Image

What to do with yourself, with your person, with your body and
soul, when you have fallen madly in love with Love? What to make
of the conversion that has pounced upon you? Pray, of course, pray
without ceasing, tell God that you love him. But God does not show
himself, you find him only in silence and solitude.

At certain moments Francis felt an urge to roll on the ground
screaming, to rid himself of that excess of joy that overwhelmed him.
Still, life had to go on, one has to earn a living—by selling cloth, for
example. It is perfectly possible to love God while selling cloth. Francis
seems not to have considered that option, any more than he thought
of becoming a religious, although religious orders were in plentiful
supply. There was a Benedictine monastery in the region.

One day when he was walking in the country, trying, like a good
merchant, to get a clear picture of the situation, he pressed on as far
as an ancient church that was falling into ruin, San Damiano. It was
there that God had been waiting for him all along. A large, tragic
crucifix, painted with touching naiveté, hung above the altar, and it
caught his attention at once. The figure of Christ, with his arms outstretched, had a faraway look, as if his eyes were searching along the
road for someone who had been long in coming. Francis immediately
fell on his knees.

In all Italy there were so many crucifixes, and from seeing them so
often people had become blind to what the crosses were striving to say.
But for Francis that day was not like any other day, and for the first
time, perhaps, he saw the crucifixion. Then he had a sudden revelation
of what the death of Jesus meant. It was as if no one had ever told him
about it before, and his heart was torn with compassion and love, of

love for the man who had let himself be nailed to the wood out of love for him, Francesco di Bernardone, now on his knees, speechless, his face wet with tears.

And amidst a sort of cosmic immobility affecting everything—time, the air, creation itself—the painted image began to speak. How terrifying it must have been, a talking image in an empty church. Frozen with terror and surprise, the young man felt as if he had been snatched from himself and lifted off the ground. How could a picture talk? But he knew that he wasn't dreaming.

The voice said, "Francis, repair my house." From the heart of Christ to the heart of Francis love went back and forth in an indescribable exchange.

When he came to, the young man experienced the desolation of the soul that finds itself back in the created world. After a moment he blessed himself and left, carrying away in his head a phrase he had misunderstood and in his heart the indelible imprint of the crucifixion. It made him suffer so much that when he returned to Assisi he groaned loudly and unrestrainedly over it. But now he realized what he had to do. At last God had clearly revealed his will: He must repair the walls of his imperiled church. The only mistake lay in that lowercase "c": he should have thought "Church," but how could he have?

To Rome, to Rome

Francis got the idea of making a pilgrimage to Rome. Perhaps he wanted to get stirring, to be in motion, body and soul; or he may have felt a mysterious urge whose message he couldn't grasp, an impulse from grace that would lead him up and down the roads of the world. No doubt his father was away on a trip. The opportunity was ripe. Leaving the store in the hands of the clerks, or perhaps of his brother Angelo, he set off on his way. Probably not on horseback—one rather imagines him walking, as he would never cease to do later on. Celano tells us that he borrowed a poor man's rags for the journey, wearing them like a uniform. The army of the have-nots had a new recruit.

Once he arrived in Rome, we can assume he didn't waste his time sightseeing, but went straight to the parvis of Saint Peter's which was thronged with beggars. The church was the long basilica of Constantine, built on the tomb of the apostles Peter and Paul. It had won the admiration of all Christendom with its mysterious shadows, its ornate pavements, and Byzantine mosaics. Francis was now among the poor. He mingled with them as if to be commingled with Jesus Christ; and he was happy, even joyful, our chronicler tells us. He must have found this new situation quite strange, but he congratulated himself, thinking it a windfall. How interesting life was, and how he delighted in the freedom of his heart, which had been released from all the cares of the world. Once so greedy for delicious food, he now ate with pleasure the scraps from his beggar's wallet.

Having finished that little feast, he went into the basilica, up to the altar of Saint Peter, where the faithful lay their offerings—scandalously stingy ones, he thought. Was that how the Prince of the apostles was treated? And with one of those lordly gestures still dear to him, he emptied his purse with a loud clatter into an opening beneath the altar. What generosity! The people stood around him in admiration. A bit confused, he took to his heels and rejoined his friends, the paupers, with whom he spent the rest of the day. One would think that he wanted to disappear among them, vying with them in raggedness, stretching out his hand, his mind possessed by a nameless joy. But why didn't he give that money, or part of it, to the poor who were with him? That is the first question one thinks of, but Francis was full of such contradictions.

A Kiss for the Leper

Once back home, he took up again the way of life that must have seemed so peculiar to his family and friends, to his mother, and also to that person we seldom hear about, his brother Angelo—who did not approve. What had become of the brilliant, self-assured young man whose songs once delighted the neighborhood? What freakish notion had led him to wear the modest outfit he now affected to find to his liking? What did his father think—and what could he do about it? Raising the roof did no good. At the age of twenty-five his son was free to dress as he pleased, provided that he kept a good appearance in the store. But the store already belonged to the past.

We can imagine the confusion caused by this eccentric among a family ensconced in comfort and the bourgeois conventions. Closeted in his room, he spent hours praying when he wasn't going out to visit his new friends, the poor. Wasn't he aware of the uneasiness he stirred up all around him? In the eyes of the world, playing the saint was tacitly condemning people less passionately devout—good Catholics, perhaps, but not given to making a show of it. But then Francis smiled, and his charm disarmed the critics.

Every now and then a cloud would come to darken the young convert's happiness: thoughts that he immediately dispelled but that kept returning anyway with suspicious persistence, arousing a sudden nostalgia for the good life he had been living only yesterday, "in the time of my sinful life," as he would later write. And when an Italian, even a saint, speaks of his sinful life, we know what that means. Where, then, was this sudden distress coming from?

At other times a crazy idea would cross his mind, and stay there. The old hunchbacked woman of Assisi . . . Her deformity made her monstrously ugly, and Francis had gotten it into his head that if he persevered in his life of continence and mortification, one day he would be like her. A more absurd notion could hardly be conceived, but this fixation would not budge. Where did it come from, Francis finally wondered, if not from the devil? And as often happened in his hours of spiritual desolation, the Lord made his voice heard.

Did it ring in the silence like a human voice, or did it speak in secret to the heart of the predestined one? Did he perceive it as a sound coming from the outside or did he grasp it inwardly, like a thought, but so strong and so sweetly imperious a thought that it created the illusion of resounding in the air? Did it make a difference? He knew that voice so well, it had comforted him so many times. It was the very voice of Love, whose inflections were so dear to him. That day it told him about the inner transformation that God awaited from him: "Replace what you still love carnally and vainly with spiritual goods. . . . Prefer bitterness to sweetness if you wish to know me. . . ."

Bitterness? Francis was ready for anything to follow the Lord on the

most disheartening path. At a stroke the demonic temptation faded like
a bad dream, and he was seized with loathing at the memory of the
sensual pleasures with which he had stupefied his youth. This wor-
shipper of beauty, so delicate in his artistic preferences, this aesthete
had overcome the revulsion he once felt at the stench of beggars, their
foul diseases, and the vermin crawling over their flesh and tattered
clothes. Or had he?

He must have had some sort of warning that he could go much
further in facing repugnant things than he already had. Yet he would
not be asked to do the impossible—and it was better not to think about
it. One day when he was riding in the country around Assisi, he heard
the all-too-familiar muffled, leaden sound that put the most stout-
hearted to flight. As if stepping out of the oldest stories in the Bible,
a leper came toward him shaking his clapper. Francis's whole being
revolted, but an irresistible force made him leap down from his horse
and march right up to that bringer of horror. We cannot envision that
moment because we don't know what goes on in a soul subjected to
such an overwhelming trial. We are told that Francis approached the
leper, whose face was one vast sore, took his hand, and placed his
mouth—that once so squeamish mouth—on the leper's rotting flesh.
An immense joy swept over the young man, and his kiss of peace was
immediately returned. Turning back to his horse, he remounted and
wished to glance at the leper but, Celano tells us, he looked in all
directions to no avail: He could see no one. With his heart pounding,
Francis began to sing.

San Damiano

Here begins the great adventure. The contemplative turns to action.
Money—he needed money, and a lot of it, to repair the church. Francis
ran to the store where, luckily, he found his father absent—a detail of
some significance. Bernardone no doubt was away at one of the fairs
to which he used to take his son. In any event, Francis grabbed several
bales of carefully chosen scarlet material, then mounted his horse and

galloped back to Foligno. There he sold both the fabric and the horse and set off on foot without delay.

At San Damiano the priest in charge, a poor old man, was in the church when he saw the door open and Francis appear. The priest knew him well: a good lad who sometimes gave him alms very graciously, but an incorrigible roisterer, living in sin. Assisi blinked the sin, but complained when the young man flung his money around every which way and gave one party after another, when the whole country was ravaged by famine and so many people had barely enough to get by on. Francis bowed, then went up to the priest and kissed his hand. His respect for the clergy was as well-known as his riotous behavior. This time the priest could not help feeling that he looked bizarre. Dressed very simply—where was his usual elegance?—he seemed a bit overexcited and abruptly plunged into an explanation of his visit: He wanted to repair San Damiano. He had all the money needed for that, here, in his purse. Would the lord priest accept it? This hastily delivered speech left the priest flabbergasted. Caught off guard by this sudden invasion of charity, he flatly refused, given the sum involved, which struck him as suspiciously large.

Changing his tactic, Francis revealed to the priest that he had undergone a conversion, that his life had become completely different, and that his plan should be trusted. Here too the priest was recalcitrant and remained skeptical about these sensational but short-lived conversions. Then came pleas and supplications: At least he should let Francis take refuge for a while in the church that he wished to repair. He begged until the priest, out of weariness, agreed; but the priest didn't want any money. Francis's story sounded jumbled and incredible to him. That mattered little to the new convert, who was overjoyed to have won the day. As for the fat, gold-filled purse, he cared no more for it than for a bag of dust. If God wanted none of it, neither did he, and with a final gesture befitting a great lord he tossed the purse disdainfully into the corner of a window.

"Bernardone's Way"

Back home the family was getting worried. Where was Francis? He had disappeared several days before, and while at first they could think this was some escapade quite in line with his eccentric character, by now it seemed too drawn out. When he returned from his trip, his father was informed about what had happened. He went straight to the store, where one quick look told him he was missing some remnants of cloth and, above all, precious scarlet fabrics. In a thundering voice he demanded an explanation. The frightened clerks recounted how signor Francesco had taken it all, rolling it up into bundles and carrying it off on horseback. On horseback! Where? How could they know? He appeared to be in a great hurry—and he left. But where? That way. By now Bernardone was storming about like a hurricane. He did that often enough, but this time his fulminations attracted a crowd of passersby. Young Bernardone was up to his old tricks again. He had taken advantage of his father's absence to ransack the store. And they thought the lad had become so sensible, even pious, always haunting the churches. That's when he was planning his move. Robbery? What else could you call it, even if it was more a question of unscrupulous treatment of a family member?

When the clothier's head cooled, he decided on a course of action and went to rouse his friends and neighbors to scour the countryside and find the thief. That required time. Meanwhile Francis had a good idea that some action would be taken against him, and he was seized with anxiety, especially when he learned from a friend what his father was planning and doing. Who was that friend? Probably the mysterious confidant who had accompanied him to the cave where Francis wept so bitterly over the sins of his youth. He didn't feel secure at San Damiano so, like a hunted animal, he took shelter in a kind of cellar dug behind the apse and hid there for a month, dying with fear. Like a second (preconversion) Saint Paul, Bernardone ranged all over the country outside Assisi, breathing threats and promising slaughter.

Francis came out only when it was strictly necessary. From time to time someone brought him food, which he consumed in the darkness of his den. He prayed, fasted, and begged God to deliver him from his pursuers. We may wonder what sense there was in this pleading—sooner or later he would have to leave his hiding place. Perhaps he was making a sort of retreat there. One day he happened to hear the cries of Bernardone's friends, who were circling San Damiano, convinced that he wasn't far from there and furious because they couldn't unearth him. But grace was working on Francis, who had put his trust wholly and unreservedly in God. This, he realized, was the surest way to solve his problem. It would take a Péguy to explain how the trust we place in God is the Lord's weak point, and that there are weapons he can't resist. But he answers our prayers in his own peculiar way, and that morning his way began by flooding with joy the heart of his beloved child and by making a man of him.

Francis had had his hour of cowardice—here too God was lying in wait for him. He looked upon himself as chicken-livered, and so the new Francis left his refuge and walked back to town, a weakened, emaciated Francis, clothed in rags and almost unrecognizable. As soon as he appeared in Assisi, he was greeted with a volley of insults, followed by a volley of rocks and mud that smeared his face. At the same time the cry rang out that would soon take on a prophetic meaning, "Pazzo! Pazzo!" Madman. He was God's fool presenting himself to the world. As the one whom he loved so much had done, he kept silent in the face of the human hounds baying at him; lost in prayer, he marched forward. Such was the glorious entrance of Saint Francis of Assisi into his age.

Bernardone: The Author Tries to Understand

Bernardone was home waiting for news and champing at the bit. The whole affair had been going on for a month. He had bled himself white (but then he was a very full-blooded man) for that boy who was turning out so badly. All that money spent to revel with the young lords, to mix with the nobility, because that would shed some luster on the plebeian family name. But it wasn't enough. Then came the suit of armor, indispensable for Francis in order to become a knight and invade the upper classes. And he had gotten his armor—and sold it by fraud—groaned the eternal provider of funds. The price of a large farm. But, however stupidly that fortune had been squandered, one hope still remained: the cloth business. That swindler Francis was, despite everything, a born salesman, with his exquisite manners, his aristocratic airs, and his knack for inveigling clients without seeming to, giving the impression that he was doing them a favor parting with the rare and beautiful material he had set aside for himself. A special favor . . . What a thrashing *he* had saved up as a favor to Francis, if he could ever get his hands on him.

It was a sort of consolation just to think about it. Because he couldn't forget those bales of fabric impudently stolen from the store. Heaven owed him vengeance. That was his state of mind when he suddenly heard a loud buzz of voices from a nearby street. Shouts. A riot? Everything was peaceable in Assisi at the moment. The sounds of angry people came closer. Bernardone glanced outside.

What he saw took his breath away. There was a man in rage being followed by young people and even children who were throwing stones at him and shouting, "Crazy!" Francis. There was no mistaking him: It was he, that horrible beggar, that miserable wretch, now publicly dishonoring his father. That was the limit. Swept by a gust of anger that sent the blood rushing to his head, he flung himself down the stairs, rage agreeably unleashing his energies. A kind of savage pleasure seized him at the sight of his victim only a few steps in front of him. He was going to "punish" him. The saliva ran down his chin —what does the wolf do when he sees the sheep? He drools.

What followed was horrible. Perhaps without knowing it, the clothier had made himself the instrument of the devil, who was furious at the escape of a chosen soul he had been so patiently besieging. Bernardone made a path for himself through the crowd and charged his son. He began by staggering him with repeated slaps in the face, then took him by the hair and dragged him all the way inside his house. There, as Pica watched in horror, he threw him into a closet, chained him up, and beat him unmercifully, "to reconvert him to the charms of the world by bruising his body," as Saint Bonaventure remarks. We rub our eyes, but the text is there, with its heavy-handed innocence bordering on black humor.

Nevertheless, his father soon realized such methods were of little use and, besides, he had business calling him up north. He left the key to his domestic dungeon with his wife and went off. We can't help thinking of Bluebeard. Once she was left alone with her beloved son, Pica set about reasoning tenderly with him—through the door. She so much wanted to see everything come to an amiable conclusion, even after those agitated preliminaries, but Francis showed a meekness tempered with iron. Finally, overcome by love, Pica give him his freedom and supplied him with some clothes to replace the tattered ones he was wearing.

Leaving his childhood home forever, Francis went back to his first refuge near San Damiano. What plans did he have in mind? The future was still hidden from view, but he knew one thing with certainty: He could no longer live except entirely in God.

Time passed, then Bernardone reappeared on the scene like a nightmare, demanding to know where Francis was and raining a storm of insults on his wife for letting him go. That must have given him a little relief. But he still had a score to settle with his heir, and he rushed to San Damiano. It was now known where the solitary was living, but the Francis he confronted was a new man. Calmly and firmly the gentle rebel declared that all violence was useless: He would never go back home. This time the clothier understood. Still he pounded away at the old sore point, shouting with the intensity of a man who has sustained an injury to his property: "My money!"

Yes, of course, the purse full of gold that Francis had thrown into a corner at San Damiano, on the window ledge. It was still there. The priest hadn't touched it. A long sigh of relief issued from Bernardone's fatherly chest.

Let us try to see the situation from the clothier's standpoint. He is usually charged with having been an extremely malicious person, and sometimes he was, but not always. A puny child, Francis was very dear to him and, along with Pica, he surrounded his son with loving attention. With an indulgence that bordered on weakness, he smoothed the way to a happy adolescence and young manhood for Francis, because he was proud of him. He overlooked Francis's craziest whims (there were a few of them) and troubled himself over him well past his legal majority at age sixteen. He had paid out gold to get him out of the prisons of Perugia; later on he was unstinting with his presents to him. He grumbled but, with that unpredictable generosity peculiar to misers, he always paid. And it must be said, in his own way he loved his son. This had lasted until Francis's twenty-fifth year, and what did he have to show for it? Suddenly he found himself face to face with a semimadman, an incompetent, in short—the word must have had its equivalent in Umbrian—a loser, a not very honest failure who took off after grabbing some bales of precious fabric to turn them into cash at Foligno. Pica maintained that her son was a saint, but women were idiots.

Bernardone had resolved on dragging "the saint" before the town consuls, to make him appear in a court of law and renounce his inheritance. There was no excuse for his fit of sadistic fury, but how could he understand a man as profoundly inscrutable as his own son? The people on the street cried, "Crazy!" They had a point.

For the moment we are still at San Damiano, and the gold-filled purse is still there on the windowsill. Whom did it belong to? Here the difficulties began. Thomas of Celano, in the first volume of his biography, tells us that when he went to Foligno and sold "all his merchandise, as usual," including his horse, Francis "sold all his property and lost all interest in money." We would like to believe it, because that jibes with the conventional idea of a saint, but the priest of San Damiano "refused the money for fear of his parents" (from Celano's second volume). Later the bishop of Assisi declared that this ill-gotten money could not be used for any sacred purpose and advised Francis to restore to his father the sum he had wished to devote to repairing the church.

Saint Bonaventure saw the situation differently. According to him, the father "found the purse in the corner of the window, which calmed him down. But it was not enough to have stripped Francis of his money . . . he wished to drag him before the bishop. . . ." Perhaps Francis considered that what belonged to his father also belonged to him—and from a legal point of view he was partly right—or perhaps he wasn't thinking about anything in particular when he made off with the cloth, except that he needed the money to restore the church, whose walls were caving in, as the Lord had asked him. But he certainly never thought that he was stealing. And the purse was there, keeping its secret, on the ledge of the little window.

The Great Refusal

Still drunk with rage and, as he believed, sure that he was right, Bernardone had decided to act, and he hastened to the palace of the commune, where he registered a complaint with the consuls against his son so as to force him to return the stolen money. On the order of the consuls, a herald went to advise Francis to present himself before them. "By the grace of God," Francis answered, "I am now free, and the servant of the Most High God alone." And he refused to appear. His sublime response threw the human system of justice into a good deal of confusion. But since he was in God's service, strictly speaking he was no longer under the jurisdiction of the civil authorities; and the consuls yielded. The bishop was the last resort. Bernardone had carefully considered that possibility, and he must have hesitated. With those churchmen you never knew what theological muddle you were going to get tangled up in, especially since the case involved fixing up a church. But he had no other recourse.

To the bishop's palace, then. Bernardone registered his complaint. He wanted no more and no less than that Francis renounce his rights as heir and restore what he still possessed. A wise and prudent man, but deeply attached to the goods of this world, Monsignor Guido, the bishop of Assisi, formally summoned Francis. He was only too willing to obey, because "the lord bishop is a father and master of souls," and Francis was the most dutiful of Christians. The prince of the Church received him with joy and delivered a short speech that was a model of tact and good sense. "You have scandalized your father. If you wish to serve God, return to him the money that you possess. Perhaps it was ill-gotten" (a fine touch, that "perhaps") "and God does not want you to use it for sacred things. Have confidence, act like a man. As for San Damiano, God will provide. *Dominus providebit.*"

There could not have been a better way to transform Francis into an ardent soldier for Christ. His head was spinning a bit as he stood before the crowd of curious onlookers assembled to watch the scene in the public square, not far down from his father's house, in front of Santa Maria Maggiore, the site of the episcopal palace, which had been built over the ancient resident of the poet Propertius, that voluptuous admirer of beauty. But what in the world did Francis have to fear? Without a word he tore off his clothes in hot haste and threw them, one item after another, at his father's feet—everything including his breeches and, to top it off, the damned purse that he had simply brought with him, hidden in one of his pockets. Now he was as naked as on the day he was born. Naked today for his second birth.

After the uproar of a moment before, the spectators fell silent. Then they saw something that moved them to tears—the hair shirt that this erstwhile dandy was now wearing against his skin. He would keep it forever. It was a hideous penitential device of horsehair for killing the instinct of sensuality and chastising the flesh day and night.

The whole episode was somewhat theatrical, of course, but Francis could not resist the urge for spectacular gestures that made him the center of attention. He had been that way since childhood, when he had to be first, the cynosure. And now this weakness was at the behest of a furious sincerity that came close to insanity. Lunatics suffer from a compulsion to strip themselves naked, and he too felt like a lunatic, crazy with anger and love; and in a delirium of enthusiasm he cried out, with a master's authority: "Listen, listen, everyone. From now on I can say with complete freedom, 'Our Father who art in heaven.' Pietro Bernardone is no longer my father, and I am giving him back not only his money—here it is—but all my clothes as well." And the last words he shouted had the sound of the Magnificat, "I shall go naked to meet the Lord."

Just as stunned as the crowd, the bishop wept and, taking the young man in his arms, wrapped him in his cope. Thus the Church took possession of one of her greatest sons. While the crowd looked on in disapproval, his father left with his property, but with sorrow in his heart. It was April 10, 1206.

They could find no better clothes for Francis than a gardener's shirt and torn overcoat that had been thrown in the rubbish, but he gratefully accepted them and later traced a cross on his new outfit with a piece of chalk.

Where to go now? He decided to leave Assisi for several days and to seek refuge at Gubbio, where he had a friend, no doubt from his prison days in Perugia. He had a choice between the highway and a path through the forest; and he chose the trees so he could sing of his overflowing happiness beneath their brotherly canopy. He sang, naturally, in French, the language that poured from his heart at such moments.

Then, as if in an opera, some brigands sprang out in front of him. They had heard him singing far off, and they were extremely disappointed to discover, not a rich man but a sort of beggar. Since he didn't have a penny to his name, they ripped off his cloak, leaving him nothing but his shirt, and asked him who he was. "I am the herald of the great King!" That grandiose reply gave the scoundrels a hearty laugh. Then several of them took hold of our herald and with savage gaiety threw him into a ditch full of snow. Francis prudently waited till they had gone off, and finally clambered out of the ditch. Then, trembling with the cold, he burst out laughing and began to sing again, his heart full of mysterious joy.

A Brief Parenthesis

In one of the secrets that he shared with others (many of which have come down to us), Francis revealed that from the day of his conversion he was continuously sick. Maybe that was the price of an extraordinary grace, but he had had more than one conversion before this one. He had given himself and taken himself back until the crucial moment when he stripped in the public square. Then the sinner faded, giving way to the saint. Till now it is the sinner whom we have tried to follow and understand. We had the feeling of coming close to his truth because we were at home with his weaknesses. We were part of the family, but from the moment when God seized hold of him, the man underwent a kind of simplification, and we sometimes lose sight of him. To borrow a phrase from Dante, he hides himself in the light. He is quite close to us because of his charity, and infinitely far off because of his indescribable inner transformation. Still, the hand he stretches out to us keeps all its human warmth, and his gentle Italian voice infallibly finds its way to our heart.

To get back to the scene of the stripping, in an age when shame had not yet been confused with prudery, this act was one of the forms of public penance. To strip himself of the external signs of wealth, of the clothes in which he had tasted all the pleasures of the world—and the pleasure of a fine appearance meant a good deal to him—to abandon the pride of his youth, showed everyone that Francis violently repudiated his entire past. The renunciation in the presence of the crowd was in itself, according to the medieval mentality, a juridical act. From now on, Francis, with nothing to his name, was taking sides with the outcast and the disinherited.

The Benedictine Welcome

Naked again, except for the shirt the brigands had left him, perhaps from some vestigial sense of humanity, and frozen to the bone, Francis nonetheless sang the praises of the Lord in the forest. Would he go all the way to Gubbio dressed like that in such cold? The countryside had suffered from late winter floods that year, and the roads were covered with water and the last of the snow. He remembered a Benedictine monastery thereabouts. The monks would surely welcome the drolly clad wanderer, but his period of disillusionment was beginning. Francis made a bad impression on the monk who opened the door. But wasn't admitting a poor man the same as receiving Jesus?

They gave him a crude smock, practically a long stableboy's blouse, and they sent him to the kitchen to wash the dishes. There at least he wouldn't be cold, but at the moment it was hunger that tormented him. They offered him a piece of bread to dunk in a little greasy water reserved for the pigs. That would enable him to hold on for a few days, then he decided to leave, and the door was opened wide for him. History reports, to the honor of Saint Benedict, that not long afterward the prior apologized for himself and for the monks when he learned that he had been sheltering a saint. One hardly knows which is sadder, the welcome or the excuses, but Francis generously and lovingly forgave them.

At Gubbio, Francis found the man he was looking for, an old friend who showed some humanity and dressed him in a tunic and belt, put sandals on his feet, and gave him a pilgrim's staff. Was he an old fellow reveler? One would like to think so, but more likely they had met as captives in the dungeons of Perugia.

We have only thin evidence of Francis's comings and goings in the subsequent weeks. He couldn't stand still. It was as if, wanting only to follow the Lord, he adopted an invisible itinerary that led him where he was sure to meet him and, just as he had kissed him in the person of a leper that day out on the road, he now went to a hospice for lepers to find him again. He was taken on as an attendant for poor invalids.

The supernatural joy that possessed him when he washed those tortured creatures who frightened everyone is something we can't conceive. It went beyond the abnegation and devotion common in those who consecrate their lives to human suffering. Saint Bonaventure, who spares us no detail, says that Francis removed portions of rotten flesh, stanched the flow of pus, and went so far as to kiss the wounds the way he would have kissed the wounds of Christ, placing his mouth on mouths eaten away by the dreadful disease; but it was on the Christ in them that he lavished those marks of love, which were repaid a hundredfold.

Here we feel ourselves to be in an unimaginable world, simply because we belong to a different species of soul, and the notions we have of sanctity are foggy ones. But there is some value in pressing as far as the frontier of mystical horror to grasp the personality of the man who sent shock waves through Christendom.

San Damiano Revisited

Francis didn't forget the poor church that the Lord, as he thought, had told him to repair; so, leaving the lepers out of obedience, he went back to San Damiano to begin work there. But the purse full of golden coins was no longer on the window ledge, and building materials cost money. That was a problem, but not for him. With a simplicity that still amazes us, Francis followed the evangelical counsel to the letter and, trusting in God's promise, he asked so as to receive. But how does one go about begging for stones?

He began going up and down the streets of Assisi, crying out, "Whoever gives me a stone will get a reward from the Lord. Whoever gives me two will get two rewards. Whoever gives me three, will get three rewards." The first response was stunned surprise. So, to start things rolling, he sang of God with that charming voice known to everyone in town. There may have been some smiles and snide remarks, but the unexpected question and the sweet, joyful melody finally took effect; and the stones appeared, one here, another there. A short while ago they were throwing stones to insult and hurt him—with a perhaps obscure sense of revenging themselves on someone who had long gotten the upper hand on everybody with his foolish escapades and his charm—and now they were bringing them to him like presents. Big ones and little ones, he accepted everything, returning to San Damiano with his harvest of rocks on his shoulders, exhausted but happy. Once again the Gospel, taken literally, showed the effective power of prayer. The method was so simple, he wondered why people didn't try it.

The rougher work of repairing crumbled walls was still to be done, but here Francis showed he was an old hand, having been well trained by the people of Assisi when he helped build the town walls after the fortress had been demolished. He had, so to speak, done his apprenticeship as a mason and navvy. And as he sang then in the exultation of victory, he sang now of the joy of obeying what he thought was the Savior's wish.

Too old to lend him a hand, the priest was nonetheless moved by such rare and zealous faith. He was a Benedictine from the monastery of Subasio, and it may be questioned whether he was any less decrepit than his church. In any event, he took it upon himself to feed the volunteer who at first was grateful to receive that sign of charity, but when he noticed that the old religious was preparing fancy dishes for him, he politely refused and decided to go beg his bread like a true son of Lady Poverty.

People were hardly fond of beggars, but as a sop to their conscience some of them often gave him whatever leftovers they had; it was highly unappetizing stuff. Francis accepted everything with effusive thanks, but one day, looking at what had been thrown into his bowl, he thought he would vomit. Nature had not yet been overcome. He bravely got hold of himself and ate. His reward was instantaneous: He had barely touched that filthy food with his tongue when its taste became delicious.

Meanwhile at San Damiano curious passersby would stop to watch the busy worker who sang all by himself as he laid the stones in place. They belonged to that race of humans who find nothing more interesting than seeing their neighbors work. But this particular neighbor had

other ideas, and with that uniquely engaging manner of his he invited
the loafers (speaking in French) to do a little manual labor for the Lord.
Some laughed and went on their way. Others, astonished to recognize
in this pious, jovial mason the elegant libertine of bygone days, felt
gripped with emotion, as if in the presence of a mystery, and came over
to help him. Francis even managed, it is said, to form a team of volunteer workmen, but that's giving a lot of credit to casual generosity. Soon
the walls had been raised again. He had started work in the beginning
of September 1206, and by the time he was finished, he felt he had put
things to rights with God on the score of the church. In reality everything remained to be done.

Naturally he had to continue his job of restoring ruined churches.
With a beaver's instinct he would go wherever the walls were threatening to collapse. First San Pietro, a chapel near one of his father's properties, in the plain of Assisi where, as a young man, he often went to get
some fresh air on the hottest summer afternoons, a spot we can locate,
thanks to the testament of his nephew. And the narrow path that led
to this chapel led in the other direction to San Damiano, as if the happy
days of his youth were bracketed by those two churches. Later there
would be la Portiuncula. The first, San Damiano, and the third, la
Portiuncula, were each destined to play a critical role in his great
human adventure.

At Home, Continued

In strong contrast to all this was the atmosphere in Bernardone's
home, where old Pietro raged in his heart from morning to night, now
in somber silence, now giving vent to sudden bursts of indignation.
Given the disaster that had struck the family, it was cold comfort to
have recovered his money. His son, for whom he had hoped such great
things, had become an object of scandal, the laughingstock of the
whole town. Still more irritating than any of this was the pity Francis
had aroused in a handful of well-meaning souls and (the last straw for

the exasperated clothier) the remarks now beginning to go around about the virtues of that good-for-nothing—and what else was Francis? At twenty-five, and counting, he was behaving like a hysterical brat.

His young brother Angelo took a calmer and much more ironic view of the situation. He was a sarcastic type. For him Francis remained the family scatterbrain, the reveler, now pretending to be converted and playing the saint. So Angelo bided his time until the day when he would meet Francis in the street or elsewhere; then he would deflate that windbag with a sharp little arrow—nothing mean sounding, just a little innocent phrase, in the devout style, but with a lethal edge to it. Actually this whole business had done Angelo no harm at all, since the ousting of his elder brother had made him his father's sole heir.

As for his mother, she was crying her heart out. To Bernardone, whimpering was a woman's affair, and Pica did not stint herself. Those stifled sobs were aggravating but only to be expected.

Encounters in the street with Francis were inevitable. When their paths did cross, one would like to think that Bernardone had an abrupt, unexpected change of heart. Quite the contrary, as soon as he caught sight of his son, he vigorously cursed him. We don't know what Francis said in reply. Perhaps he kept silent and moved on, but the incident was repeated several times. Francis, who was dressed like a pauper, was met by his father's curse in the presence of scandalized onlookers, and he must have suffered from it, because he finally thought up a way to diminish the sadness of those painful scenes. He ordered a beggar named Albert, chosen for his venerable appearance and paid half the alms Francis took in, to adopt him as his son and to accompany him on his rounds through the town. Every time they ran into the clothier and Bernardone uttered his usual curse, Albert would make the sign of the cross over his adopted son and give him his blessing, thus turning aside the evil words of the unnatural father. Francis would then say to Bernardone, "Do you think that God can't give me a father to bless me and undo your curses?" That strange scene surprised the people of Assisi and touched them.

It didn't touch Angelo at all, however. He was waiting to shoot his poisoned arrow, and he got the chance one winter morning when he met his brother, clothed in rags and shivering as he prayed. Speaking in a loud voice, Angelo said to a neighbor, "So ask Francis to sell you some of his sweat for a farthing!" The answer came back in French without hesitation, joyful, smiling: "I have already sold it to the Lord."

The Narrow Way

Francis knew well that the way to God does not pass through consolations. The shortest path is suffering, which leads right to him. The supernatural joy that welled up in him was accompanied by sickness and inner mortifications, which he accepted as a grace. Not that he didn't have to do battle occasionally: The old Adam took forever to die. Self-love in particular had at least nine lives. One day when Francis went to beg oil for the little church of San Damiano, he found himself in front of a house where he was about to knock on the door when through a half-opened window he saw (with a jolt) a group of men among whom he recognized some old fellow revelers. For them the feast was still going on—without him. They were singing and dancing and getting ready to play after having enjoyed a sumptuous dinner. He saw all that, and as he watched, a flood of memories swept over him with extraordinary force, especially when the music did its part. Overcome with shame, he didn't dare to enter the house and, blushing violently, he went off. How close that moment of weakness brings him to us.

In the moments of cruel uncertainty that followed, he accused himself of cowardice and, making an about-face, he ran all the way back to the house. There he humbly made admission of his fault. We can imagine the scene: the amazement of the passersby who had no idea what was going on, the little man in rags with his heart pounding as he struggled valiantly within himself against the demon of pride. When he had regained his composure, he walked into the midst of the players and made his request in French—because he was Francesco, the Frenchman, and speaking French with his erstwhile companions was the natural thing to do.

They heard him out in silence. It must have been extremely awkward. They could not believe their eyes: this beggar, the prince of youth, the *dominus* of yesteryear, was now asking them to give him some oil for the love of God. They could hardly refuse it to him, but then what could they say to this peculiar character whose presence stirred up in them a world of memories? Beneath the rags his charm was as powerful as ever. He took the oil they gave him after a moment's delay; he thanked them with his habitual courtesy and withdrew. God, who asks us to do hard things, gives at the same time the courage to accomplish them.

The repercussions of the great scene before the bishop and the crowd in Assisi had not yet faded into oblivion. That spectacular farewell to the goods of this world made the young Bernardone someone exceptional. They watched his every movement, as he went about town with a beggar's bowl, singing the praises of the Lord. Others got their bread by hard work; he humbly asked to be given his. And once again they began to laugh and, worst of all, to smile, because there can be indulgent gaiety in a laugh, but a smile harbors contempt. His clothes, his walking stick, his sandals, that belt around his loins made him a target for the irony of the skeptics. He had, of course, repaired the walls of a little church, but not all by himself; he had gotten help. He had good intentions; he did good work. Now they wondered where all that was leading. So did he, perhaps.

Why not restore the life of another church, one as badly off as San Damiano? There was no shortage of them in the region. He resolved to take them one after the other, like a doctor going from patient to patient. The first was San Pietro, near the ramparts, a modest church and still standing. Some biographers think he had some architectural talent, and he may have—Italians are often gifted that way.

One day Francis was walking in a forest of oaks when he discovered an old shrine, twenty-three feet by ten; used only by foresters and vinedressers, it lay deserted. This chapel belonged to the Benedictines under the name of Our Lady of the Angels, later to be called Our Lady of la Portiuncula; that is, "of the little space," or "of the little benefice," because it was an oratory for a handful of the faithful. God, who was waiting for him everywhere, was waiting for him here to speak explicitly to him. But did Francis realize that he was placing his foot on the threshold of the human glory he no longer wanted?

With his usual energy he set to work, and out of devotion to the Holy Virgin he decided to live as a hermit in the very place where she was venerated. The repairs were all but finished. A monk from Mount Subasio came, at Francis's request, to say early morning mass. One time, on the feast of Saint Matthias, the priest read to him the passage from the Gospel where Jesus sends his apostles out to preach and gives them a rule of conduct. "Take no gold, nor silver, nor copper in your belts, no bag for your journey, nor two tunics, nor sandals, nor a staff. . . . And preach as you go, saying, 'The Kingdom of Heaven is at hand.' " Those words made Francis tremble as if a voice had fallen from heaven into his ear. When mass was over, he asked the priest to explain Jesus' discourse point by point; and as the meaning of those brief, peremptory phrases became clearer, he felt enfolded in joy. The message he had waited so long for had finally arrived. And he cried out, "That's what I want; that's what I desire with all my soul!"

Suddenly he threw away his walking stick, his sandals, his cloak, his leather belt. The Gospel had been revealed to him in all its dazzling brightness. At once he became the disciple of Christ. But hadn't he known the Gospel? He had heard it many times since his childhood, but the book has a peculiar feature: You can listen to it year after year, and then a moment comes when from out of its pages comes a soundless, but deafening, voice that you will never be able to silence.

Conditions in the Church

Francis's filial love for the Church of Rome remains one of the most striking aspects of his character. From his youth till the day he died, his fidelity to it never wavered. He may have hesitated on the road to his conversion, but he had no doubts about an institution that Christ himself said was on the point of collapsing—an idea the young convert couldn't understand. Paradoxically, his very faith resisted such a message. That San Damiano might come crashing down was evident, but not the Church. That was unthinkable. It was there forever, until the end of time. The Church was the Church as permanently as the sky was the sky.

Yet he couldn't have been blind to the facts. Any picture one draws of the Church in the year 1200 would have to be, by and large, very dark. There is no need to look for proof of this among the Church's enemies; we have plenty of evidence from within Catholicism, beginning with the many papal bulls issued by Innocent III against the most scandalous abuses. But if the pope was worried about the general decay in Europe, his comminatory bulls could do little to stop the usury, the venality, the gluttony and sexual excesses of many priests, even in the monasteries. Scandal was everywhere. There was unheard of luxury in the Church, luxury and lust. People sang songs mocking lecherous monks. Defrocked clerics gadded about and burst into song, blasting church dignitaries. The Latin verses of these goliards were often admirable. The *Carmina Burana* found an echo in Dante's *Inferno,* if only in Canto XIX, which deals with simony. Faith itself was stricken. Cardinal Jacques de Vitry turned his eyes toward the Eastern Church and asked some troublesome questions.

There were plenty of faithful Christians, to be sure. Francis knew some perfect priests, but he was also aware that the Church was passing through a period of critical disturbances. If he hadn't noticed it himself, then the itinerant preachers from the north, from Lyon and Milan, would have enlightened him, with their constant complaints about the damage done to the episcopacy by the taste for riches, to which they opposed evangelical poverty. There was no gainsaying them on this point, but Francis held on for the same reason that the common people, for the most part, would not give in on the essential item: For all its excesses the Church still had the power of the keys, to open the gates of paradise by absolving sins. Francis remained unshakably Catholic all his life.

He had known at least three perfect priests. In his childhood there was the old canon of Saint George's, who told the story of Saint George and turned the attentive youngster toward the ideal of chivalry that he never abandoned. Then came the priest of San Damiano, who knew the young man so well and who was the first to realize that the Francis who stood before him, searching for Christ, was a transformed person.

The third one was that Benedictine from Subasio who came to say mass for him every day at la Portiuncula. It was dawn on February 24, 1208. The murmur of the Latin words barely broke the silence in the little Romanesque church lost in the midst of the oaks. The priest read the Gospel by the light of two candles. Francis noticed the verses, still a mystery to him, about the first disciples' way of life. Soon the monk would reveal their meaning to him. Now the decisive moment had come; the mass was over, the candles snuffed out, the door opened, and Francis was on his way.

The Other

From that moment on Francis was a different person. All the theologians in the world put together couldn't describe this transformation of the inner man, which is not subject to the canons of classical psychology. Francis gave way to Christ. He remained a human being but he was possessed by Christ. Yesterday's Francis, dying of love, had surrendered.

What we usually mean by "conversion" is simply a change in attitude. Someone renounces this or that—not without a struggle—because he has accepted a credo that excludes all wrongful acts, but the inner man hasn't changed. He controls his concupiscences, but he remains a man of concupiscence. There has been no substitution of one person for another. In the case of Francis there was.

And now, what was this new Francis going to do? His first concern was to make himself a plain tunic out of coarse material and, to spell out the meaning of his mission, he cut it in the form of a cross. Thus clad in something like the armor of God, barefoot, his loins belted with a cord, he returned to Assisi and began to speak. In his high, clear voice that carried so far, he addressed the whole town. The words surged up by themselves from his heart, which was full of the love he wished to share with everyone. God was mad with love for each one of the people met by this little man with burning eyes.

They listened to him with astonishment. He expressed himself so simply and so passionately, with words so direct and right that everyone took them as meant for himself. Many people followed him, marveling that Francis spoke a language so different from the sermons condescendingly dropped on them from the pulpit on Sunday. No more throwing rocks at him and shouting, *"Pazzo!"* He was saying something new. Where had he learned all that?—once all he knew was love songs. What had happened to him?

He was on familiar ground with the people of Assisi. He wasn't speaking to frighten them, but to announce the peace and joy of the Good News—*"Pace e bene!"*—like the fanatic they used to hear crying in the streets. And yet, when he looked at them and urged them to repent—and quickly, because the time was short—their hearts beat with a vague unrest. No one judged himself guilty, and paradoxically they all felt targeted because of that man who moved about among them and, with the most ordinary, everyday words, not the discourse of learned theologians, repeated to them that God loves sinners and hates only sin.

Admiration soon turned into enthusiasm, which is contagious. It may have been at this time, or later on, that a young man whose name we shall never know, perhaps a boy barely in his teens, one of those simple, mysterious souls who never argue with grace, wanted to take the same path as Francis and find peace with him. This was really his first disciple. The biographers scarcely mention him, but he was the first, and he remains next to Francis like a luminous shadow.

By the Ways of the World

It was still wintertime, but there was Francis out in the streets and on the roads, greeting people, wishing them peace and joy, and preaching. The word *preach* is ill-chosen and smells of boredom. To begin with, preaching required a great deal of study. There were many preachers in Umbria, including Cathars and Waldensians, some of whom were talented. And there were always audiences curious to hear them. These peripatetic preachers had their heads full of theological controversies. For his part, Francis knew nothing except for some

words of Christ he had lovingly remembered and would repeat to
anyone willing to listen, with a fervor and humility that brought tears
to the eyes of men and women because they had the impression that
the words were coming not from that man's mouth, but from the
mouth of of the one who had uttered them in Galilee for the very first
time.

It seems evident, however, that for Francis, speaking to the people
as he walked along was not enough. He had to give a sermon—in a
church. Out of instinctive fidelity to his childhood, he selected the
chapel of his school where the old priest used to talk to the class about
the life of the saints and Saint George in particular. How does one go
about giving a sermon? He didn't know, but his natural eloquence
helped. He had fallen in love with God, and what should a lover speak
about if not his love? If he speaks dully, he bores his audience; if he's
inspired, he makes them love too. This is what explains Francis's immediate success. We may doubt that he got up into the pulpit. The pulpit
was made for the learned and their lofty style, but Francis didn't use
big words. A child could understand him. Everybody understood him
when he spoke very simply of the greatest mystery of all, God's love
for everyone in the world. No one was excepted, even the wicked, even
the worst of them. He believed what he said, and he believed it with
such force that the people hearing him were overwhelmed. Sunday
sermons didn't disturb anyone, while this little man so miserably
dressed, with nothing remarkable at all about his appearance, but with
a gleam in his eye as if his soul was on fire, captured their passionate
attention because he seemed to make everything change around him.
The world was no longer the same; nobody was the same or felt the
same. Something had happened. When the parish priest spoke, venerable as he was, nothing happened. It was impossible to explain. And
when the little man went away, they wondered if it was really the
clothier's son or someone else whom they had heard. And it *was* someone else.

A Witness Above Suspicion

After the very first companion, who has remained unknown (almost as if all those who would love Francis down through the centuries should recognize themselves in that vanished face), the first disciple we know about was a rich citizen of Assisi, Bernard of Quintavalle, an important person, a doctor of both civil and canon law at the University of Bologna. He lived in an imposing manor; he was a member of the lesser nobility, but highly respected. His conversion was far from sudden, which is what makes it interesting to us. He was hit by a bombshell, but in slow motion, as it were.

All the stir caused by Francis and his conversion fascinated him. The new self-made pauper had endured affronts from the mockers and cynics. He had not been spared insults nor rocks nor the mud that was sometimes hurled along with them. He accepted it all with the incomprehensible humility that exasperates the world and provokes contempt. Bernard observed these things and wondered. If Francis was pretending, where did he find the strength to persevere? Nagged by doubt and feeling pity for the poor "fool," he offered his house as a refuge one evening and asked Francis to dine with him.

The invitation was so courteous that Francis accepted. It must have been repeated several times because a friendship ripened that would later blossom magnificently when Francis began to preach. But here too Bernard de Quintavalle was very prudent, not the sort of man to make commitments lightly. In one of those turnabouts so frequent with the masses, hostility toward Francis gave way to respect and then to infatuation and almost to love.

How to get a clear perspective on all this? Bernard had undoubtedly had long conversations with "his" poor man, who spoke from the heart with overwhelming sincerity—but it was so easy to get carried away; to present, without realizing it, a flattering, even edifying image of oneself; to be fooled by empty words.

A serious character and Francis's elder, Quintavalle wanted to make a personal, rational judgment about his guest; and so a little after

Francis's first sermon he had recourse to one of those pious stratagems that first alienate us from him, but whose results would prove him right. When Francis slept at Bernard's house, his host used to put up a bed for him in his own room where at night a lamp was kept burning.

Curious by nature, distrustful, an attentive observer, Bernard was at last in a good position to discover the whole truth about Francis. After a reasonable amount of time, he pretended to fall asleep. Some people listen behind doors or look through the keyhole, which is an inexhaustible source of information—the best, according to one English novelist. Quintavalle took a different approach: He began to snore. Then he saw Francis slip out of bed and kneel down, his eyes raised to heaven and his hands lifted in prayer, and then he heard him murmur, "God! God!" In the soft light of the little lamp Quintavalle watched that man whose body was already worn out by austerities. Beneath the crude garment that he never took off there was not much left of the "king of youth." And now those stifled cries—they were not meant to be heard by anyone but God, and each time they struck the indiscreet witness full in the chest like a loud knock on the door. He was listening to a dialogue of love. The answer was contained in the exclamation itself. The cry of love of man for God mingled with God's cry of love for man. Everything else faded away around that exchange which was penetrated with the terror of a mystery. "I love you," said the creature and his Creator together, united and fused, so to speak, into each other. Bernard was afraid. "God!" Francis repeated, in a sort of drunken ecstasy.

This lasted until daybreak. Neither Francis nor his host had slept, but Quintavalle had felt his heart change. That morning, in a few words that have come down to posterity, he declared to Francis, "I am completely resolved in my heart to abandon the world and to follow you in whatever you bid me."

A stunning conversion, even more so than Francis's, which had been long and laborious, with hesitations and flights from Love, distraught returns followed by fresh betrayals, and then the final capitulation wrung from him by main force. Quintavalle surrendered at the first stroke, like a child. This rich man and prominent citizen sent everything packing, entrusting his will to the hands of a poor ignoramus who knew nothing but God.

And suddenly prudence shifted to the other side. Now it was Francis who decided to reflect on such a serious and difficult decision. Wouldn't it be better to take counsel? With whom? With the Lord, of course, who would tell them what he wanted through the Gospel. They would open the book at random three times. This form of bibliomancy was very common in the Middle Ages and has survived to our own day.

A friend of Quintavalle, also a jurist but much less wealthy, Peter of Catania—whom certain texts call a cathedral canon, which might be purely honorific, because his name hasn't been found among the canons in the cathedral register for those years—expressed the desire to join them, as they were about to leave for the nearest church, San Nicolò. There they heard mass, and when the church had emptied, they asked the priest for permission to consult the Gospel that was still resting on the lectern.

The book was opened first to Saint Matthew: "If you would be perfect, go, sell what you possess and give to the poor, and you will have treasure in heaven; and come, follow me" (Matt. 19:21). It was a crucially important verse that left no room for qualifications. The second time the book gave the necessary details: "Take nothing for your journey, no staff, nor bag, nor bread, nor money. . . ." This was the same verse (Luke 9:3) that the Benedictine had commented on at la Portiuncula; the reiteration must have had a powerful effect on Francis. Everything had been foreseen on the practical level. Finally, the third time, came the most difficult, one might almost say the most impossible, counsel: "If any man would come after me, let him deny himself and take up his cross daily and follow me" (Luke 9:23). Here we leave the realm of earth to grapple with the absolute. Abandonment of self, the ultimate form of wealth, and the most tyrannical.

Francis then had a burst of inspiration that proclaimed his whole spiritual ideal: "Here is your life, here is the counsel Christ gives us, here is our rule and the rule of all those who would come with us."

If we admire Francis's enthusiasm over the discovery of a Gospel he had doubtless heard many times before but now took in with a sharper ear, we are equally touched by the modesty and humility of Messer Bernard and Peter of Catania, who listened like good schoolboys as that simple priest explained verses to them that they knew by heart. But with Francis they recaptured a freshness of soul they had long since lost in worldly life. "How can a man be born anew?" Nicodemus asked

Jesus. Quintavalle and Peter of Catania now knew the answer. In the time that it took to get rid of their property and to put on the coarse Franciscan habit they would become Brother Bernard and Brother Peter. The former leading citizens were dead.

I wonder if there is any one of us who hasn't dreamed for at least one minute of parting with all his property at a stroke. For Peter of Catania that must have been quickly over and done with, but it took longer for Quintavalle, and the operation was not without a certain picturesqueness. In public, on the Piazza San Giorgio, on April 16, 1208, Francis helped his disciple give away his gold to the unfortunates who had come from all around. And as there had to be a shadow hanging over this unexpected feast, a miser showed up in the person of a priest who had just recently sold quarry stones to Francis for San Damiano. Seeing all that money being scattered every which way, he decided he had been underpaid. His name was Sylvester. One can imagine Francis's smile and his hand reaching into the sack of gold pieces to compensate the gentleman. "Are you satisfied now, lord priest?" he asked. And Sylvester went away, content with what he had gotten.

Returning home, Sylvester had a dream that night: He saw an enormous dragon threatening the city; then Francis appeared with a golden cross in his mouth that rose up to heaven and stretched out over all the earth, putting the monster to flight and restoring peace. A few days passed, Sylvester did penance in his house, then went off to find Francis—a new Sylvester, conquered by grace. He not only brought back with him the gold he had coveted, but he too gave up all his property and took his place in the newborn brotherhood.

He was its first priest, and that created a new situation. It was not so easy for a cleric who had an ecclesiastical benefice to abandon his property. Similarly, those who were heirs to property owned by nobles had to submit to the complexities of medieval law. These problems soon landed on the bishop of Assisi, who had Francis in his jurisdiction.

Brother Giles and Others

Did the spiritual unrest sweeping through Italy in that period ever touch Francis? Even in his youth, when he was addicted to pleasure, could he have ignored the open-air semons where preachers exalted the ideal of evangelical poverty? At what point did he become aware of what the Lord really wanted of him when he asked him to repair his crumbling Church? It's not easy to date the events of the inner life. Most likely he preferred to keep silent on such a serious question. All we know, and this may be enough, is that he always had a profound respect for what Maritain called the Church's personnel, from the lord pope to the humblest village curate. The heresies that swarmed about never troubled his faith, but that wind of mysticism blowing from southern Italy must have at least brushed him lightly. What *was* that reign of the Holy Spirit announced by Joachim of Floris, except a great renewal of love? And what else did he, Francis Bernardone, have to preach but the love preached by Jesus?

Many people had their doubts about the problem of salvation in a world that was almost as perplexed as ours is today. A rustic named Giles wondered too. This pious illiterate, whose simplicity was perfect, had heard about Francis and his great fervor, and he dreamed of joining his companions. On the April 23, 1208, he bade his parents farewell and went off to look for the saint. We have very few dates from the early history of the Franciscan adventure, so they are all precious. This one matters because it marks the arrival of one of the souls who followed the founder's spirit with the purest fidelity.

Giles went first to the church of Saint George, whose feast they were celebrating, then he took the road to la Portiuncula and met Francis near Rivo Torto as he was coming out of the woods. Without launching into any explanations, Giles knelt down and made his request. Then one of those spiritual thunderbolts crashed that would become so common in the history of the order. The newcomer's heart was transparent. Francis received him joyously, raised him up, and delivered a little speech to him: "Ah, my dear brother," he said, "if the emperor came to Assisi to choose a knight or a chamberlain, and he cast his eye upon you, how proud you would be. Now it is God himself who invites you to his court in calling you to serve in our little militia." And taking him by the hand, he introduced him to his companions: "Here is a good brother whom God has sent us. Let us sit down and eat to celebrate his coming."

Given the absolute poverty in which they lived, we can envision how frugal that feast must have been, but the lordly style of the welcome shows us in a flash the Francis of old and his fine aristocratic manners.

That same day he brought Giles to Assisi to find him something to make a habit out of. What about the color? The documents of the time speak of a gray material, like the kind worn by lepers; but that color drove people away. It was put aside in favor of brown, and Franciscans later dressed more or less like the sparrows. Francis's tunic, which is kept in the lower church of Assisi, is brown shading off into black. In any case, on the way to town they met a poor woman who asked them for charity. "Give her your cloak," said Francis to his neophyte, who joyfully obeyed him on the spot. Eventually Giles revealed that he thought he saw the cloak fly off to heaven with him.

A few days later the brothers split up to go preaching, two by two, all over Italy. Francis took Giles as his companion to the Marches of Ancona. Full of exultation, they sang at the top of their voices. On the way Francis made predictions about the future and about the enormous number of fish he would catch in his bow net. Giles, who knew well that there were only six fish in all, listened in silent wonder.

Sometimes Francis stopped to speak in the public squares of towns and large villages, urging his audience to repent. Giles, who stood nearby, waited for the right moment, like a partner in a theatrical routine, and then interjected, "Well put! You can believe him." Such utter ingenuousness defies commentary. One might think, one would like to think, that people were touched by these improvised sermons, so unlike the usual sort. An echo of them reaches us from the dim distance of the thirteenth century, and it moves us still.

But the passersby were not the least touched, they were surprised and hostile. Who were these two men in rags? Here opinions were divided. Some suspected there was mystery and real religion in the whole thing, but many took them for fools, and the young women fled, fearing their madness might be contagious. It wasn't—not yet—for no one thought of following them. Finally, their rounds accomplished, Francis had a desire to see all his brothers again and, not knowing how to reach them, he prayed God, "who had reunited the scattered children of Israel," to bring them together. He returned with Giles to la Portiuncula, and to their complete astonishment they found everybody gathered in a cabin they had built. There—and elsewhere—they felt they were in paradise.

From that first year on they were gripped by a kind of longing to see their enthusiasm spread over the earth. They had already gone around the Marches of Ancona and Umbria in paris, but they wanted to go farther. In a group of seven, they went southward by the road Francis would have taken after Spoleto if he had pursued his adventures as a warrior.

At Terni they went upstream along the Nera to the shimmering waterfalls. That mountain of spring water fascinated them for an instant, but they had not come there to enjoy the solitude. They were supposed to convert Rieti where, they had been told, the people were turning to paganism because of the sweet luxuriance of the earth in that happy valley.

When, after going along the shores of the lake of Piediluco, shut in between the Reatine Mountains, they came to the pass that looks down over the valley, the light seemed to caress their eyes. The whole landscape was spread out before them with its checkerboard of water, fields, orchards, and forest. Some of the mountains shone, their crests covered with an early snowfall, but all the colors of autumn warred merrily with each other among the vines and trees in a golden haze.

They had first gone straight to the mountain, where at the very top the blue of the sky seemed to cut out the patterns of the summit. The village of Poggio Bustone was perched dizzily on the heights above the valley. There they had greeted all the villagers whom they met with a joyous "Hello, good people!" and were immediately adopted by them. But they went up higher to repair a little hermitage, built on top of some concave boulders, a place given them by the Benedictines.

Later in the season they went down into the valley. Rieti was splendid with its belt of low ramparts, crenelated like a royal battle crown drawn by a child. As pagan as they were, the inhabitants were only too happy to welcome them and listen to them; and they brought the brothers fish and fruit. The gentleness of the climate inclined their souls to be gentle. One day Francis met a superb armed knight who greeted him courteously. Then he told him: "Up till now you have served the world magnificently with your sword and buckler. You are a perfect knight. But from now on you will wear a tunic of rough wool and a cord about your loins, and you will be the knight of Christ."

Thus it was that, leaving his armor right there, Angelo Tancrede of Rieti followed Francis. Having started out with seven, they returned with a new companion; and the valley of Rieti was henceforth always a privileged place where Francis loved to seek refuge, even in times of great suffering.

Barefoot Beggars

What mysterious force drew men to that little group they saw passing by, singing in the streets of the hill towns of Umbria or wandering through the fields and woods? Barefoot, dressed like paupers with a robe resembling a sack and a cord for a belt, but joyful like children, they seemed to have come from another world where sadness didn't exist. Could one own nothing and live happily on this earth? Had the Golden Age returned? Assisi watched with a vague admiration, but a bit uneasily, the ragged fellows who were upsetting convention—in the name of the Lord.

One after the other, four newcomers from Assisi presented themselves: Sabbatino, Morico, John della Capella, Philip the Tall. Sabbatino would remain obscure. Morico was a religious who took care of lepers; stricken with those white spots of dead flesh, he had called on Francis for help and was cured by an electuary concocted for him by Francis: bread crumbs soaked in oil taken from the lamp that burned continually before the altar of the Virgin. Then came John della Capella, so named because he wore a cap over his cowl and who was, some say, the Judas of the band. On that point a doubt arises: Why did there have to be a Judas? To establish a resemblance with the Gospel story? This idea certainly did not come from Francis, but legends don't come about all by themselves—and we must be wary of them. The accusation looks like a settling of accounts from the time of Saint

Bonaventure. Giovanni della Capella created a community of lepers and had the idea of founding a parallel brotherhood, but interference from the Roman Curia stirred Francis to tighten things up when he got back from Egypt; and there is nothing to indicate that John did not immediately submit to the man whom he had joined with as a youth. Philip the Tall, who came from a village on the other side of Mount Subasio, would leave the reputation of a gentle lover of Christ. He understood and interpreted the Scriptures without having had any formal education.

Meanwhile the ten brothers set out in different directions. Without being disappointed—how could Francis ever disappoint them?—they knew a joy sobered by experience. The bitter fruits were not slow in coming. In the streets of Assisi these vagabonds were greeted with sarcasm and, occasionally, some rather pointed questions: "Yesterday you had plenty to live on, and now that you've sold everything, you come to ask us for bread. Aren't you crazy?" They answered meekly, invoking the love of God and wishing peace and happiness to everyone. In the end they carried away, along the jibes, a few crusts of bread and some indescribable leftovers—unwanted garbage from the kitchen —but they considered themselves fortunate because the joy that swept over Francis's soul lived in theirs as well.

Moreover, Francis never stopped encouraging them, because when they faced the world's hostility, some of them couldn't help trembling a little. They were taken for hopeless boors, and the blasphemers sneered when they spoke of God. But as for that, said Francis, they must reply serenely by preaching repentance and never forget that the Lord himself was speaking through them to the proud and wicked. Gradually the consensus grew that they weren't ordinary beggars. If they met people still poorer than themselves out on the road, they would rip a sleeve off their wretched habits, a broad swatch of coarse cloth, and give it away in the name of Christ.

And they traveled across the country in pairs, because that was how Jesus had sent his disciples.

About the Chroniclers

When the chroniclers are not busy contradicting one another, they are either abridging or else overextending their accounts to make them more attractive or more plausible. They have no great horror of lying. One can choose the version offered by this or that chronicler, depending upon one's sensibility. As an example of what I mean, compare the various accounts of the first interview between Francis and Innocent III.

Some of the witnesses of Francis's life followed a different method. The important thing with them was recognizing the saint: In that regard they never hesitated and they never made a mistake. There were the hunted animals that fled for refuge at the feet or in the arms of Francis, because they knew the wickedness of men wouldn't reach them there. There was the hare that nestled against Francis and refused to leave him, the kid that rushed to Francis's side and to which he gave an affectionate lesson on how not to get caught. But the little animal would have none of it and shadowed his steps. There were the birds that perched on his shoulders as if on the branches of a protective tree, the fish that listened to his counsels of prudence. Finally there was the famous wolf of Gubbio, an obedient convert that renounced meat eating and became a Christian wolf. None of these creatures were ever wrong about Francis. They had no need of Celano's volumes nor of Saint Bonaventure (a master in the art of careful portraiture), nor even of the Three Companions or of the honest Anonymous of Perugia, thanks to whom the voice of innocent Brother Giles has come down to us through the babble of the centuries. They didn't even need the Lord Pope Gregory IX, who knew him and loved him and eventually canonized him. The wild animals and his very simple brothers didn't wait to learn what they knew before everyone else did.

Once he became the leader of a little troop that asked only to obey him in gladness, Francis must have felt the weight of his new responsibilities. Faced with the problems of life, the enormous trust of his disciples posed a challenge to him. He had eleven beggars on his hands,

men who didn't even know their trade. He had to teach them everything.

The vow of absolute poverty was not without its problems. The
only thing they could count on was the charity of their neighbors—a
virtue that all too often remained an abstraction. His assurance was
never shaken, but Francis plunged deeply into prayer to ask God what
he wanted of him and his followers.

One day when he withdrew into solitude, Francis experienced the
terror of contemplating "the Master of all the earth," and the memory
of the time he had wasted in his early years put his conscience on the
rack. Soon, however, he was filled with a supernatural joy that restored
his inner peace. Suddenly he went into an ecstatic trance, carried off
in a pool of light that grew larger and larger. He saw the immense
crowd of his future disciples stretching to the far corners of the globe.
When he regained consciousness, he returned to his brothers, transformed by the idea that he had been given a mission.

Would he convert the world? That may have been his dream, one
of the many dreams that had guided him since childhood. But for the
moment he had to instruct his disciples. He began by describing his
vision to them. It took their breath away: a multitude coming from
every country to live their way of life. "And I can still hear the sound
of their footsteps."

One readily imagines the enthusiasm felt by the little group: From
France, from Spain, from Germany and England, a crowd that spoke all
sorts of languages was hastening toward them. Then he gently informed them of the price that would be exacted for those graces: First
the delicious fruits would be gathered, then others less sweet and
pleasant, finally still others that would be bitter and inedible. In a word,
they were going out to beg, but they must not forget that one day the
Lord would make them into a great nation.

Standing Fast

"My Church is crumbling into ruins," Christ had told Francis in the little church of San Damiano. What was true of San Damiano was far more true of the Church he had founded, which was spiritually destroying itself. The prevailing evils had been the same for generations: simony, avarice, gross immorality, and contempt for the demands of the Gospel. It was a catalog of things that ought not to be done. Thousands of Christian souls longed for the ideal that God offered in the Scriptures and, seeing that the Church didn't give it to them, wandered off and searched for it elsewhere. Touched especially by the fervor of people like Pierre de Vaux or the Catharist preachers who contrasted the Gospel with the pagan luxury of clerics who had lost the sense of their vocation or were unprepared for it, these Christians now followed new shepherds. No doubt there were exceptions. Saints were not lacking; sometimes they could be found in isolated places, as if they were the true Church all by themselves. There were even saints of a kind never seen before, who flourished all through the twelfth century, men and women—particularly women—who rank among the great visionaries and mystics. With the energy so characteristic of women, they stood fast for the whole century, like larger-than-life statues, from Saint Lutgard to Elizabeth of Thuringia, from Mechtilde of Magdeburg to Elizabeth of Schönau, in the depths of monasteries and next to the thrones, from Saint Hildegard to Elizabeth of Hungary.

Still, the general disorder made a picture so spectacularly vivid that the Church was threatened with disaster. But it was the only Christian church in the West recognized by the majority of the people. Breaking away from it because it was no longer truly evangelical would mean swelling the ranks of the heretics who appealed to the Gospel pure and simple, but without the Church. And what else did Francis want except the Gospel, with his rule made up of three peremptory verses?

Francis could see what everybody else saw. But as degraded as the

Church was, he still considered it the house of Christ. One day a heretic pointed out to him a priest living openly with a concubine and posed the insidious question whether a mass said by that man with polluted hands could be valid. Francis's only reply was to go up to the priest, kneel down before him, and kiss the hands that held the Body of the Lord at mass. This feeling for the Church kept Francis from drifting to anything like a nascent Protestantism, as happened with the "Brothers of the Free Spirit."

Manichaean Influences

The mockeries and insults of the people of Assisi gradually gave way to a respect bordering on admiration when Francis's beggars humbly asked for something to eat and sang the praises of the Lord. Their incomprehensible happiness aroused envy and won them followers. Unexpected conversions multiplied among the rich and learned as well as among those less favored. But they knew what awaited them. Everybody knew about the mortified life led by the *Poverelli.* Renouncing the good things of life, the delights of comfort, sensual pleasure; going hungry, enduring the cold, and praying, praying, praying—that was the cost of such bliss. It didn't seem too high. Even today we wonder what kind of inner miracle it took to recruit those souls who gave themselves to God.

Francis's presence had a great deal to do with it. He was a permanent invalid but that didn't lessen his joy, and he communicated to everyone a unique peace of heart and, above all, a love of brother for brother. He and his companions were children of God; they had won the freedom of those whom the world can no longer seduce and who rejoiced to own nothing any more. What a sense of lightness that gave them, but what trials too, because, after all, the body was always there with its lusts, though they had been mastered. "The enemy," said Francis, "is the body." For that reason it had to suffer.

"The body is the devil," said the Catharist preachers, whose pure morals astonished even Saint Bernard. And long before their time, in that mysterious Orient where shadow and light commingled, the flesh had been likened to evil and consigned to darkness. Among the Zoroastrians, the body, once dead, was abandoned in the towers of silence. Could it be that a little of such pessimism clouded the limpid joy of the Franciscan soul? The fact is that it took some time before Francis was willing to give his poor flesh, tormented by mortifications and sickness, the affectionate name of Brother Body. He and his body had made peace. But even before then he had forbidden the classical sorts of ascetical self-torture. The instruments designed for that—whips, belts bristling with sharp points, etc.—were thrown onto a pile and burned. No doubt he had noticed that the Gospels never mentioned them: Poverty, chastity, and obedience were quite enough.

Teaching the Brothers

What is striking about Francis is his delicacy. He knew very well how to command, but the imperious tone was not his style. In the early days he could tell that the brothers, for all their zeal, were ashamed to beg. That lingering trace of vanity didn't irritate him, he simply decided that he would give the example and left by himself to go from door to door. He returned in the evening with everything they needed. This went on for several days, but his strength gave out; and the brothers, undoubtedly a little ashamed, listened to his instructions in the art of begging, then submissively went off in their turn. Pride overcome gave way to childlike gaiety. When they got back to la Portiuncula, they compared the results of their individual expeditions.

So deep was Francis's love of poverty that one time, meeting a wretch still more totally destitute than himself, he felt a spasm of sorrow and of something near jealousy. "The world says we are the poorest of the poor for the love of Christ. Well, that's false, and this fellow here proves it!"

Such was Francis's teaching in its gentle rigor and naked simplicity. He gave his brothers everything he had in his heart.

One day the brothers said to him, as the disciples had done with Christ, "Teach us to pray!" How could he improve on what Jesus did? He taught them the recite the Our Father with all their soul, and here is the specially Franciscan quality of the story: The brothers felt so much joy that, in their simplicity, they began to sing it.

Part Three

FACING THE WORLD

The Pope and the Beggar

Now that his companions had a rule and discipline based on the Gospel, Francis realized that he had founded an order—unwittingly, because he had had no such intention. Perhaps he understood that, instead of acting, he had been acted upon, and that grace was leading where it wished without consulting him, ever since he had sacrificed his freedom. Sooner or later he would have to go to Rome—everything was heading him that way—to win acceptance for the simplest of all rules, because he wanted the pope's approval. Up until this time the authors of monastic rules had not submitted them to Rome: Approval was tacit, unless the rule was explicitly rejected. But in Rome a severe trial was awaiting him. He was about to confront one of the greatest figures in the history of the Church and surely one of the most redoubtable characters of his day.

Innocent had particularly shown his mettle the year before, when Europe had been shocked by two acts of violence coming like the murderous swipe of a wounded beast: the deaths of Pierre de Castelnau (in January) and Philip of Swabia (in June).

Pierre de Castelnau had not wanted to leave his monastery, since he felt some repugnance for dealing with heresy. Innocent III had told him, "Action is better than contemplation!" and had sent him as his legate to Languedoc. There Castelnau tried the weapons the pope had supplied him with (in lieu of an army), interdicts and excommunications, in order to force Raymond VI of Toulouse to stop protecting the Cathars. On January 14, 1208, the legate was assassinated with a hunting spear, like a wild boar, near the Rhone, by a squire of the count of Toulouse. This gave the pope the chance he had been dreaming of, to launch a Crusade of extermination against the Albigensians, as if no one could govern except as the Church saw fit. The spiritual power began to look a lot like ordinary human power.

In June, Philip of Swabia, the freshly victorious master of Cologne, who was practically assured of becoming emperor, was assassinated by a partisan of his rival. The murderer, Otto of Wittelsbach, may have been in the pay of both Otto of Brunswick and the pope. To disguise this political crime as a crime of passion, rumors were spread that a suitor for the hand of his daughter Beatrice, mad with rage after being turned away, had stabbed the monarch in a corridor of the bishops' palace at Bamberg. The killer was wisely executed at once, and the Diet of Frankfurt made Otto sole emperor. The pope thought he finally had a submissive emperor, but he quickly had to admit his mistake. Once again he was about to use his favorite and most devastating weapon, excommunication, which made crowned heads see things Rome's way. But that point had not yet been reached.

In 1209 Innocent III was in the prime of life. Born at Anagni, where one of his successors, Boniface VIII, was destined to receive the slap heard round the world, he was descended from the noble family of the counts of Segni, which gave nine popes to Christendom. He considered himself the Lord's anointed, the absolute master of the temporal as well as the spiritual order, less than God but greater than man (the word *superman* had not yet been invented), the judge of all, judged by God alone. He saw no limit to his power as the overseer of kings. If a sovereign proved headstrong, he excommunicated him. To chastise Philip Augustus for living in adultery, he invoked a clause of the feudal system subjecting him to the king of England. These details may give some notion of the terrifying impression he could create when the opportunity presented itself. But, on the other hand, he was a highly spiritual man, and as soon as he was elected pope, he undertook a thoroughgoing reform of the Church. In fact, he saved it.

The portrait we have of him in a fresco at the monastery of Subiaco shows us a narrow face with compressed features, the eyes almost touching; a fixed, imperious expression; a fine, long nose; a small mouth; and protruding ears, as if to hear all the rumors in the universe. One curious habit: He loved to eat lemons.

By one of those ironies that history seems to adore, on the day when Francis wished to introduce himself to the pope, he could not have found, from the heart of Sicily to the borders of northern Italy, a man more occupied and preoccupied than this personage who styled himself the prince of all the earth. And one of the ideas that most obsessed the brain beneath that golden, pointed tiara was to make an end of the disorders in the Church by starting a Crusade of renunciation and poverty all across Europe. In addition, he had just flung his anathema at the Cathars, and the war against the Albigensians was getting organized.

On that spring day in 1209 he was walking up and down in the Lateran palace, in the so-called Mirror Gallery. The moment he caught sight of Francis and his eleven companions, he had them shown out, thereby driving from his presence the supremely providential man who could best assure the triumph of his ideal. But every monarch has his phobias, and one of Innocent III's phobias was heresy; because heresy was revolution. He mistrusted the "Good Men of Lyon," the ragpickers of Milan called Patarins (two years earlier he had ordered the houses of their fellows in Viterbo put to the torch), as well as all those exalted characters who made a commotion over the Gospel and attacked the morals of the clergy. What was the Church good for, they said, unless it adhered literally to the Gospel? So there had to be a reform, reform at all costs. Their reasoning was beyond reproach, but dangerous. What was the point of having churches, if the Gospel was enough—and who would have dared to say that it wasn't? The argument was specious but strong; it contained the seed of all the modes of Protestantism that would flourish in the soil of the future. So, that little band of tatterdemalions pleading for an audience were just more harebrained *illuminati* who were unquestionably planning to lecture the head of Christendom. Out!

We would like to know what happened afterward, but the accounts we are given have an official, contrived quality to them, except for one that comes from England, dated 1236, and that has been judged absurd. We shall see.

So now Francis and his little troup of paupers were asking for an audience from the most political of Saint Peter's successors. But it wasn't so easy to get to the foot of the throne to address the servant of the servants of God. Fortunately, Guido, the bishop of Assisi, was in Rome at the time. He was quite surprised to see Francis there, and still more amazed at the petition of the man he had once covered with his cope. He agreed to help him. He went to find a saintly friend of his, Cardinal John of Saint Paul, a member of the Colonna family, who had recently been assigned to do a pretrial investigation of the Waldensians, and who was well acquainted with all the problems of heresy. Monsignor Guido explained Francis's plan to him. The Gospel again! But the bishop reassured the cardinal that one couldn't find a more obedient Catholic than Francis. Shrewd diplomat that he was, the prelate had the inspired notion of putting up that entire little "evangelistic" crowd in his own palace for a few days. A bit more information would be useful: Francis would be able to talk to his heart's content, and so disclose what he really had in mind.

Cardinal John of Saint Paul was, in effect, the Curia. He went to great lengths to show Francis that his rule, though very beautiful, was out of touch with the present-day world. Why didn't he choose to follow Christ's law in a religious order, of which there already were so many? But Francis had no vocation of that sort; Christ had told him what he wanted, and that was enough. He understood that he was there to fight, and to fight for Christ. The cardinal stubbornly resisted but to no avail. One cannot help being touched to see how this expert in heresy was won over by Francis's passionate words. He got him his audience with the pope.

At this point the accounts diverge. Francis must not have made a very good impression in his wretched clothes, and his ragged companions, all clustered round him, didn't help the situation. If we can trust Roger de Wendover, a monk from the abbey of Saint Albans in England, the pope observed him with disgust but listened nonetheless to his reading of the new rule. His commentary was brutally simple: "Brother, go herd pigs. I should compare you to them rather than to men. Roll in the dunghill with them, offer them your rule, and be their preacher. . . ." Thus spoke the superman of Christendom.

Francis, the narrator continues, bowed his head, and went off in a great hurry to look for a herd of pigs to roll in the mud with, till he had smeared himself from head to foot. Then in that foul-smelling state he came back to see Innocent III. We are not told how he made his way to the pope—legendary reports scarcely worry about trivial details. Faced with such overwhelming simplicity, the pope was full of wonder and in a gentler voice ordered the pig-preacher to go wash and then return. The second interview took place without delay, where the pope conferred the office of preaching on this model of obedience and his brothers.

A highly edifying story, believe in it who will. Perhaps we can retain this much from it: Innocent III had a violent nature, he instinctively distrusted novelty in religion, and Francis of Assisi was very persistent.

What actually happened was, I think, altogether different. The night following the afternoon when Innocent III was walking in the Mirror Gallery and had the ragged little monks thrown out, he had a dream-vision. If we edited all the dreams out of the history of the Middle Ages, the whole thing would grind to a halt. So, the pope dreamed that a palm tree was growing slowly at his feet until it attained a fabulous size; and God revealed to him that this tree was none other than the beggar in the ash-gray robe whom he had refused to see.

Now, without hesitation, he had his servants fetch the unknown pauper. For his part, Cardinal John of Saint Paul, finding that he couldn't bend Francis from his goals and won over by his enthusiasm and decisiveness, asked him to accept him as a spiritual brother. He could see no other solution now except to obtain an audience with the pope. Innocent III listened to the beggar explaining his rule and admired its simplicity. But the cardinals from the Curia who were on hand for that interview declared that the proposals of the *Poverello* were beyond human capacity. Their objections were strong: "Mysticism leads to politics"; An assembly of beggars outside the bounds of a religious order would spread a certain dis-order; there were enough monastic rules for them to pick from; and, if they wanted to found a new order, how could they live without any money?

Then the cardinal had an inspiration: To argue that this rule was impracticable was to reject the Gospel and blaspheme against Christ. Even today, eight hundred years later, we may wonder if there is any answer to the cardinal's adamant logic. In any case the pope must have felt its power, because he said to Francis: "My son, pray to Christ to reveal his will to us; then I shall be able to grant you what your generosity desires."

The Power of Dreams

Skeptical historians have an easy time of it when they challenge the oneiric element in traditional biographies because, as they ask, where is the proof that all such things haven't been invented after the fact? But this approach grossly misreads the psychology of medieval people, who acted so often on premonitions and saw in dreams a divinely chosen method for communicating with them and, at times, for revealing God's will. The same was true of visions. They were mental phenomena, no doubt, but so vividly detailed that people had the certainty they were seeing images outside themselves. In their eyes illusion was impossible and, setting all reasoning aside, they followed their dreams straight into action. There were no psychoanalysts to disturb this system of dynamic ideas come from another world. For human beings in those distant times, sleep offered a source of spiritual energy and even mystical revelations. Have we changed all that much on this score?

Scientific investigations into the depths of the sleeper's brain provide interesting evidence on the intermittent patterns of dreaming. One can deprive an individual of his dreams by awakening him at the very instant when the dream begins, but at the end of a certain number of dreamless nights he will die. We need our dreams to live. That magnificent truth was discovered in our time, but it leaves intact the secret of that strange sphere of life where the soul moves for a third or so of our earthly existence. Once they have played their role, dreams fade. The ones that remain sometimes maintain an appearance of hallucinatory reality. Medieval people made no mystery of dreams and followed their guidance when they were thought to come from on high. But for us the slightly spectral imagery of dreams is like the recollections an irresponsible person has of his trips, and we reject the testimony of a traveler who is not guided by the goddess Reason. It is nonetheless true that this vital phantasmagoria plays a part in our destiny.

The dreamer of the twelfth and thirteenth century, who was closer than we are to a world of instinct, knew, perhaps better than we think, how to take into account the fleshly and spiritual factors in those nocturnal confrontations with himself. Scripture provided him with a great abundance of examples that we still consider historical: the dream of Jacob, who saw angels going up and down a ladder that reached to heaven; pharaoh's dream about the fat cows followed by the lean ones, which Joseph elucidated. Such revealing dreams were always bursting into the dark night of history, even as late as modern times. It is interesting to note that, on the eve of his tragic death, President Lincoln, at a meeting with his cabinet, told of a dream he had the night before. He saw himself in a boat floating over the high seas, "without oars, without a rudder, over a limitless ocean. There was no one to help.

I was drifting, drifting, drifting!" And he concluded: "But, gentlemen, this has nothing to do with our work, let's see the business of the day." Five hours later he died at Ford's Theater when John Wilkes Booth fired his revolver.

The exchange between Innocent III and Francis of Assisi took place from vision to vision, one dream answering another, like ships that pass in the night on the high seas.

The Beggar and the Pope

When Francis returned to see him, the pope was still thinking about the remarks made by his cardinals and, with them still present, he took up their point of view, making himself a sort of devil's advocate. "How will you live? What will you live on without money? And with what money?" It was good common sense speaking its everyday dialect.

To these simple questions Francis replied simply, "Lord, I leave it up to my Lord Jesus Christ: If he has promised to give us eternal life, he will certainly not deny us, when the time comes, the indispensable necessities for our material life on this earth." But the pope refused to yield, even if at the bottom of his heart he felt moved by the words of this obviously uneducated man. "Man by his nature," he said, "is unstable and never perseveres for long in the same paths. Go, ask the Lord to inspire you with more sensible plans for your future, and when you are sure of what you want, come back to see me and I shall approve your rule."

Francis withdrew. As he prayed in silence, God inspired him with a parable. He came back at once to see Innocent III. It was the third face-to-face meeting between the pope, dressed in red and gold like the setting sun, and the little man in cloth the color of earth.

Looking at the gentle but obstinate petitioner, the pope remembered a dream that had come to him shortly before this and had filled him with disquiet. He saw himself sleeping in bed, with his tiara on his head, and the Lateran basilica tilted to one side at a dangerous angle, when fortunately a little monk who looked like a beggar, leaning against the Church with his shoulder, held it up and kept it from collapsing. He recognized the beggar as the same man who was talking to him. And so how could the pope not listen to Francis tell his allegorical story when he himself was thinking back to that dream?

An extremely rich king had married in the desert a very beautiful and very poor woman. She gave him many children, but she remained in the desert. When her sons were grown, they complained that they had nothing. She told them: "You are children of the king; go to his court and he will give you what you need." Then they went to the palace of the king, who was astonished by their beauty. "Where did you come from? Who are you," he asked. "The sons of the poor woman who lives in the desert," they said. "Have no fear, you are my sons. Those who are nothing to me are nourished at my table, all the more reason why I shall take care of you." And Francis added: There is no danger that the sons and heirs of the eternal king will die of hunger, for the king in the parable was Christ, who would provide for everything; and it was he, Francis, who had given birth to them.

This speech succeeded in persuading the pope, but not quite enough to extract a formal approval from him. He gave Francis some friendly advice and invited him to come back and see him when the number of his brethren had increased. Then, and only then, could he grant him more. Meanwhile he would allow him to preach.

Forty-seven years later, Saint Bonaventure described the scene a little differently—for the sake of ideal hagiography. He shows us the pope, "amazed by Francis's discourse," agreeing without reserve. "Not only did he grant all that Francis asked, but he promised to give him still more. He approved his rule, gave him a mission to preach, and had all Francis's lay companions given little tonsures to permit them to preach the word of the Lord God without being disturbed." One interesting note here, the Curia added that the brothers had to elect a leader, which would make them one more order in the Church, thus averting the specter of a heresy like that of the Good Men of Lyon.

But there was no written approval of the rule.

After prostrating himself at the feet of the lord pope, Francis took his leave and, with his brothers, left the city immediately by the via Salaria. What was he thinking of? Despite his rediscovered innocence, he still remained very much an Italian; and his natural shrewdness had taught him the value of kind words. But how could he argue with a personage wearing a tiara, he who was nobody and knew nothing?

What sort of figure could he cut before those staggeringly learned men? The pope had given him his verbal consent. The pope's word was enough—but what if either of them died? *Verba volant.* When the *Poverello* heard his brothers exult and sing victory, he must have felt a secret pang. He had a foreboding not of failure but of illusory success, which was worse. The cardinals had grumbled too much. They didn't want his overly simple rule, and he didn't want to found an order.

At this point the documents fall silent, fearing to spoil the pretty picture they have painted. Francis at the court of Rome was like a child, but he had a supernatural grasp of the hidden meaning of events; and he must have caught wind of the hesitation in those compliments and blessings that committed no one to anything specific. The approval won by force was only a permission in principle. Jesus was the only one he would count on, and Christ gently restored to him the joy that the world has never been able to give. In a vision he had one night he rediscovered all his courage: He saw a gigantic tree to whose top he was carried up and, seizing it with both his hands, he managed to bend it effortlessly all the way to the ground. The tree was the pope.

The Trap

It was hard walking to Spoleto in the hot sun, and the brothers, utterly worn out and dying of hunger, found their only consolation in discussing the happy outcome of their Roman expedition and all its promise. But when they could go no farther and they stopped in a deserted plain, a stranger came up to them and gave them some bread. When they turned to thank him, he had disappeared. Who was he? There was no point in asking; miracles were ordinary fare among the first Franciscans. With new vigor they continued their journey and arrived near Orte, a place so pleasant they spent fifteen days there.

They didn't see anyone at all pass by, but they would not have been Franciscans if the beauty of the landscape had left them unaffected. They went to beg their food at Orte or on the road to Narni and hid the surplus in an old Etruscan tomb. They all felt so happy that they

decided never to leave that charming Thebaid, where they were perfectly at home, far from men, praying to God and giving themselves
to contemplation in a state of absolute destitution. There were rocks
with springs gushing from them, waterfalls, caves for shelter, tall pines,
marvelous natural beauty.

Francis saw the trap. Their vocation was calling them elsewhere.
The world had to be converted, not just their neighborhood, Spoleto
and then Assisi, but the whole world. And so they left without complaining, with the gaiety of obedience, because everything was a joy
to them as they followed the bidding of their guide.

The pope had allowed them to preach. Francis used that permission
with extraordinary success. Without at all realizing it, they were re-
placing a lukewarm, stick-in-the-mud clergy who, with a few exceptions, limited themselves to the drudgery of Sunday sermons and never
thought to announce the word of God on the highways and byways.
Such methods were good only for heretics. But Innocent III had had the
idea of a prudent Catholic counteroffensive when he verbally granted
Francis and his companions what they so passionately desired.

The Brother

We have a hard time imagining the enthusiasm Francis stirred up
in a country as spiritually weakened as Italy was in those days. Sensibility was paralyzing the flow of grace. People were often misled by a
purely formal, ostentatious piety. The period also felt—thereby resembling our own era—a void that pleasure couldn't fill, a hunger for
something different, a restlessness of the heart. The Church had forgotten how to speak to the soul, because it was bogged down in the
material world.

Then in the piazza or at a turn in the road, there appeared a man
with bare feet, dressed like a beggar and crying in a joyful voice, *"Pace
e bene!"* One listened to him despite oneself. The fellow knew how
to talk, and what he said was so simple that everything seemed new
in his language, which had no hard words, those words that make

thinking a muddle. No need to have studied to follow him—and they did follow him, first of all because he spoke as he went along, and especially because he believed everything he said. He believed it so strongly that they believed as he did and along with him. They felt that all the things they had learned as children and almost forgotten were now beginning to come true in a terrifying fashion.

You had to save your soul at all costs, you had to go to paradise. They knew that already, but they had never known it the way they did now as they dogged the footsteps of that little man. Everything that makes an Italian heart beat with love pounded in each one of their hearts with great, muted strokes. It was incredible: He was in love with God—and that wasn't all, because he went much too far, this madman with the lilting voice. He said that God was in love with us all; he would suddenly weep, weep for love, and some people would begin to weep too, the women first, with the talent they have for that, then the men, starting with the young ones. He went on, apparently not noticing that a crowd was right behind him. People left their work, came out of their houses. One would think he had bewitched them and that he was going to make them leave this world to lead them straight to God.

How did he go about turning them from love to uneasiness? By conjuring up before them in a flash the wall of black fire that cut them off from the heavenly garden and eternal bliss. Miser, throw your gold in the devil's face, as if it were the most nauseating ordure, if you want to enter paradise. Libertine, drop all your women and all your pleasures that keep you from seeing death hot on your heels.

They felt terror from the secret sins their lives were full of, without Francis's having to tell them. But he told them anyhow, not with the trumpetings of righteous indignation, as the clergy did, or with their threats of fire and torment, but with an unconsolable sorrow and bursts of searing tenderness, as if he were about to lose his beloved children. And, no longer able to find the words, he began to gesture, his face streaming tears. What eloquence could match those hands stretched out to them? They felt like throwing themselves on their knees to comfort him and to promise him they would return to the Lord. There were women who did this at once, un–self-consciously, carried away by love of God, of heaven, of everything, no doubt including the preacher. Some of the men imitated them, the young ones especially; they were all moved.

Priests who happened to be passing by watched in silence.

Rivo Torto

The chroniclers never stop reminding us how weak Francis was: An extraordinary flame animated that delicate body. One of the mysteries of his destiny is that he was deprived of physical strength when he needed it most to accomplish his vocation. Inner energy made up for everything.

After the spiritual victories he had won, those mass conversions that cast him into an abyss of humility and adoration, he had to find the disciples a place to stay. They looked for one. A first attempt with the bishop of Assisi failed. Finally they opted for a very modest cabin next to a streambed that was ordinarily dry but a fearful torrent after rainstorms, Rivo Torto. It had once belonged to a leprosarium, but it was no longer owned by anyone, and the little band settled in there as best it could. It was more a shelter from the sun and rain than a real house, but Francis declared with his usual good humor that as a jumping-off point for paradise it was better than a palace. They had to squeeze together to get everybody in, and they could neither sit down nor stretch out. Each brother had his name inscribed on a beam. Lay people would never have tolerated this absolute lack of comfort, of even the idea of comfort; and yet what unforgettable hours the brothers enjoyed there, basking in the presence of Francis, who brought God to them. The summer of 1210 passed, then the winter. What did the heat of the day matter, or the freezing nights? Francis was in their midst, watching over his children with love.

Love was the gift he gave them. He gave them God. Those completely liberated souls were dazed with joy. Francis had been right to insist on a state of perfect poverty. No mistake about it: Poverty is the very first of the Beatitudes, however awkward that may have proved for a society that wanted to be, and thought of itself as, Christian. But Francis was an extremist who accepted no subterfuges. Lady Poverty has an entourage of indispensable virtues, whose absence constitutes a betrayal of the Gospel: charity, humility, purity of heart, and all the others; take them away and see what remains. It's quite easy to envision a pauper hungry for wealth, rotten with pride, obsessed with luxury, ruthlessly ambitious, or haunted by the desire for power. The world is full of such people who are *not* the poor in spirit.

The truly poor person is someone who is hungry. This is the character Francis modeled himself after. The truly poor person has nothing, wants everything that God is willing to give him and nothing more, beginning with his daily bread. The truly poor person is Christ, because Christ made himself poor for all people.

The rich are another story. The Magnificat tells us that God sends them away with empty hands. This is bothersome for capitalism, even if it disguises itself in the lineaments of totalitarianism, like the wolf in sheep's clothing. Two thousand years after the coming of Christ the search is still going on for a system to tranquillize everyone. So far we have found famine and war—along with atheism. Francis believed he had found the right answer in the Gospel pure and simple. The pope had looked at that stubborn little man and asked him to think things over. All hope was not lost.

Two huts separated by a screen and covered with leafy branches by the brothers made up the settlement at Rivo Torto, a place of delight for the soul, but a purgatory for the body. One night Francis heard a voice gasp, "I'm dying." It was a brother groaning. Francis asked him what was wrong. "I'm dying of hunger." Quick, everyone up. Prepare a meal, for the whole company. A brother must not die of hunger, but neither should he be embarrassed by having to eat alone: Francis was always well-bred. It was no doubt an austere midnight supper that broke their fast—crusts, turnips found in the fields, perhaps some eggs ... what else? Water from the stream. Gaiety in lieu of dessert. Francis's charm must have transformed it all into a feast, touched lightly by the fleeting memory of old times.

The joy that reigned among those men might seem to defy explanation. They sang, they prayed, they listened to the teachings of the man they called simply "the brother." From the distance of eight centuries this fervent little community looks strange to us, not because of the ideal that inspired it, but because of all the questions raised by its way of life. The rule was strict and work obligatory. "If anyone will not work, let him not eat." In exchange for their work the brothers could get all the necessities except money. And when the necessities did not arrive, they went begging just as poor people did. Francis had a phobia about money, which he compared to excrement. There was an absolute prohibition against accepting any, and he added: "Let us be on our guard, we who have abandoned everything, lest we lose the kingdom of heaven for so little."

They did whatever kind of work they knew best. Caring for lepers in a nearby lazaretto was deemed one of their most useful contributions. Lepers were even brought into the hut to be attended to. There was, however, one leper so repugnant that Francis himself asked that he not be allowed to enter. It happened that one of the brothers, John the Simple, took it upon himself, out of thoughtlessness or overzealousness, to bring this stinking piece of human flesh into the home of the tiny brotherhood. Far from losing his temper, Francis felt ashamed. He seated the beggar at the place of honor next to him, and gave him food and drink, while he himself drank from the same bowl where the sick man had placed his oozing lips. Such acts of charity were past counting.

It goes without saying that they were utterly chaste. If a brother was tormented by impure desires, the remedy was simple, and Francis, having tried it himself, guaranteed its efficacy: One plunged oneself immediately into the freezing waters of the stream until the temptation went away. Later, shivering but calm and controlled, the brother would return to the hut, which felt like a kind of warm nest.

One day in September 1209, the emperor passed through the neighborhood with all his dazzling retinue. Otto IV was on his way from Perugia to Viterbo to have himself crowned by the pope. What was an emperor? Francis and his brothers remained in the hut, all except one, who was dispatched to the great man to remind him that all triumphs are ephemeral. A few months after this Otto would be excommunicated, and his string of victories began to run out. Francis's indifference to the pomp of worldly power made an enormous impression on the people of Umbria.

Sermon in the Cathedral

Great as it already was, Francis's popularity reached prodigious new heights when it was learned that the pope had approved his rule. Francis himself didn't have to spread the word, his brothers took care of that. The permission to preach granted by Innocent III was only verbal, but that didn't weaken it in the least. Who would have thought to challenge it? Francis's presence all by itself breathed new life into the religious hopes and dreams of every social class, but his listeners were impelled as much by curiosity as by a thirst for the Gospel. Assisi wanted to hear the man who had scandalized the town some years before now preaching Christ, and preaching him in a church where the people could get a good look at the saint, as they now considered him. The church of Saint George, they decided, would be too small to hold the crowd, so they chose the cathedral. And it became the scene of a thrilling face-to-face encounter—which for some reason nobody ever writes about.

The only part of the church of San Rufino that remains more or less as Francis knew it is the facade. It still has that slightly cyclopean majesty of the Romanesque style, simple in its overall effect, but singularly rich in detail. A gallery of small columns crosses it from right to left beneath the three rose windows, which seem to spin in place like wheels above the portals. There are many enigmas to be read on that tall page of gray stone. On the tympanum of the great central portal Christ is enthroned as a bearded king between the sun and the moon. One one side his mother sits nursing her child; on the other there is Rufino, bishop and matryr. So much for heaven, but strange things are happening on the rounded architrave of the gate, which is guarded by two fierce lions hard at work devouring, respectively, a Moor and the Jewish ram. The most curious item can be found in a saraband of highly suspicious beasts chasing and biting one another all around the entrance, encircling it with a weird, malignant garland that the artist has rendered so vividly it seems to wriggle. Released there by the devil, they sound that infernal note so common in medieval art. They animate the stone with a hallucinatory, lifelike quality and give the spectator an indefinable malaise. But that isn't all. Around the central rose window, which is protected by the symbols of the evangelists, the lion, ox, eagle, and man, prowl the shadows of some sort of animals mutilated by time and worn so thin that only their paw prints are left.

Assisi was a half hour's walk from Rivo Torto. Francis had to be helped, weakened as he was from fasting. No doubt they brought him on the back of an ass all the way to the cathedral and, as is still the custom in certain Italian churches, they had him get up on a platform rather than imprison him in a pulpit. That gave him the freedom he needed, because he had to pace back and forth as he spoke with his usual gestures.

When he looked out and saw practically everyone from his native town gathered round him, thousands of faces turned toward him, his physical weakness disappeared, giving way to a sudden fiery energy that restored his youth. We can only guess what he said, but he had nothing in his heart except the Christ of the Gospels, and what burst from his burning prophet's heart was a pure cry of love. His words had an overwhelming simplicity that went straight to everyone's conscience. The tenderness of God flowed into that voice, moving people with the mysterious seductiveness of a song. But it was not just a matter of bringing joy to restless souls worried about their salvation. The whole town was guilty: Avarice had locked up its heart like tightened purse strings; luxury was killing love; political hatred was driving the Gospel out more effectively than any sword thrusts. He knew all that because he knew all the inhabitants of his town, having lived among them as one of them.

And they knew him. The confrontation must have been startling. This coarsely dressed monk with a cord around his waist who made his audience weep and sigh was someone they had seen four years ago when he was the king of youth, wasting his father's money in aristocratic style and living in disorder and sensuality. They all remembered that perfectly well, and he had not forgotten either, of course; but a peculiar shiver went through the crowd to see how the Lord had seized hold of this man of pleasure and had taken his place to speak to each one of the citizens of Assisi. God had disguised himself as a poor man and was proclaiming his Gospel, as he had long before in the Holy Land. It was as if Francis had disappeared behind the person whose language he spoke.

Upon hearing the call to repentance, groans and laments arose from the crowd, which was on the brink of the religious frenzy so widespread in the Middle Ages. For those few hours at least Assisi was duly chastened and ready to convert. It had its prophet, it embraced its saint and would not let him go. We may hope that Pica was still alive and could listen to the son whose spiritual glory she had predicted. We have no idea where Bernardone was. Perhaps he stood behind a pillar, wondering to himself.

The brothers were not on hand for that triumph. They stayed back at Rivo Torto, but they tasted a rare consolation in the form of a stunning vision. Francis had not yet returned when they saw a chariot of fire come in the door, pass through the hut, leave, reenter, leave again, come back one last time, and then disappear, leaving the brothers terrified and ecstatic because in that supernatural light they had received the grace to see clearly into each other's conscience, and had seen, we may be sure, only goodness. Thus the soul of their brother Francis made amends for his absence by sending them this proof of his love.

Peace, Assisi!

The groans of repentant Assisi in the cathedral of San Rufino were fully justified. The town was badly in need of conversion, not just because of its shameful deeds—on that score, its neighbor Perugia was more than its match—but because the hostilities among the common people, bourgeois, and patricians led to bloodshed every day in the streets. The situation was hopelessly tangled: Perugia was the vassal of the pope; Assisi was theoretically still under the protection of the emperor, like the communes of Lombardy. The citizens of Assisi would not forgive the nobles who had returned home after the war with Perugia: They were traitors. And despite the accord they had signed, they kept pressing claims for their property that had suffered damage during their absence. These conflicts were utterly ferocious and had been going on for ten years.

At Perugia in March of 1209, with the slightly reluctant consent of the pope, Otto had reinstated the old imperial commandants, notably the duke of Spoleto, and restored their rights. This forced the people of Assisi to unite. They abolished serfdom, while on the other hand they returned some of their property to the nobles.

What role did Francis play in the pacification of his home town? Placed under interdict by Innocent III and with its podestà excommunicated, Assisi finally tried to have the warring parties come to an understanding. It was high time—the once prosperous town was in great distress. With all his eloquence, Francis called for peace. It didn't come, only its poor relation: the truce of November 9, 1210, one of many. Concessions were made on both sides. Perhaps the saint's impassioned voice had awakened echoes, but we can't say for sure.

That same year a son of one of the noblest families in Assisi, the Offreduccio, entered the brotherhood. One wonders whether Francis may not have had a tendency to plague people—plague them in a "superior" (and possibly unconscious) fashion. This idea suggests itself when we read about the ordeal that Rufino Offreduccio had to endure from a spiritual whim Francis once had. Rufino was small and delicate and, it should be noted, a cousin of Clare's. He had very little talent for preaching and a slight stutter to boot. One day Francis got the very peculiar notion of asking him to do the impossible. "Go preach at San Rufino." In consternation Rufino humbly begged to be excused from a mission he was sure he couldn't accomplish. This wasn't a refusal to obey, but Francis was pleased to view it as a tepid sort of obedience, and he ordered Rufino to go preach in the cathedral half-naked, dressed only in his breeches. This time Rufino bowed and left for the church of San Rufino, Martyr, climbed up on the platform, and began a sermon on penance. That strange apparition was greeted with a chorus of laughter. Was this a joke? Not at all, the poor fellow with the rebellious tongue tried to speak about God, but amidst all the hilarity he couldn't be heard.

Meanwhile back at la Portiuncula Francis suddenly came to his senses. Why had he given that absurd order, causing a model brother to suffer pointlessly? Delay was unthinkable; he would go at once to atone for his lack of humanity. Accompanied by Brother Leo, who had an extra habit draped over his arm, he went to the cathedral, took off his tunic, and in this semi-naked state took Rufino's place. There was a new explosion of laughter. Had the brothers lost their minds? But

Francis began to speak of the nakedness of Christ in his Passion, and all of a sudden there was silence. Emotion gripped the faithful as they listened to his heartrending words. Tears flowed down the faces that a minute before had been contorted with vulgar merriment.

Rufino would become one of the three brothers who always accompanied Francis and took care of him until his death.

La Portiuncula

In the spring of 1211 the Franciscan community was driven from Rivo Torto ("the tortuous stream") in the most unexpected way. The brothers were praying one day when a peasant roughly pushed his ass into what he called the shanty: "Let's go, get in there, you!" Francis immediately decided to leave together with his companions, and he felt as bad about it as they did. However humble the ramshackle cabin may have been, they were attached to it as one of the places that the Lord had blessed with his presence. No doubt there would be other hours of grace, but none quite like the times here when the earth had seemed to stretch up to heaven and touch it.

That peasant shoving his burro into the "shanty" might well have been given a shove by Providence to drive the brothers on to a better place. Francis made another appeal to the bishop of Assisi, but the lord Guido still had nothing to offer, so he went to the Benedictines of Subasio. For a yearly rent of a few fish the abbot generously let him have the chapel of Our Lady of the Angels, a very modest building surrounded by a little slice of land but, O wonder, located in the middle of a forest. Francis knew it well: He had set out from there to conquer the world, and he had returned there afterward. The little company enthusiastically settled into that ideal refuge. A thatched cottage was put up in a few days beneath the great oaks, then all around it huts were built for the friars. Each one had his own. It was a rustic monastery where Poverty was at home. Francis couldn't have dreamed of anything better, and he and his brothers lived through a period that came straight from the *Golden Legend,* a time whose enchanting image we rediscover in the *Fioretti*. The Middle Ages never presented all the freshness of the Christian faith in more delicious pages than these. They are packed with miracles, but one can find plenty of historical truth in the portraits of the earliest Franciscans.

At la Portiuncula prayer and contemplation took turns with work and preaching. Francis dismissed a "brother fly" for incurable laziness. For all the other religious there was a plethora of opportunities to put charity to work, whether by helping the peasants or caring for the lepers in the nearby lazaretto. Needless to say, the only recompense they would accept was food. Money was refused except when they had to buy medicine for their sick.

Later on, those six years spent at Our Lady of the Angels would remain as a foretaste of paradise in the brothers' memory. There they had followed Christ and lived the Gospel. Like Christ, his only model, Francis gave his followers what he had received from God. By a special grace his mere presence turned them into saints, without changing their personal characteristics. If holiness can be eccentric, theirs was some-times eccentric in the extreme. They were all individuals. One never tires of hearing the stories of their fantastic doings, where buffoonery goes hand in hand with a mind-boggling simplicity that reveals souls with not a shadow to darken their crystalline transparency.

They came from practically everywhere, from the fields and towns; from the nobility, the common people, the universities, the rich bour-geoisie like Bernard of Quintavalle, or the Church like Sylvester. By accepting them Francis simplified them. By living close to him they became Francis's sons forever, without losing anything of themselves, priests and laymen alike, because after Sylvester other clerics came too. Francis, we must not forget, never wanted to be a cleric. Besides, his complete lack of theological studies would have necessarily kept him from becoming one.

You Won't Find What You're Looking for in Books

Some of the brothers gladly sacrificed all their wealth, including a few luxurious manor houses. Others among the less fortunate, but with equal generosity, renounced humbler forms of property, for example the rustic brother who bid farewell, not without a pang, to his cow. Still others endured the difficult trial of giving up all the cultural riches they had acquired over long years of study. Such was the case of Bernard of Quintavalle, who offered whole libraries to God—great learning consigned to oblivion. Nonetheless, his reputation as jurist remained strong at his alma mater of Bologna, and it was to Bologna that Francis was inspired to send him, in the name of obedience, to found a convent.

Bernard didn't hesitate for a minute. He went out there, revisiting the streets he knew so well, the palaces surmounted by their proud towers, and the turbulent crowd of students who walked around the town squares day and night. In the largest of these, the Piazza Maggiore, the erstwhile doctor, now barefoot and dressed in that strange tunic of his brotherhood, was taken for a madman and with the ordinary cruelty found in all ages was hooted at by the street urchins, "*Pazzo! Pazzo!*" Bernard listened to that cry, so familiar to Franciscan ears, with a joyful smile on his face. He could have escaped, but he sat down on a corner post. Men joined the children in throwing dirt at him, then rocks, and in roughing him up. He didn't move.

The next day he returned to undergo the same treatment, and again the day after, a martyr to the loving obedience that typified Francis's sons.

Meanwhile, such singular perseverance had caught the attention of a curious onlooker. Bernard's face, aglow with joy, was not the face of a madman. The observer was intrigued; he came up and asked him who he was and what he was doing there on the Piazza Maggiore. By way of an answer Bernard drew out from beneath his tunic a copy of the rule of Saint Francis and handed it to him. The man read it and was filled with astonishment at its high spiritual quality. The jeers fell silent, as people watched and waited. The opinion of this passerby was, in fact, not without importance: He was a learned doctor of the law, Nicholas dei Pepoli. He turned toward some friends who were with him and declared, "This is the most sublime religious state I ever heard of." Then he offered Bernard a house where he could set up a convent. Bernard wanted nothing better, but things went too well for his taste. After a certain amount of time, when the convent had been founded, the founder, who had once been so vehemently insulted, became the object of widespread admiration that was fast turning into veneration because of the austere life he led. Before long they would be calling him a saint. Without hesitation he took flight and returned to Assisi. "Brother," he told Francis, "the convent is established. Send some brothers to it. As for me, they honor me overmuch there, so that I fear I have lost more than I gained."

Some time later the learned doctor, Nicholas dei Pepoli, entered the order he had admired from the first.

John the Simple

There is no end to the tales about Francis's first companions. The word *delicious* irresistibly comes to mind, whether on account of their freshness of spirit and naiveté or their purity of heart. Brother Giles would be a favorite if we had to make a choice. We also especially like Brother John the Simple who was out plowing his field one day and, having learned that Francis was in the village, ran off to look for him. He found him sweeping the church—Francis insisted that the house of the Lord should always be clean and attractive. Without a moment's hesitation John grabbed Francis's broom and set to work cleaning the church. Afterward he sat down alongside the saint and roundly told him that the Lord had arranged their meeting, and so he was ready to do whatever Francis wished. Moved by this enthusiasm, Francis asked him to strip himself of all his worldly goods if he wished to join the brothers. Instead of answering John the Simple ran to the fields and returned with one of his oxen, his share of the family inheritance, which he was prepared to sell to give the money to the poor. But, back at his home, the family had heard what was going on and they were all in tears. The children in particular, his young brothers, clamorously voiced their grief. John was going away; John was leaving them for good. And then on top of everything, the ox.

Francis couldn't endure such despair. With the gentleness that had won him the love of others ever since his earliest years, he proceeded to arrange things so as to satisfy everyone. He ordered a meal to be prepared. "We're going to eat together; don't cry anymore." He spoke to the family so affectionately and merrily that there was no resisting his charm. Within a few moments their good humor had been restored, and the meal became like a feast. Then Francis explained that God was doing John and his family a very great favor in choosing him to follow him. "To be God's servant is to be a king." To be a king! Now there was something to be proud of. Good cheer all around. Still, Francis was quite aware of how poor these people were. "Don't worry," he told them, "I'm taking your brother, but I'm leaving you the ox." And, the chronicle naively adds, "They rejoiced, especially because they had gotten the ox back." Francis was too bright not to have guessed that the ox meant more to them than the young man.

So John put on the habit of a Franciscan, and from then on he applied himself to imitating Francis as faithfully as possible. It was, he thought, the surest way to become a good friar. If he saw Francis genuflect, he did too. He went so far as to copy all of Francis's gestures. If Francis raised his hands to heaven and sighed while praying, he could be certain that two steps behind him John the Simple would be raising his hands to heaven and sighing in exactly the same way. Francis, who had immediately taken a liking to him, was amused at first, but finally got tired of this scrupulous mimicry; and one day he reprimanded him. "Father," said John the Simple, "I have promised to do whatever you may do, and that's what I want, to do what you do." In the face of this ingenuous soul, uncorrupted by the world, Francis gave in. Besides, John was becoming so obviously holy that one could only admire him in silence. Not long afterward, around 1213, he died. His religious life, as brief as it was perfect, left an enduring memory. When Francis spoke of him, he felt, not sadness, but a marvelous joy; he always called him Saint John.

Along with Francis, who receives one of the loftiest places in the

Paradiso, Dante brings Bernard, Giles, and Sylvester, the first three brothers known to history, into the realm of the blessed. In all likelihood those were the only ones he could glorify, since he had no sources other than the *Legend* of Saint Bonaventure. Presumably he was unable to read either Celano or the legend of Perugia, which were already being hidden away in some convents to evade the ban of destruction laid on them by Bonaventure—a saint, but also the minister general of an order who wanted a portrait of the founder that matched his own ideas.

Life at la Portiuncula

One is tempted to view la Portiuncula as a kind of paradise, an uncomfortable paradise, to be sure, but a paradise nonetheless, because the comfort that we cling to with horrible cowardice becomes quite ridiculous when measured against the inner joy that the brothers lived on. Amidst the prayer, mortification, and poverty reigning there was a merriment such as few brotherhoods have known on earth. Freed from all their materials goods, which they had discarded as so much ordure *("tanquam stercora"),* they cast themselves upon God. Francis had told them how to go about it, and they recognized in his voice the inimitable accents of Christ.

From their earliest days, when they numbered only a dozen, Francis had led them into the woods of la Portiuncula and there he had told them they were called to work for the salvation of many others. Now that they had shaken off the burden of their property, their vocation was commanding them to beg their bread and preach repentance. And so, two by two, one behind the other, on the roads and in the villages, they went about, constantly meeting with insults and mockery; but at the end of the day they got together again in a mood of childlike gaiety. "They loved one another with an unspeakable love," says the anonymous writer from Perugia, who collected Brother Giles's reminiscences at the end of his life.

After Francis died, Giles sought refuge in a life of solitude, which he never abandoned. The only person whose presence he could tolerate was Brother John, his confessor, who wrote down everything he still recalled. Thus, of all the witnesses to the history of the Franciscans, Anonymous of Perugia touches us the most because his account has such freshness and absolutely no literary artifice. In it we can hear the voice of a man who never learned to lie and whom Francis cherished, calling him his knight of the Round Table. For chivalry, the very oldest mirage on Francis's horizon, still had in his eyes all its magic and irresistible appeal, to the point that if we set this ideal aside, we will never understand the man.

Like all the boys of his day, Francis had grown up admiring King Arthur and the knights of the Round Table. That protean myth gripped the imagination of all the young people in Europe. It showed honor in a heroic light, armed with a sword or lance, ready, as Hamlet says, "greatly to find quarrel in a straw," whenever it detected an offense. Served and venerated like a queen, the knight's chosen lady was raised to an unreal level of perfection, and defending that inaccessible creature was his bounden duty, like that of battling for the Christian faith and cleaving in twain as many infidels as could be reasonably wished.

There was no way this immense medieval dream could fail to excite a mind like Francis's and to shape his ambitions, whether in a literal, this-worldly sense or in a mystical vision of his destiny. As devoid of pride as he was, he always kept his chivalric instincts, faithful to his lady, whom Christ had chosen for him. We remain what we are till death—turn a glove inside out and it's still a glove. The saint and the sinner are reunited in the same coffin. They try in vain to go their separate ways, but they are forced to cohabitate, even if they are no longer talking. They have the same address in life and in death.

In 1211 Innocent III discovered that Otto made light of his commitments. Of the treaty recognizing papal supremacy over the emperor's Italian holdings, Otto cynically remarked, "It's a good document for your archives." We are just around the corner from Bethmann Hollweg's "scrap of paper." The pope excommunicated the emperor. And, in accordance with custom, after the bull of excommunication was read, the candles were turned upside down and the church was plunged into darkness. In reply Otto simply declared that he wasn't frightened "by the threats of a priest," And he continued to seize territory in southern Italy. He was then deposed upon order of the German bishops, and at the Diet of Nuremberg Frederick was elected in his place, at the age of seventeen. Having only meager possessions, the so-called "beggar emperor" already had something in common with Francis: He had been baptized over the same porphyry font in San Rufino. Later on he would display the same understanding of Islam.

In any case, Francis couldn't turn a deaf ear to the noises of the world. Among the greatest scandals of the time was the presence of the infidels in the Holy Land, the fact that Jerusalem was in Muslim hands. Francis had not forgotten that on the day of his conversion he had traced a large cross on his tunic with chalk. He was already a Crusader, and ever since childhood the passion for great adventure had never ceased to haunt him.

The first three Crusades had failed, the fourth had fallen short, and Jean de Brienne was preparing the fifth. Arise, then, Christian knight! If he couldn't exterminate the unbelievers, he would convert them; he would go into their midst, preach the true religion to them and win the precious grace of martyrdom, a second baptism that would fling wide the gates of paradise. A great many religious nourished in their souls the secret hope they would be tortured, thus wiping away the sins of a lifetime. The glory would redound to the whole Church for, according to Tertullian, the blood of martyrs is a seed. Numberless Christians would come forward to replace their martyred brothers and sisters. Thoughts like these raced feverishly through Francis's head. His brotherhood had been founded, the convent in Bologna was getting a steady stream of converts from every corner of Italy and even beyond. His mission in his homeland accomplished, he could now spread the kingdom of Christ with his blood and carry off the most coveted palm of all.

Together with a companion he left for Ancona, the nearest port. The trip from Ancona to Syria was not a mere junket. To go down the Adriatic and around Greece took a good three weeks, if the winds were favorable but, as the Psalms tell us, the wind has a peculiar feature: It accomplishes the word of the Lord, whether in the case of the Invincible Armada or of the boat carrying Francis of Assisi. And that boat now ran into contrary winds that absolutely thwarted the travelers' wishes and blew them toward Dalmatia. They had to take refuge in the port of Zara, where there was nothing for Francis for to do. We can't help thinking of the night in Spoleto, when God had blocked the way to the battlefield for Francis, who was wearing his fine armor and armed with a lance and buckler. You can't argue with God. Sometimes he uses sickness, sometimes he turns the wind into a brick wall. Francis was disappointed, and his only recourse was to go back to Umbria, but with what? He didn't have a penny. Regardless, he and his companion stowed away in the boat when it set sail for Italy. They thought—mistakenly—that they wouldn't be discovered at the bottom of the hold. The captain threatened to deposit them on the nearest shore, but one of those providential strangers appeared to take pity on them and give the sailors an imposing amount of provisions. At that price they were more than willing to bring the two monkish passengers home. This time the wind behaved the way it was supposed to, and within a few days the would-be Crusader could take the path back to Saint Mary of the Angels, obedient and crestfallen.

There was no shortage of comic incidents. Laughter was not forbidden; on the contrary, Francis felt that melancholy came straight from the devil. One day he had a difference of opinion with Brother Bonaparte, who was in charge of the kitchen, and who told Francis, "I do my best to prepare you dishes you can eat, and what do you do? You mix in water and ashes."

"Brother Bonaparte," Francis replied, "it's the intention that counts; yours is pure and so is mine. God will reward us both."

In the face of Brother Bonaparte's indignation some questions inevitably suggest themselves. Francis's ascetical practices went much further than this appalling dietary whim. Various kinds of mortifications, as well as prolonged and repeated fasts, must have affected Francis's health, which was already seriously undermined. Today we know for certain that Francis suffered from bone tuberculosis and malaria. His Testament confirms his sickly condition, without providing any details. How, we wonder, did he manage? It's natural to think that heaven gave him the strength he needed when he needed it—I myself believe this is so—but we should not forget that living in the outdoors helped him. He drew his breath in the healthful environment created by the trees of la Portiuncula and the forests of Mount Alverna, which were to him like mighty friends. Add to this the fact that he always sought sanctuary in places where the ozone-charged air gave him new vigor, in the woods and near springs, witness the hermitages of the valley of Rieti, Fonte Colombo, La Foresta—names that speak for themselves—and the deserted island in Lake Trasimeno. Still, the way he defied all sorts of weariness and strain is a sort of miracle in itself.

The *Carceri*

Somewhat later that summer Francis received yet another gift from his Benedictine friends. They offered him the *Carceri* (the prisons), the caves where in the earliest period of his conversion he had come seeking solitude, under the protection of his mysterious friend. They were spots of greenery hidden in the woods on the slopes of Mount Subasio, where the silence was broken only by the sound of a flowing stream. Bernard and Sylvester were the first of the contemplative Franciscans to seek out these "prisons"—escape hatches for the soul. Then the brothers built a little hermitage there.

From the beginning there were two distinct currents in Franciscan spirituality: the active life and the contemplative life. The active life was lived in good works, or the apostolate, preaching and, of course, charity in all its forms. It aimed at reawakening the Christian faith of people all too often ready to backslide into paganism, and at helping the unfortunate.

The contemplative life is almost impossible to summarize in a few sentences. Without risking any confused explanations, one might propose this minimal statement: Contemplation asks the individual to leave himself behind, to give way to God and be united with him. As far as I can see, it's not simply a matter of giving up habits that pose an obstacle to the inner life, but of breaking away from the cares of the world in solitude and silence, of driving away what the seventeenth century called diversion, in all its forms, whatever the eyes can see, the ears hear, and the senses experience. That's just the beginning: Contemplatives must also reach a state of absolute inner silence, must quiet the tumult of their own thoughts, dispel all their ideas, especially the ideas they form of God, because they are almost invariably false. In this mental nakedness the faithful soul will have the best chance of approaching its Creator. And to do that it must take the humanity of Christ as its point of departure to ascend to the mystery of the Trinity . . .

From the heights of Subasio, down through the openings in the firs and the beeches, the viewer contemplates the whole plain and, still higher up, above the dark forest, the mountain displays its tonsured crown. The landscape helps us understand better what men like Sylvester and Bernard were looking for in those caves where the sounds of the outside world couldn't reach them. "Here are my knights of the Round Table," said Francis, "the brothers who hide in deserted places so as to give themselves up all the more fervently to meditation. . . . Their holiness is known to God, but most often ignored by the brothers and by men. And, when their souls will be presented to the Lord by the angels, he will reveal to them the result and the reward for their troubles: the throng of souls that have been saved by their prayers. And he will tell them: 'My sons, here are the souls saved by your prayers; since you have been faithful in little things, I shall entrust great ones to you.' " This is the language of the great mystics. As for Francis himself, he plunged at nighttime into the abyss of the quest for God and during the day he took part in the life of his community, but he had the special graces that are indispensable to living both kinds of life.

Love Story

When Francis was preaching in the cathedral of San Rufino, he had no idea that a young girl, seventeen years old, accompanied by her mother and sister, was listening with passionate attention to the great seducer of souls who spoke of God's love. Francis was not what is called handsome, and he was twelve years older than she. But that didn't matter because, as unsurpassingly beautiful as she was, she welcomed each of his words with an indescribable emotion. He wrenched her out of herself. Together with him she fell in love with Love—and how can you separate Love from love for Love's messenger? Had the two kinds of love interfused? We have only one heart to love God and his creatures. If Clare had been told that she was in love with Francis, she would have been horrified and would not have understood. But after she got home, his voice, at once gentle and vehement, kept following her, preaching penance, scorn for riches, mortification of the flesh.

She could no more resist the impulse to love than he could. It was their nature, hers and his, but this was the first time she had heard him extolling Love, and he revealed to her that their passion was the same: the infinite desire to be one with God.

All during her childhood, she had listened to people talking about him, before and after the war and her family's exile in Perugia. No doubt she had at least spotted him during her walks—the whole town knew about the antics of that lad, the king of youth and the lord of rumpus. What did they think of him in her house, in the very noble family of the Offreduccio? Perhaps they expressed some ambiguous amusement over him, while disapproving of the way he threw away his father's money on banquets. Still, they weren't too hard on the scamp, who was always singing, day and night, especially night. His high spirits led almost everyone to treat him indulgently. The little girl listened.

She was twelve years old when the incredible news broke: The king of youth had converted and sought refuge—stark naked—beneath the bishop's cope, after disowning his father. Clare had surely not witnessed the scene (she never mingled with the crowd), but she must have been struck by what she was told about it. At a stroke the young man had cut his ties with the world, with all its vanities and all its wealth, to follow Christ. Clare too loved Christ, but as for leaving the world . . . People were already talking about her marriage prospects.

Young Clare was very pious. That's putting it mildly—she was, a great many witnesses report, already a saint. From childhood she had led a quasi-angelic life. One of her most characteristic traits was her desire not to be seen by anyone. Beneath the extremely elegant clothes her family dressed her in she wore a rough woolen garment like a hair shirt against her skin. She managed to put aside, and later give to the poor, the delicious meals served at her parents' table. One had to watch her very closely to discover that she spent hours and hours in prayer, that in her own way she was already living like a nun. Francis couldn't have dreamed of a listener more fervent or more totally dedicated to God.

Did he know her in 1210, when she was such a reticent young girl, so resolved never to show herself to other people? It seems doubtful.

Yet she must have heard something about him from her cousin, that same Rufino whom Francis had sent to preach half-naked. It wasn't long before the inevitable happened.

We know perfectly well what Francis thought of women after his conversion. To say he avoided looking at them is an understatement. He forbade his brothers to speak to them and, as for himself, he simply removed them from his world which, we may note, suggests how much they fascinated him. In a word, he feared their presence.

And now young Clare, as she faced the growing threat of marriage, the very idea of which horrified her, longed to ask his advice, to open her heart to this brother who spoke so marvelously about Christ. With the stubbornness of the elect, she decided that she would go to him whatever it cost. And so she did, in secret though not alone, accompanied by a very safe relative, Madonna Buona di Gualfuccio.

Francis, meanwhile, had been informed of Clare's intentions by Rufino, who served as intermediary, and agreed to meet her. Brother Philip the Tall, a pure soul if ever there was one, was chosen to be present at the interview. But where did it take place? In the woods? That hypothesis cannot be ruled out since they wanted the family to know nothing about it.

So many precautions! Without wishing to make any insinuations, we can't help being reminded of those old-fashioned novels where the code of outer respectability stands like a dragon on guard over the first permissible transports of eroticism. Let me press on and ask if that was what was actually going on here. This was love, mystical love, two souls flying toward each other above and beyond the demands of the flesh. Here too they had to be careful. The terrain was dangerous. Can we imagine the ancient adversary, as Dante calls him, passing up such a rare opportunity? A man facing a woman, both of them saints, but neither of them disembodied spirits. Don't tempt the devil, the proverb says. Did they realize that they were doing just that? Francis was in his thirtieth year; as he looked at that young girl in her exquisite beauty, how could he not fall in love with her? A fall would have been an incalculable disaster, because it would have hurt the millions of souls who were to find salvation under their guidance. But miraculously there wasn't even the shadow of a fault. With Francis we see the problem more clearly because in his case we are, so to speak, on familiar ground. Grace was visibly at work on his humanity. He had desires and passions like ours, but with this girl who in utter candor revealed to him the prodigious call of God's love, we have the feeling of running up against impenetrable light.

Let's try to visualize the scene, to get a better understanding of Francis's attitude. It was no accident that he chose Philip the Tall to accompany him. A serious, reflective man, Philip was a sharp-eyed observer who missed nothing and had no scruples about speaking his mind. His presence would make Francis doubly prudent. Would Francis distrust what he was going to say? He may have been a saint, but he was still impulsive, and while he wanted never to look at a woman again, he was about to see one of the most beautiful women, morally if not physically, at his feet. Let Francis beware of himself! He was going to have to fight.

Clare too was moved. Lovers have no psychology because they are out of their heads. Clare was in love with Christ—and, perhaps, with Francis too, but not consciously, because she couldn't make the necessary distinction between them. She was overcome with the joy of surrendering her soul to the man who gave her God; and it is quite possible that, in her extreme euphoria, she fell down at his knees and blurted out her desire to leave the world and its riches to follow Christ. After being long contained in the silence of meditation, the words burst forth from her heart. He listened, and suddenly, as if delivering a sword thrust at an enemy, he said, with a strange brutality, "I don't believe you." Had she heard him rightly? She didn't flinch. Francis continued: "Still, if you want me to have faith in your words, you will do what I am going to tell you: Change your clothes, put on an old sack, and go about the town begging your bread."

Did she suffer from this unexpected demand? Not the least in the world. She was delighted to offer Christ a proof of her love. It was wonderful to obey this man who spoke to her for the Lord.

Francis, rather, was the one who suffered. How could he have ordered her to do that? But he had felt inspired to do it, and little by little its meaning came to light. By telling Clare to become a beggar for the love of Christ, he had given Lady Povery the living face of a young girl. It was the triumph of the highest kind of courtly love. There was no suspect desire to be feared any more. The chosen maiden was now inaccessible, except in the mystical sphere where souls are reunited in a foretaste of paradise. One cannot dream of a purer love.

Clare dressed herself in rags and went to beg on the streets of Assisi.

It was easy to ask the impossible from someone of her breeding. We are told that she dressed herself in a sack and put a white veil on her head, leaving the house stealthily as if for a tryst, a meeting with that stranger, total poverty. No one had any idea of this, but then who, once he had seen her in that getup, could have believed his eyes? No one, except Francis.

This was the beginning of one of the most magnificent dreams of love humanity has ever had. But it's more than doubtful that they saw things that way. Their love was swallowed up in the love of Christ, and words don't exist to give any notion of such mystical bonds. The flesh could play no role here, but of course it was still present, though hidden in the depths of the unconscious and never manifest. We can grasp something of this in the vision—one of the strangest bequeathed us by the Middle Ages—that Saint Clare had of Francis later on. It reveals above all what might be called an abysmal innocence, precisely because of its astonishing concreteness. Quite evidently, she didn't understand the meaning of what she said. And how is one to find a language for the soul without using carnal expressions? Modern-day amateur psychoanalysts could obviously have a field day with this document, but the theologians who read it in the thirteenth century were not fooled: Purity of heart burns steadily and brightly in the frankness of her avowals.

It's certain that Francis never learned about this—one trial, at least, he was spared. And as for Clare, she would have been scandalized if she had been told that even in such supernatural love nature couldn't be absent, since the soul is united with the body. And how could this love express itself, except in terms of earthly love, with its inevitably sensual vocabulary? The vision, as reported by the sisters to whom she entrusted it, recalls the Song of Songs, that supremely beautiful love poem in which the Church has always seen the soul smitten with God. Clare spoke the language of desire because she had no other kind to translate the excess of an ineffable passion.

Sister Clare

Naturally, Clare's parents knew nothing about the secret comings and goings of their daughter. She was nearing eighteen and, ever since she was twelve, they had been looking for a husband for her. This couldn't go on; and she decided to leave her father's house.

On March 18, 1212, Palm Sunday, Clare went to mass with her parents for the last time. She would run away that night, thwarting forever their plans and hopes. There could be no question of saying good-bye to them, and that idea troubled her so much that she neglected to go take one of the palm fronds being distributed at the altar. So Bishop Guido came down the steps, personally carried a frond down to her, and placed it in her hand. The gesture might seem unusual, but it was important. It symbolized the Church's approval of Clare's vocation. The bishop, who had been informed by Francis, knew all about Clare's proposed flight.

At dawn, in the deepest silence, Clare and her cousin Pacifica, who also wanted to become a nun, left by a jib door, which served as the door of the dead, never used except to give passage to coffins. Perhaps Clare and Pacifica saw themselves as already dead to the world, called to a new life. They made it to Saint Mary of the Angels, where Francis was waiting for them. Everything was ready. It was the hour of matins and pitch black outside. The postulants were welcomed by the light of candles held by the brothers who came out to meet them, while the woods of la Portiuncula resounded with hymns of joy. Like a true Italian, Francis knew how to summon up all the poetry needed for the first steps toward paradise taken by these brides of Christ. On his own authority he gave them both the tonsure. Then they took off their rich clothes and exchanged them for the coarse Franciscan frock.

Normally it would have been the bishop's job to confer the habit and especially to cut the girls' hair, but Francis took charge and quietly did things his own way, as usual. He must have felt a surge of joy as he passed the scissors over the head of the woman who was now Lady Poverty in person, his lady whom he had snatched away from the world. It was like a spiritual takeover, a seizure by the Church of what belonged to it.

Once their first vows were pronounced, Francis led his spiritual daughters to the Benedictines at San Paolo di Bastia, on the road to Perugia, a few miles away. As had to be expected, Clare's parents were shaken by her disappearance and went scouring the countryside till they had found her. One thinks of that famous scene at the wicket of Port Royal, where the father of Angélique Arnaud raised a storm, demanding the return of his daughter. Clare's uncle, at the head of a band of armed companions, came in shouting and cursing, which drove the young nun into the convent chapel, where she seized the altar cloth with both hands. The shouting stopped when she bared her shaven head. Then Uncle Monaldo, the head of the family, realized she would never give in, and he withdrew.

Eight days later it was Catherine's turn. She was fifteen years old, and she too ran away, rejoining her sister among the Benedictines. This time Uncle Monaldo, in his role of elder brother, was resolved to use strong-arm tactics at whatever cost and barged into the convent with a dozen or so knights. He did make an initial effort at gentle persuasion, but it got him nowhere: little Catherine was as determined as her sister, whom she called to her aid. Overcome with rage, one of the men beat her unmercifully and dragged her by the hair toward the mountain, followed by the fierce gang of myrmidons. At this point a miracle occurred. Monaldo struck her with great violence and immediately uttered a cry of pain: His arm had been gripped in an agonizing paralysis. And Catherine, whom her abductors were still struggling with, became as heavy as a massive piece of lead.

Meanwhile Clare ran in and began to harangue the men so forcefully that they abandoned their prey and went back sheepishly to Assisi, while the two sisters returned to their cells. But these dramatic events may have frightened the Benedictines, because Clare and Catherine had to seek refuge elsewhere. After fleeing to the Benedictine of Sant'Angelo on the other side of the mountain, they were given San Damiano by the generous bishop of Assisi. Here, just as Francis had predicted when he was repairing that church, the first monastery of the Poor Clares was established. Catherine received from Francis the name of Agnes as the symbol of purity safe from the clutches of the world. He always liked to give each one of his people the name that defined them in his eyes.

Vocations would not be slow in coming. With a fatherly eye Francis watched over his spiritual daughters, especially his beloved Clare. Still, memories of his restless youth and the nearness of the two monasteries started him thinking. One day when he had to preach to the Poor Clares at San Damiano, he began by kneeling down and praying for a long time. Then he had ashes brought to him, drew a circle with them around himself, put some on his head and, still kneeling on the flagstones, went on with his prayer. The astonished sisters looked on expectantly. At last he got up, recited the *Miserere,* and left the church. And that was all—a sermon woven out of silence.

Deep down he was as apprehensive as ever about women. Perhaps he noticed a little too much enthusiasm in the charity his brothers showed toward their saintly neighbors. One day he dropped an ironic and revealing remark: "It is the Lord who has preserved us from taking wives; but, who knows, it may have been the devil who has sent us these sisters."

And in his first rule, he wrote: "Let us be careful to keep all our members pure, because the Lord says, 'Everyone who looks at a woman lustfully has already committed adultery with her in his heart.' " And he decided that those among the brothers who displayed a certain repugnance toward visiting the sisters would be assigned to that task.

Life Must Be Reinvented

In those days the Franciscan ideal shone with something like the splendor of the dawn, gradually scattering the darkness of the emerging sects. The brotherhood was flourishing everywhere in Umbria. In towns and villages all across the region people saw these gay companions appearing, dressed in habits of coarse homespun, singing aloud or even performing tricks to attract crowds and announce the Good News to them. We can almost hear the Salvation Army tambourine jingling in the distance. Francis called these alert missionaries God's jugglers, as if the Lord were snapping up souls through sleight of hand. Begging their bread, but offering their work in exchange—haying, sweeping, washing or, if they knew how, making wooden tools—they never accepted money and lodged wherever they could, sometimes with the local priest, beneath a lean-to, in a hayloft or a barn. Often enough they spent the night camping outdoors.

People got used to them. However warm or chilly the reception given them, they preached with the fervor of neophytes, and their faith stirred a responsive chord deep within their listeners. They were the prophets of a new world where disgust for riches and passion for the Gospel changed lives and brought happiness. What good was it to listen to the Waldensians and those strange *Perfecti,* whose language was becoming incomprehensible? Franciscan simplicity was wiping out heresy. Down the roads marched the new brothers, two by two, one following the other, the very men whose steps Francis had once heard in a prophetic vision.

These beginnings of Franciscan life, so sweetly anarchic in appearance, had to give way to an order. Each year saw the number of brothers double. They were coming in now from all directions, and some of them were destined to play an important role in one of the greatest adventures of Christian thought. Even more sensitive than the men to a mystical call, the women at San Damiano sought the inner peace that a turbulent, violent world threatened to destroy. The light Francis shed reached the first convents of the Poor Clares, who loved Christ as he did. A song of joy went up to heaven. This was a moment never quite recaptured later: The bolt from the blue can't be repeated.

The Children's Crusade

The great scandal of the day was that Christ's tomb remained in the hands of the infidels, while the Crusades that had successively tried to deliver it had all been fruitless. There had already been four, and the fifth was being prepared in Germany and Hungary. This was the business of kings and knights, among the common people everywhere in the West the rush to the land of Christ crossed over the Church's dogmatic frontiers. It was like a stampede of souls, out to storm an ideal world where the Gospel was triumphant. For Catholics especially the person of the Savior had a magnetic power whose profundity we have lost because, except in isolated cases, our twentieth-century faith has become feeble and formalistic. We have lost the essential thing, which is the enthusiasm we call fanaticism. Without realizing it, Francis was followed by crowds of people harshly dubbed heretics, who resembled him in his love for Christ. Some of their number had been seen mounting the stake with the certitude that Jesus was speaking to them. It should come as no surprise that within the bosom of the Church children proved to be among the most accessible—one might almost say, the most vulnerable—to divine love. It was only too easy to make them lose their head. Like Francis they had the heart of a Crusader.

But what sick brain could have begotten the idea that where men had failed children could succeed? The movement seems to have taken hold almost immediately, and without any concerted efforts, in France, Italy, and on the banks of the Rhine. A Cistercian monk, Alberic of Trois-Fontaines, from a monastery near Châlons-sur-Marne, has left us an account dated 1241 of the French contribution to this doomed effort. Stephen, a young shepherd from a village in the Touraine, believed he had been chosen by God to lead the youth of the country to a holy war. A sort of mystical delirium gripped the children of all classes, rich and poor. Thirty thousand came, from the age of eight and older; and the eight-year-olds inspired the teenagers to join them. It was as if Jesus Christ were calling for help. Their parents let them have their way, overwhelmed by the mysterious, infectious power of the group. The children went down the Rhone Valley, singing and carrying crosses, the smallest riding on the shoulders of the older ones.

This army of innocents arrived in Marseilles. There two shrewd privateers, Hugues de Fer and Guillaume Porc (Iron Hugh and William Pig), names one might describe as invented by the devil, embarked them for Palestine free of charge on seven vessels, of which two sank. All the survivors were sold to slave dealers. A few of these victims, driven insane by fear, managed to escape, but many perished. The others served the whims of their masters in one way or another. And behind harem walls one sometimes heard sad songs sung in French.

Germany had its share in the horror. In Cologne a young boy named Nicholas gathered twenty thousand little Crusaders of both sexes. He got them across the Alps, not without horrendous difficulties, but he had promised them that they reached Jerusalem, they would see all the gates of paradise open wide to welcome them. When they finally got to Genoa, where they were supposed, not to embark for the Holy Land but, as they firmly hoped, to walk all the way to Jerusalem as the Mediterranean dried up beneath their feet, people ridiculed them. Profoundly demoralized and utterly exhausted, they had to break up and go home as best they might. The ones who did, when all was said and done, could consider themselves lucky, but they had had to bury many small corpses along their way through the mountains.

In Italy the bishop of Brindisi tried to prevent the embarkation of this army of dreamers, but he couldn't save the girls who were carried off to houses of prostitution or sold as servants—for slavery still existed, even in Assisi. All of Europe was downcast by these expeditions, which it lacked the courage to forbid. Innocent III had cried: "These children put us to shame. While we sleep, they joyously leave their homelands." But what had he done to keep them?

Francis must have been moved by this terrible disorder, which cast such dishonor on Christendom. We would like to know what he thought about it, but the chroniclers of the day have deemed it wiser to maintain a modest silence—assuming that the evidence hasn't been destroyed.

One generation of historians follows another and contradicts it. Refuting their predecessors seems to be a pleasure of which they never tire. And so new errors are added to the venerable ones of earlier times, but the game is not without profit, because it clarifies certain truths. Sometimes history has to be restrained from taking the dizzy plunge into legend, but it's possible to go too far in this direction. In our own day, for example, we have seen writers question the fact that Joan of Arc was burned in Rouen. In the case of Francis all the texts concerning his youth came close to being done away with. Down through the ages documents have been thrown into the fire. Alongside the history that says its piece stands the mute specter of history reduced to ashes.

As for the so-called Children's Crusade, we have sketched in the bare essentials, trusting a document from 1240—but it was reworked twenty years later. This doesn't exclude the possibility that other documents may have vanished in a pious holocaust designed to safeguard the reputations of certain cities that were eager to exploit the Crusade or of certain personages like King Philip Augustus of France, who had the young Crusaders driven away from the outskirts of Paris.

In any case there is no suppressing the evidence that has come down to us. Some years later what is called human justice took its course: Hugues de Fer and Guillaume Porc, the Marseillais flesh merchants, were hanged by order of Frederick II.

A Mountain All His Own

In the spring of 1213, thanks to one of those inspirations that so often guided him, Francis left Spoleto for the Romagna, together with Brother Leo. Along the way he stopped at the foot of the castle of Montefeltro, where they were celebrating a feast set off by a tourney in honor of one of the counts of the family who was being knighted. "Let us go to that feast," said Francis, "for with God's help we will do some spiritual good." There is no doubting his lofty intentions, but Francis was also attracted by the word *knight*, because to the end of his days he would wear the imaginary armor of his youthful dreams. So festivities like those at the castle were not to be missed. The Lord had thought of it all beforehand.

A banquet was being given in the great courtyard, attended by a throng of gentlemen. The scene must have been as glittering as it was noisy. Francis didn't hesitate; he walked into the castle, found the place where the merrymakers were gathered, and climbed atop a low wall so that the whole fashionable company could get a better look at him. One can imagine the lords, great and little, watching that beggar perched on the stonework as if on a platform, lifting up his voice—a beautiful voice, a clear, strong tenor—to harangue them about the martyrs and all the saints who suffered for the love of Christ. His language was so simple and so vigorous that they listened and were overcome with emotion. Certain strains always found an echo in the soul back then.

When Francis fell silent, a man came forward and took him aside. It was Messer Orlando du Chiusi, a well-known person of high rank and great wealth. "Brother," he said, "I would like to speak with you about the salvation of my soul." To this tremendous question Francis gave an answer that reveals all the courtesy of the Middle Ages and of a born gentleman. "That pleases me greatly, but go and do the honors to your friends who have invited you; and after dinner we shall talk as much as you like."

With complete humility the great lord obeyed the beggar; then, when the feast had ended, he returned to Francis and confided to him his desire for a life of perfection. Francis showed him that the external world was no obstacle, since everyone bears his own solitary place within him. After which Orlando told the man of God: "I own a mountain in Tuscany that would be ideal for your brothers: Mount Alverno. It is covered with woods and far from the world. If you like, I will give it to you and your companions, for the salvation of my soul."

Filled with joy Francis could only accept his gift. God does things royally: Francis had been seeking a perfect spot for prayer, and now God was offering him Mount Alverno. Francis would have his magic mountain.

Once he got back to la Portiuncula, Francis informed his brothers of the providential donation that crowned his wishes for a retreat. Still, he would have to explore the mountain a little, and at the moment he didn't have the strength for it. Bouts of illness left him too weak to do anything, so he sent two companions in his stead. They first went to Lord Orlando to tell him about their mission. He supplied them with fifty or so men at arms as all-purpose helpers, because in that lonely area there was always danger from wild animals.

After a careful search they fixed their choice on a level stretch of ground just beneath the mountaintop; and there, aided by their troop of men, they built a hut of boughs and took possession of Mount Alverno in the name of God. And so Francis became, horror of horrors, a landowner. Did he think about this? We may wonder, but no doubt he saw the matter in a different light: Even if the deed of gift came later on from the heirs of the count of Chiusi, Mount Alverno had passed from the hands of Messer Orlando into God's hands, and Mount Alverno belonged to God.

Despite his weakness Francis decided to visit the site and took to the road, together with Brother Masseo, whom he named leader of the trip; Brother Tancrede di Rieti, a noble knight who had abandoned the glory of arms to become a friar; and Brother Leo, to whom Francis so often opened his heart.

The first evening they stopped at a convent to sleep, but the night that Francis spent all by himself in the church must have been down-right hellish. Satan attacked him with his most violent demons, who tried everything to unhinge him. They raised a horrible ruckus—which apparently woke no one else up—subjecting Francis to a trial like nothing he had known before. But the knight of Christ stood firm. "Damned spirits," he told his enemies, "Do with my body whatever God lets you. I will gladly endure it, for I have no worse enemy than my body." Then the demons dragged him all over the flagstones of the church and vied at tormenting him while Francis thanked the Lord for what he called a sign of great love. Disheartened, the demons finally left him, and he went off to the nearby woods, where he conversed with Christ, not without shedding abundant tears as he recalled the Passion.

The brothers awoke to find him raised up from the ground and "enveloped in a shining cloud." By morning he was incapable of taking a single step. If he still wanted to climb to Alverno, he would have to ride on the back of an ass. His companions went off to fetch one, and found a peasant willing to lend them his beast when he learned it was for Francis, the man everyone was talking about. And so, broken with fatigue, Francis was hoisted on top of the ass.

Here occurred one of the most moving incidents of his life. Having gone a little way by his side, the peasant had the far-fetched idea of giving a bit of a lecture to this exemplary character who happened to be indebted to him; and an incredible dialogue started up:

"Tell me, are you Brother Francis of Assisi?"

"Yes."

"Well, try to be as virtuous as everybody thinks you are, because many people have a lot of confidence in you; so I advise you not to have anything in you out of line with what they expect."

Instead of replying, Francis let himself drop down to earth and, kneeling before the man, he kissed his feet and thanked him for his charitable warning. Overcome with emotion and reduced to silence, the peasant lifted him back up onto the ass, with the help of his companions, and they continued their ascent until they reached the foot of Alverno.

There Francis stretched out in exhaustion beneath a bush. And hundreds of birds flew in from every direction, singing and beating their wings around him as if sent from God. Many of them rested on his arms, his legs, and his head, uttering little cries of joy. The peasant and the three brothers couldn't believe their eyes, and Francis himself was ecstatic over the way the Lord had shown him through his brothers the birds that the choice of Alverno was a good one.

Thoroughly refreshed, he was able to continue his journey and after a little exploration he discovered the place where God was waiting for him in the crevice of a rock: It was there that Francis would relive the Passion of Christ in his soul.

Thus the great problem had been resolved, and the chosen place pointed out. Was Francis happy? Yes, but he was still indecisive. The question arose in his mind: Was his vocation to give himself to contemplation or to work for the salvation of his neighbor? As if contemplation were not action on a higher level . . . Did he sense a new temptation after the assaults of the night before? From whom could he ask advice? Upon reflection, he sent Brother Masseo with a companion to see Lady Clare at San Damiano, then he dispatched Brother Sylvester to the solitude of the Carceri. And the answer came without delay, the same in both cases: Act. This advice from two contemplatives was just what Francis had been waiting for. Contemplation would come later, in due time.

The Man with Wings on His Feet

Francis made one trip to Spain, but all we have is a brief account by Celano and a handful of conjectures. Perhaps he went to Santiago de Compostela, but his ambition was to get to Morocco and to convert its sultan, whom he called the Miramolin—a plan that fit in well with his perpetual desire for martyrdom. Such was his ardor to reach the goal of his journey that his companion could barely keep up with him, because at times he broke out into a run. But once again, as in Spoleto, the road was barred. He fell sick and had to return to Italy.

From a distance we can understand what might be called Francis's hesitant joy when he saw the ideal place for solitary life shown him in the rocks of Alverno. Similarly, we feel his unmixed joy when the two contemplatives advised him to choose the active life. To borrow one of Baudelaire's favorite expressions, there was in him a double drive, not toward God and the devil, to be sure, but toward moving and staying put. Or rather contemplation and action. In Spain he rediscovered the energy of his youth to hurry down the roads, running not toward pleasure but to martyrdom. One never transforms oneself completely. Francis remained true to his nature, the only thing that changed was the direction.

In any case it was clear that Providence wanted him back in Italy. He returned to la Portiuncula, finished his convalescence and, incorrigible as ever, gave in once more to the lure of the open road. There was no hope of martyrdom in Umbria, but there was action, preaching, visiting little groups of brothers scattered through the countryside or withdrawn into hermitages, as more men, rich as well as poor, kept joining up. They left the world behind and traveled about in pairs, one behind the other, praying as they walked along. These strangers, whose steps Francis had once heard, were now a great many. He had to see them, to teach them a little. It should not be forgotten that Francis was a man who lived in the open air. He was never locked up in a convent cell for very long. The road, the highways, the word of God borne like a seed on all the winds . . . Contemplation couldn't be put aside, of course: It found its place in the heart of the night. But in the day they had to act. And beneath all this lay the nostalgia for martyrdom. That would come later, the supreme reward before the entrance into paradise. It would, but not the way he thought.

While waiting, he went off with Brother Leo to spread the Gospel once more in the valley of Rieti, which would not abandon its pagan ways. Walking in this paradise was the reverse of doing penance. Italy has nothing that speaks more directly to the heart than those hills with their shady slopes where the cypresses stand like watchmen over the villages, fields, and deep grassy meadows. We are hardly surprised that this landscape harmonized so profoundly with the soul of Francis of Assisi; the surprise would be if at some point in history or other a Saint Francis had *not* arisen from the soil in that enchanted nook of the universe.

A natural scene with such a gently spiritual appeal drew the man who lived close to heaven to make him listen one day to the ecstatic song of the earth. Francis glanced around him like a lover who is forever wonderstruck. Habit meant nothing here, everything kept its primeval power, everything stayed new, as new as God.

And so Francis carried within him the land of Umbria, borrowing its color for the clothes he and his brothers wore. It was a far cry from the days when the crowds threw mud and rocks at them. Now when he came to a town, he was welcomed by cries of joy; and as the bells rang out he was led in procession by people singing psalms and bearing leafy branches in their hands. He preached of returning to God and obedience to the Church. He was never a reformer. The throng surrounding him cut off so many pieces of his tunic he was left almost naked.

"The saint! There's the saint!" they shouted. What did he think of these cheers? We know very well. "Don't canonize me too soon," he said once during a triumph of that sort. "I am still perfectly capable of fathering children." A valuable remark that sheds light on a whole aspect of his inner life, his deep humility, the total refusal of all human glory, and that sanely ironic view of himself that permitted him to maintain his balance in the face of stunning success.

Perhaps too he wondered about the serious problem for the future: how to organize and govern his brotherhood. Could he do the job? He had his doubts, but in this as in everything the Lord would guide him. Patience. Time would tell.

They say that Saint Bernard made a trip on foot from one end of Lake Geneva to the other without even realizing that there was water alongside the road. With his hood lowered over his head he followed the path and his train of thought. This is a character trait one can admire, and it illuminates what the Germans would call Francis's *Weltanschauung.* The most beloved of all the saints was simply a great lover of both the visible and the invisible world. When he turned his brotherhood into an order, he must have suffered because he saw a brother in every living being, and he had his heart set on the word *brother.* Everything found its way into this brotherhood, because everything came forth from the hands of God the Creator, who is Love. Francis enrolled the sun and extended his domain to the last blade of grass and the least of the insects. In winter he had wine and honey set out for the bees to keep them alive during cold snaps. He spoke to flowers, breathing their perfume with delight and inviting them to praise the Lord in their own fashion. We are amazed to see that a more or less uneducated man was capable of giving Italy its first great poem in the vernacular. Yet it would have been still more astonishing if that cry of love had not burst forth from Francis's throat. He had had it in him ever since his childhood.

The stories of his relations with animals have brought joy to generation after generation for eight hundred years. By what instinct did they recognize in him the brother par excellence? We don't know, because we are almost completely ignorant about their affinities with the human race and especially about their rapture in the presence of the mystery of holiness when it manifests itself in an exceptional man. The life of Francis of Assisi provides so many examples that we don't know which ones to choose. The wolf of Gubbio is a character apart, who will be treated in a little while, but let us stop for a moment by the lake of Rieti, where a fisherman offered Francis a tench that he called brother, advising it, as he always did in such cases, not to let itself get caught, and then releasing it back into the water next to the boat. Instead of disappearing, the tench began to wriggle joyously before the man of God. It would not go away without Francis's leave—and his blessing.

Stories of this sort still have all their old freshness, charm, and plausibility. The skeptics are free to smile at them, to wriggle joyously in their doubts. When they encountered Saint Sergius of Russia, other animals displayed the same love for human holiness.

Francis couldn't have asked for a more affectionate companion than Brother Leo, nor one more attentive to his every word. Those words were later to be recorded on little rolls of parchment, the famous *rotuli* scholars are still hunting for in every corner of the Franciscan world. One hopes they will discover them some day buried in a library or hidden in a wall: They might give us a Francis whom we shall never know well enough otherwise.

While awaiting that day, let's follow him up the slopes of Monte Rosato to the convent of Poggio Bustone, which he had founded during his trip to the region, at an altitude of twenty-six hundred feet. The valley lay beneath him in all its splendor, washed by a tender, golden light that filled him with happiness. It seemed an ideal place to lead the contemplative life. Perhaps it was, but Francis wanted to go higher. He was a lover of beautiful landscapes, like Saint Benedict, and he would find his favorite hermitage at thirty-six hundred feet on the same mountain, beneath a wall of high cliffs. He would be intoxicated by its utter loveliness. What did it matter that his body suffered almost continually, when the pain was overcome by the indescribable joy in his heart? The invisible universe was so close in the silence of those heights and in the dazzling far off vistas of a promised land.

But he had to tear himself away from all that, to go back down and share with people the divine good cheer he received in those moments of pure love. He had the gift of bringing peace and making others smile. Through his hands something was transmitted from heaven to his brothers and to everyone who approached him. For all that solitude would always be a temptation. The mountains gave it to him, but this tireless seeker for God went to find it elsewhere, in an island of Lake Trasimeno, not far from Assisi and Perugia. Long and wooded, it seemed, amidst the chiaroscuro of its trees, a refuge still more secret than the first. Wild animals came right up to him, drawn by the magnetism he couldn't surpress. Brother Leo, who had gotten him aboard a boat for the island, left him by himself all during his retreat there.

But Francis never stayed in one place, and after a while he set off on foot along the roads and over the hills of Umbria, heading north to visit the increasingly numerous hermitages. Meanwhile in Rome the Curia was working on his rule, modifying it, and retailoring it in its own way to make it more reasonable. Francis would get a rude awakening.

Brother Elias of Assisi

He probably entered the order in 1213, a grand and mysterious character, the son of a mattress maker, who would become the third most important person in Christendom, almost equal to the pope and the emperor. Blessed by some, cursed by others, he disappears and reappears in the chronicles of the period, depending upon the whims of those who hated or admired him. But who was he?

Born in Assisi of a mother from the town and a father from Castel Britti, near Bologna, he was most likely around the same age as Francis. He first made a living as a mattress maker and also as a schoolmaster.

He knew Francis because everybody in Assisi knew everybody else, especially in the textile business. Were they intimates?

The reader will recall the young man whom Francis saw a great deal of, because he preferred him to his other companions and whom he took as his confidant at the moment of his conversion. It was to him that Francis revealed his discovery of an immense and precious treasure. The unknown friend was overjoyed—and curious to know more.

But however great his curiosity, nothing of what he said to Francis has come down to us. We can imagine the exaltation and naive verbosity of the young convert. Like a lover speaking of his love, he unleashed a flood of words, and his confidant listened. He patiently followed after that singular lad who had fallen in love with God. One day Francis led him to the cave where he would have that great storm of tears, the first in a long series that ultimately damaged his eyes. The confidant stood off a bit to the side, discreet but attentive, watching over Francis, who intrigued him because of the extraordinary quality of his soul. To put it simply, he guessed that he was dealing with someone special, and that wherever Francis was, greatness was there too. And Francis loved him. That unknown person may have been Elias, and I would say that it *was* Elias. The fact that he was a few years older than Francis, his post of consul during the first commune of Assisi, all the papers destroyed (by order of the Ministers General John of Parma and Bonaventure) that concerned him, his intelligence, and his character as a whole incline me to believe that Elias was the stranger. Especially his character, because Elias was known to be ambitious.

Leaving Assisi, he went to live in Bologna, where he became a notary, a job that didn't prevent him from getting an education in that university city, Europe's first, and the day would come when Elias was considered one of most learned men of his time.

We have left Francis behind only to rediscover him in the light of his friendship with Elias, but their relations were marked by all sorts of upheavals. No one admired Francis more than Elias, and yet he seems to have been his most formidable antagonist. He provided Celano with a large part of the first biography we have of the saint, claiming to be Francis's best informed confidant. Brother Leo would deny that claim and dispute the honor of being his most intimate friend. And so he was surrounded by incessant quarrels that threw everything into confusion. Whom should we listen to? Who is right?

As the years passed the saint and the eminent politician came to confront one another. Then there were explosions, short-lived estrangements, but also persistent disagreements broken by occasional reconciliations. Elias would experience terrible defeats and stunning successes, and his enemies would go so far as to challenge the final blessing that his beloved brother gave him at the moment of death.

When, exactly, did he enter the order? Possibly around 1213 in Cortona, but we don't know anything about it. Some of the relevant documents have disappeared. The only date that sheds a little light on the situation is 1217, because in that year Francis sent Elias as the head of a mission to Syria with four brothers. It was an important mission, the first one to the holy places. So Elias must have been a tried and tested Franciscan for some time before this. But then another question arises: Why did he enter the brotherhood whose primitive character he would do something to adulterate? Did he have a vocation? We have no right to deny it, and he loved Francis, but we can't help thinking that he saw (Francis did too, of course) the immense future of the Friars Minor, that prodigious flock of sparrows darting toward heaven, seemingly carrying with them the earth, whose color they had borrowed. Their success would be unprecedented—provided someone knew how to manage it. Glory, Brother Elias . . .

He would have his share of human glory. He remains, along with Frederick II and Innocent III, among the greatest figures of the thirteenth century. He put the Franciscan way of life on a firm footing. Absolutely speaking, he was nothing next to Francis. But let's leave him to his noble temporal dreams. He wanted glory; let him have it. Whatever his sins, his love for Francis wins him pardon.

1214

In the life of a saint, where action and contemplation are balanced harmoniously, there is an inner continuity that mocks our desire to tag events with precise dates. We want to follow time step by step, whereas the soul moves in an eternal present, but we let ourselves be mesmerized by the flow of facts behind which the essential truth lies concealed. Still, a few reference points grant us the illusion that we understand better what eludes our curiosity.

The year 1214 was marked for Francis of Assisi by two losses. First came the death of John the Simple. We have see that in speaking of John, as he often did, Francis called him Saint John. John's spiritual perfection assured his eternal blessedness, and Francis didn't mourn him.

But did he weep over the second death, which we learn of almost incidentally, when in the notarized title deeds of the Bernardone property, we find the name of Angelo has replaced that of Pietro? Old Bernardone had been a witness despite himself to the anticipatory canonization of the son whom he had so lavishly cursed. Eventually this torrent of abuse had to give way before the unanimous public acclaim for Francis; and the amiable beggar Albert, who had deflected his father's lightning bolts, found himself out of a job, though he no doubt joined the brotherhood. What became of the cloth merchant's pride? How did his heart react to the passage of time? Who could refuse to forgive him? God had taken away all his earthly hopes and given him little in exchange. One hopes that he mellowed before rendering his angry soul to God.

In the year when the battle of Bouvines was fought, when thrones were tottering once, there were a great many newcomers to the brotherhood, but Francis insisted on personally receiving them with honor at la Portiuncula and clothing them with the coarse habit in the church of the Holy Virgin. With his customary grace he spoke to everyone on his own level, which called for as much finesse as tact, because there were all sorts among the new arrivals, men of every conceivable origin and background, learned men and simple alike. Fatigue didn't matter to him, and each postulant, whoever he was, was given a loving welcome.

Francis had an inexhaustible, heavenly tenderness, and he knew how to pour it into the hearts of the strangers kneeling before him, who felt they were getting it from Christ.

My Brothers, the Birds

Nonetheless, something in Francis's nature couldn't resist the call of the open road. One day, together with several companions, he left la Portiuncula and went off toward Spoleto, singing in French, as he so often did. Just when they were nearing the charming little town of Bevagna, which was destined to play a role in the quarrel between the pope and the emperor, and whose crenelated walls still seem to be watching in a fold of the ground for any suspicious approach, they saw all sorts of different birds awaiting Francis in a vast meadow at the outskirts of the town. There were also an incredible number of birds in the trees all around. The crows and their cousins, the long-beaked black rooks, added a serious note to that colorful gathering, which was lightened by the clear notes of the wood pigeons and the orange-throated bullfinches. All the birds of the countryside were there, the birds that pilfered and those that lived only to sing and the ones that haunted the rocks or nested in the furrows. When Francis drew near, not one of them budged, not even a magpie.

He greeted them with the usual blessing of the brotherhood: "May the Lord be with you." Then he asked his brothers the birds to pay careful attention as he preached them a sermon full of good sense and love.

First, he congratulated them on the way they were dressed, leaving gaudy, floral patterns aside, so that no one would be offended, and on the sublime independence their wings conferred on them. They had all the skies to frolic in. They lived without a care for the morrow; their food was generously provided for them every day. How God loved them! And, said Francis to his brothers the birds, they ought to thank the Lord all day long.

The birds showed their joy at these words by beating their wings and stretching out their necks to get a better look at their brother Francis, but what most caught everyone's attention was their silence. And when he began to walk among them, brushing against them with his habit, they stayed near him and flew away only when he had given them permission.

After this he went to preach to the people in the public square of Bevagna. We would like to know what he told them that day.

The Fourth Lateran Council

Reforming the Church was such an urgent task that it could brook no delay. Perhaps the special mission of the heresies was to shout this at Rome in their own peculiar manner and in every language. Apply the remedy or die. Apart from the luxury and avarice that were ravaging some of the clergy, there were doctrinal errors spreading about that had to be dispelled at all costs, not to mention the new Crusade to be launched. The dream of Innocent III was beginning to look like a last warning. Did the pope really believe in 1209 that a beggar would keep the Church from collapsing? In any case he took plenty of time to make up his mind. It wasn't until 1213 that he sent out his invitation to all the patriarchs, archbishops, abbots, bishops, priors, and kings of this world. The appointed time and place were November 11, 1215, Saint Martin's day, in the basilica of Saint John Lateran.

More than four hundred bishops answered the call, along with eight hundred abbots and priors. One of the most important personages in the Church, the patriarch of Constantinople, was present. but the Greek bishops did not come. The kings sent their ambassadors. So thick was the crowd of lay people that the basilica couldn't hold everybody. The opening session put all the pomp of Rome on display. After the singing of the *Veni Creator,* Innocent III spoke on a text whose prophetic meaning no doubt escaped him: "I have earnestly desired to eat this passover with you before I suffer" (Luke 22:15). He didn't speak as well as had been hoped, and he had no premonition of his death in the coming year.

The sessions that followed were given over to organizing the Fifth

Crusade, a constant concern of the pope since the failure of the previous four. It was decided that the general departure would take place in June 1217.

Then came the great stumbling block whose disastrous importance the council couldn't grasp, the formulation of the dogma of the Holy Trinity: "The Father engenders the Son, the Son becomes incarnate, and the Holy Spirit proceeds from the Father and the Son." This was the tragically famous *"filioque,"* which still separates East and West within the bosom of Christendom, sundering a Church whose two halves have yet to reunite.

The doctrine of transubstantiation was solemnly proclaimed, and the obligation of every Catholic to receive the body of Christ during Paschaltide under pain of excommunication. Also mandated was auricular confession of all one's sins at least once a year.

What is discreetly called the Albigensian affair was likewise dealt with, after a fashion. Without returning to the subject of the cruel war that weighs heavily on the memory of Innocent III's pontificate, one is pained by the appearance of the name of the ferocious Simon de Montfort, who was awarded the lands he had unjustly conquered. We might say in the pope's defense that he never managed to get a clear picture of that grim, bloody business, because some of the letters from his legates were held up; but great men never hear the whole truth.

Finally, there remained the question of the magisterial new broom needed to sweep the Church clean. The list of abuses was so long that an abridged version will have to do. It began with prostitution and licentiousness, which was to be expected since they are found in all times and places. The sexual life of the thirteenth century included more or less all the varieties known today. But at the root of the countless irregularities lay an unbridled appetite for luxury and sumptuous fare on the part of both clergy and laity. Drunkenness was commonplace. If we had no other source of information but the papal bulls denouncing excesses of every kind, they would be enough to paint a picture of that voluptuous society: feasts, banquets dissolving in debauchery, lewd parties where minstrels performed their perverse songs, erotic dances and chants that made their way into the churches (Francis had seen that in his adolescence). The taste for beautiful clothes and precious fabrics led to the most insane expenditures. The flowing cloaks in the style Francis had worn as a young man were still

the rage, even among the clergy. It was impossible to tell laymen from
clerics who wore brightly colored clothes, green or red, and let their
hair grow long. Masses were said badly, shortened and mumbled. It
took money and still more money to give a feast, to win a lawsuit, to
gain access to the lords who set the example of the "inimitable life"
borrowed from pagan Rome. Venality wreaked its ordinary havoc
among the magistrates and even the higher clergy. Bribes, the oldest
scourge of institutions, reigned supreme. Great men and small were
susceptible to it; and the same was true of simony, an incurable disease
that even bishops suffered from. Concubinage among priests and religious had ceased to scandalize anyone. We may end with the case of
an archbishop from Lund in Sweden who had the audacity to ask the
pope if his having successively kept two concubines constituted big-
amy.

Meanwhile, the disorder among the secular clergy was matched by
that of the monasteries and convents where the very principle of evangelical poverty seemed to be in danger of disappearing. The lust for
gold, the incontinence of the monks and nuns had become the laughingstock of the people and the inexhaustible source of licentious tales
and satirical songs, whose echoes lingered long after the reforms had
restored the different orders to their early severity. It was a long, hard
struggle.

Amidst this melancholy sketch of a Church threatened with collapse, we must remember something that the modern reader might
miss: the fact that however deep the trouble, there was always faith,
undoubtedly stained with superstition and vulnerable to the contagion
of heresy, but despite everything present and strong. Chosen souls
living in silence and solitude were spared this corruption and, as in all
times of deadly peril, saints came forward.

Scholars have wondered if Francis attended the council. We might
as well ask whether he cared about the future of the brotherhood. But
what sort of figure could he cut in the Constantinian basilica, where
the princes of the Church and the legion of abbots listened to the
declarations of the lord pope? Where was his place? If his brotherhood
was now recognized, the Poverty that it stood for with its sorry tunic
of crude material was ill designed to command respect, whereas the
priors in their noble habit breathed an air of success, suggesting the
wealth against which they would soon be hearing a sulphuric blast.

Outside the basilica, the throng of lay people from all countries, intimidated by the guards, moved impatiently about beneath the portico of forty columns (carried off from pagan temples) and on the piazza, where carousing and drinking bouts alternated with songs, some pious, some not, in a blend of naive fervor and coarse gaiety. The people were waiting for something, an event, a sight, the opening of the five monumental doors that displayed all the Church's magnificence to their dazzled eyes. It still had the triumphant prestige that cast a reflection of blissful eternity onto the great holy days and transformed and illumined everyday life, filling it with mystery and poetry.

At the sessions of the council, Francis must have secretly rejoiced to hear Innocent III trampling down the insolent pomp of the higher clergy at a time when so many poor people were complaining of starvation. Was Francis, for all his resistance to it, moved by the splendor of that grandiose setting, whose purpose was to announce—what? The Gospel? A return to the precepts of Jesus? One might have thought that a faint breath of Catharism was stirring the flames of the thousands of candles aglow in the basilica, but the faith was well protected against the absurdity of heresies. There had been a great deal of discussion about the Fathers of the Church, but Francis was no student. When Rome spoke, he never argued. Still he declared that he had nothing to do with Saint Augustine or even Saint Bernard. Francis's influence, however, would make itself felt, if only through the respect that the brothers accorded the clergy and that gradually made priests realize what people expected of them. For all that, he left Rome with an unforgettable impression of secular grandeur decked in the adornments of Mammon. Those precious fabrics that pride wrapped itself in proclaimed the pleasure of owning the goods of this world, but how to judge the men who wore them? That wasn't his business—after all, he had been one of the spoiled children of the rich.

He had counted on the cardinal of Saint Paul to get him into the basilica, but his protector had died four months earlier. A Franciscan at heart, he had presented Francis to the pope and defended him for the love he bore him. Somebody else would have to replace the cardinal. God would see to that, as usual. So Francis thought and, of course, someone *was* there, a man of high standing, at once a relative and counselor of the pope, Ugolino di Segni, the cardinal-bishop of Ostia. He was over seventy years old. Tall, robust, extremely shrewd, a man whose opinions were widely respected. He also knew Francis, having met him in Rome in 1209, where he observed him a good deal. He was astounded by the simplicity of the little pauper, the *Poverello*. Whether a shoemaker or a prince of the Church, you couldn't resist that shining aura of holiness. And after bewitching the youth of Assisi, Francis's charm showed the singular power of affecting even the Roman Curia. Ugolino would take him under his wing. In his fertile, constantly active brain an idea was born that seemed to be a providential inspiration. Francis, as he saw it, represented an enormous but still disorganized force. The brothers were scattered all over Italy and beyond. They all had to be gathered together into an order.

For some weeks now a Spanish religious had been in Rome, and he too had founded a community of preaching brothers: Domingo de Guzmán was a dozen years older than Francis and different from him in many ways, except for his all-consuming love of Christ; he had very much a legal mind, which Francis did not, and was passionately determined to have the Catholic faith triumph where it seemed most threatened. In a word, he was back from a war, from southern France, which had been struggling since 1209 against Simon de Montfort, count of Leicester. In that devastated Albigensian country, cities were burning and blood flowing, but the Catharist heresy had to be put down, and the expedition against it bore the name of a Crusade. What did Francis say about all this? We don't know, but his love of France was known to everyone, and he must have suffered to see Christ imposed on people at sword point. And what did Ugolino think?

Ugolino wondered that these two great leaders of men should be at the council at the same time: The diversity of God's gifts knew no limits. There was a striking contrast between Francis and Dominic, manifest even in their physical appearance. Wearing a garment the color of earth and dust, the *Poverello* reminded the viewer of a sparrow or, as they were called in France, a *moineau*—a little monk. He was a sparrow beloved by everyone: He had the bird's humility, its spirit of independence, its relish of freedom. Christ had spoken of those little creatures, happy to be alive and at home almost everywhere.

Dominic was altogether different. In his handsome habit of yellow wool so pale it looked white, he had an air of somewhat intimidating nobility. And, since it was cold that November morning, he had draped his shoulders with the black cape of the canons regular. So he too resembled a bird, a swallow perhaps. But the swallow doesn't fly at random; it's always ready, when the time comes, to cross the sky with its companions in perfect order, in those vast triangular formations we admire.

What was Ugolino dreaming of? During a break in the council, one would think he might ask the two founders to meet at his house. Thus it takes only a simple hypothesis to bring two of the greatest men of the Middle Ages face to face. What wouldn't we give to know exactly what did happen! If they actually met, Francis, who could read souls, would have grasped in a moment that he had before him a friend of God. And as he wasn't blind, he would have noted, connoisseur that he was, the tasteful cut of Dominic's white habit and the solid quality of the cloth. Dominic might have seen things from the same supernatural and practical angles. Francis's holiness was obvious, and his wretched tunic showed the total absence of human vanity. There was only one thing you could take from that beggar, something that he offered to whoever wanted it: poverty.

Perfect Joy

durus hic sermo . . .

The happiness beyond all happiness comes from loving God and feeling oneself loved by him: No one knew this better than Francis, and he had taught it countless times to his brothers. But one had to uproot oneself from the earth, to fly from the world and oneself. And who would have the courage to launch out on such a hazardous adventure as this flight on high, this escape of the soul?

When he got back from Rome, Francis wished to speak about these things to Brother Leo, who served him as confidant, secretary, and confessor. Leo at least must understand that finding the narrow path right away, and then following it till it leads to paradise is not a pleasure trip, as most people imagine. Access to God is not so easy. This lesson is as hard as it is famous. It can't be omitted because it has the pure sound of the Gospel to it.

Did this conversation really take place on the road to Perugia, or did Francis speak with Brother Leo near Saint Mary of the Angels? It doesn't much matter. There they were, the two of them (in reality or imagination), walking one behind the other, Leo in front, Francis in back, according to the Franciscan custom Dante describes for us in the *Divine Comedy*.

It was very cold, and both were suffering from that, especially Francis, who was weaker. And then in his clear voice he began the unforgettable dialogue (which I shall abbreviate slightly here):

"O Brother Leo, even if the Friars Minor should give good example in sanctity in every corner of the earth; even there is not perfect joy."

Silence. They went on their way, and once more his voice rang out:

"O Brother Leo, although a Friar Minor might give sight to the blind, cure paralytics, cast out devils, and raise the dead, even there is not perfect joy."

A little bit farther on, and again his gladness resounded in the frosty air:

"O Brother Leo, if the Friar Minor were to know all languages and all learning and all Scripture, so that he could prophesy and reveal not only the future, but the secrets of minds and souls as well, there is not perfect joy."

He knew very well that all that was inspired by Saint Paul's sermon on charity in 2 Corinthians, but under the impulse of the Holy Spirit he added what Saint Paul had left out. Perhaps Brother Leo wondered what he was getting at, but Francis wanted him to be patient.

"O Brother Leo, little lamb of God," (that was what he called his confidant) "although the Friar Minor might speak with the tongue of an angel and know the course of the heavens and the virtues of herbs, and if all the treasures of the earth were revealed to him and he were to know all the properties of birds and of fishes and of all men and animals and of trees and of stones and of roots and of waters, there is not perfect joy."

A few more steps and Francis began almost to shout:

"O Brother Leo, even though the Friar Minor were to know how to preach so well that he could convert all the infidels to the faith of Christ, even there is not perfect joy."

For two miles Francis had been paraphrasing Saint Paul. Now it was Leo's turn to ask a question:

"Brother, I beg of you in the name of God, tell me where perfect joy is to be found."*

But after the enumeration of these choice graces came a rather rude jolt: Arriving at Saint Mary of the Angels, soaked through from the snow and frozen from the cold, they knocked at the door of the convent where they were in a hurry to dry off and warm up. But instead of opening the door, the brother within accused them of being frauds, rascals, robbers of the poor box, and told them to be gone. And so they stayed outside in the snow and wind, dying of hunger, until nightfall. But they wouldn't complain or curse the inhuman porter. On the contrary they thought that he at least knew whom he was dealing with, and that it was God who made him speak so brutally. And there, Brother Leo, is perfect joy. And if they persisted and knocked again at that silent door, and this time it opened, but they were driven away, insulted, slapped, and told to go to the hospital; and if they accepted all that with cheerfulness and charity, *there,* Brother Leo, would be perfect joy. But it was too much, they were hungry and they begged the doorkeeper to open up for the love of God. Then they were beaten with a knotty club, dragged by the cowl, thrown to the ground, thrashed in the mud, and they endured all that too by thinking of the sufferings of Christ: There was perfect joy. They had come to the narrow path that Christ said few people find. They had overcome themselves for the love of Christ; they had put up with everything; they had accepted the cross. The goal was reached, a blissful eternity would be opened to them.

Sic Transit

The mention of Perugia is not without interest in the account of this quest for perfect joy. Francis and Brother Leo turned their backs on that arrogant city when they went off in search of the absolute, and it was

---

*Adapted from *The Little Flowers of St. Francis and Other Franciscan Writings,* trans. Serge Hughes (New York: N.A.L., 1964), 62.

not by accident that the saint named the city of which he still had somber memories. After the disaster of Ponte San Giovanni, he had passed that year in the papal jails of Perugia which, though subject to the power of Rome, was conspicuous for every kind of excess. Symbolically, then, the two religious were fleeing a sort of little hell as they went to seek refuge at Saint Mary of the Angels. This gives us some idea of the aversion Francis felt toward the Babylon of Italy. The day would come when he would curse it, but well before that a sinister event took place there.

The reader will recall the plans for Fifth Crusade, which the pope was so intent on bringing off. But first there was an urgent need to reconcile Pisa and Genoa, which were supposed to join in the expedition, and above all Venice's meddling had to be foiled: In its usual fashion the republic was trying to bend the itinerary of the Crusade (aimed at Jerusalem) to its own advantage. And so Innocent III was going to work for a rapprochement between the two cities on the Tyrrhenian Sea. He decided to go to Perugia on July 1, 1216, accompanied by most of his cardinals (a little more than twenty) to settle the difficulties. That could take time. He was only fifty-four, but overwhelming labors had worn him out.

Jacques de Vitry, who had just been named bishop of Acre, was passing through Umbria and wanted to receive his consecration at the hands of the pope, but a strange surprise awaited him. On July 11 the pope had been struck down by an embolism. Because it was very hot, the funeral rites had been rushed; and there was no one to watch over the body in the locked cathedral.

The next day, in the early morning, Vitry entered with several members of the Curia and found Innocent III lying naked and stinking on the pavement, all alone in the somber, massive Romanesque church, which still lay shrouded in night. The pope's crosier, tiara, and precious vestments had all been carried off by robbers in the darkness. In a famous letter the French bishop described the horror he witnessed. "I have seen with my own eyes," he added, "how vain, brief, and ephemeral is the glory of this world."

Sic transit gloria mundi. Such was the end of that great man, the author of a treatise on contempt for the world—*De contemptu mundi*—to which death would add a masterfully cynical commentary.

Thomas d'Eccleston, a thirteenth-century English Franciscan,

affirms that Francis of Assisi was present at the pope's death. This
strikes us as quite possible, and there is no documentary evidence
anywhere against it. Francis would certainly have wanted to watch by
the corpse of the man to whom he owed the official approval of his
community, just as the Friars Minor later did for Honorius III and
Gregory IX.

The Conclave at Perugia

Under such serious circumstances the Church couldn't go very long
without a leader, and the sacred college was hastily called together.
This situation, by the way, had been foreseen by Pope Alexander III,
who decided in 1179 that the new pope would be elected as soon as
his predecessor was buried and in the same city where the latter had
died. That was because Rome was sometimes plagued by dangerous
uprisings. To constitute a legal conclave, only half the total number of
cardinals plus one were needed. Election by popular acclamation had
been abolished.

On July 18, Cardinal Savelli was elected pope, taking the name of
Honorius III. He was a very kindhearted old man who had given
practically all his goods to the poor. His piety was known to everyone,
so there couldn't have been a better choice, except for his age, which
made a short pontificate likely—something his electors may have in-
tended in the first place. He had been a legate from Sicily and a precep-
tor of the boisterous emperor-to-be, Frederick II, who benefitted from
his indulgence, the indulgence one shows a gifted and difficult child.
His temperament inclined him to conciliation, but didn't deprive him
of a keen sense of reality. He was, among other things, a first-class
financier; and when Francis came to present himself, this expert judge
of souls must have wondered, as did Innocent III, not about the mission
of the pure, simple *Poverello,* but about the grave material problems of
organizing the new order. Honorius loved Francis, naturally, and admired his idealism and the mad generosity of his heart, but . . .

One of Honorius's first tasks was to consecrate Jacques de Vitry bishop of Acre. Vitry, who was well placed for observing what went on in the Curia, got a bad impression of that nest of intrigue, where the affairs of the world took precedence over everything else. It must be admitted, however, that those affairs were in a fiendishly complicated state. In Sicily, Frederick II was ruling in the name of his five-year-old son Henry; and the pope couldn't help feeling apprehensive as he saw the redoubtable empire of the Hohenstaufen in the process of restoration. In France Philip Augustus, as usual, was confronting Rome over his troubles with women and was continuing to play the part of umpire among kings. The heir apparent, the future Louis VIII, openly supported the cause of the English barons, who were in revolt against John Lackland, upon whom they had imposed the Magna Charta. When King John died, there were difficult times: His successor, Henry III, was only nine years old, and Roman legates ruled in his stead. We can conceive the antipathy someone like Jacques de Vitry felt toward this political unrest, where the passion for power—no more to him than the fool's rattle or bells—took its grim toll. It made him all the more appreciative of the Franciscan ideal, which was all love, as in the earliest days of the Christian Church. His praise of Francis's community was unstinting: "They have only one passion, to snatch souls in peril from the vanities of the world . . . their way of life is that of the primitive Church. . . . In the daytime they give themselves to the active life and the apostolate . . . at night they withdraw into solitude to lead a contemplative life. . . ."

After the coronation of the pope, Vitry left Perugia and returned to France to preach the Fifth Crusade. He would not see Francis again until they met overseas.

Sending All of Them to Paradise

For his part, Francis set off for la Portiuncula. He too must have been wondering about all the events he had witnessed. What had he gotten from his audience with Honorius III, that kindly but prudent old man?

Words of encouragement and a blessing. That was fine; it was quite a lot in fact, but not enough.

Meanwhile, something of considerable importance was in the making. Here we must rely on the account of a Franciscan, Brother Bartholi of Assisi, describing at second hand and a century later, in 1335, one of Francis's visions. As he prayed one night in the church of Saint Mary of the Angels, in that same month of July 1216, Christ appeared to him with his Mother, bidding him to ask for a grace that would glorify God and save human beings, and with that in mind to return to Perugia and present his request to the pope.

Francis couldn't resist the desire to ask for something as immense as his own heart. Vision or no vision, he always seemed capable of going to the outer limits of daring where charity was concerned to save humanity. We can't help recalling Charles de Foucauld's prayer: "My God, bring all men to salvation!"

In a similar state of mind Francis, accompanied by Brother Masseo, went to see the lord pope. He had already settled on his plan: Strengthened by Christ's permission, he meant to ask for a gigantic indulgence.

At Perugia he got his audience. A face like his was not easily ignored, and he soon found himself at the feet of Honorius. In the presence of his cardinals, the pope asked Francis the object of his visit. There followed an incredible dialogue, from which a handful of phrases have come down to posterity. Francis wanted a very important indulgence. One can imagine the smile on the old man's face.

"An indulgence? For how many years?"

"I am not asking for years, but for souls."

His language was odd, and the pope needed clarification. "Explain yourself, my son."

"Holy Father, let each of the faithful who crosses the threshold of Saint Mary of the Angels at la Portiuncula, if he is absolved and contrite, receive pardon for all his sins and remission of the punishments attached to them."

Such a total pardon of all sins and the remission of punishment was the indulgence granted to the Crusaders who went off to fight for Christ. Francis knew that, but the chivalric ideal was still alive in his heart. He was quite ready to do battle if he had to. Despite the pope's astonishment, there was some power in Francis's mere presence that made all objections fall away. Still that amazing request called for mature deliberation. The cardinals, as expected, raised objections: This indulgence, if granted to everyone, would surely weaken the Crusaders' privilege and cause discontent, if not defections.

Francis then turned to his strongest argument: Christ himself had charged him with making that request of the pope. How could anyone resist a saint with such a prodigious mandate? Honorius gave in, but he needed the criticisms of the sacred college. The extraordinary indulgence could be obtained only once a year, on August 2. Francis asked for no more than that. Mad with joy, he could already see the multitudes entering the church of the Virgin, rescued from eternal death; and, having thanked the pope, he was speeding off.

"You simple little fellow," cried the pope, moved by Francis's ingenuousness. "You're going away without any written authorization."

Had Francis changed his mind about the value of parchments and signatures since his interview with Innocent III? His response was immediate, and wonderful: "If that indulgence is from God, the Holy Virgin will be its charter and the Lord Christ its notary."

A little later, among the lepers of Collestrada, where he stopped on his way back, he saw in a dream the Lord confirming the pope's approval. And on August 2 in the church at la Portiuncula, he himself proclaimed the indulgence. Seven bishops were on hand, no doubt feeling perplexed about it all, for the consecration. But Francis's happiness was radiant as he cried, "I shall send them all to paradise."

Of course, this indulgence has been the subject of vigorous debate over the centuries. It underwent alterations that varied with what might be called the temperature of the faith. There was an effort to extend it to a large number of churches, which slightly diminished its authority. In our time, indulgences—those that survived Luther's savaging—are no longer in vogue but, properly understood, they make up a part of the Church's spiritual treasury. Behind all this lies the incandescent charity of the *Poverello.* The rest is silence.

Whether or not we believe in it, we can always dream about that extraordinary grace on the very spot where Francis proclaimed it, but there is no way to hide the disappointment that awaits the pilgrim here. Stimulated by a ground swell of devotion, zealous architects hastened to decorate and enrich a building that should have remained in its original nakedness. It's what always happens with the works of man. We look for the Saint Mary of the Angels as repaired by Francis's hands; we try to ignore its nineteenth-century fresco, where the piety of the period has had its unfortunate say. The primitive chapel still moves us by the modesty of its dimensions. But the Renaissance forgot all sense of proportion and triumphantly encased it in a basilica. Yet Francis remains strangely present on the site where he prayed for the world. His cabin has not been moved; it stands just a few meters from the chapel, but you have to search for it beneath all the marble and gold. And where is the forest where he once found a deeper solitude in the night?

Subiaco

In the meantime, far from la Portiuncula, momentous things were taking place. In England the king was a child. A void opened up that the pope thought it wise to fill by sending legates across the channel to govern the kingdom. This was to ignore the national instincts of the English and their passionate love of independence. But how could anyone back in 1216 foresee the Lollards, Tyndale, or Henry VIII's Act of Supremacy?

In that same year, 1216, Francis paid a visit to the Benedictines of Subiaco. Their brothers on Mount Subasio had given the chapel of Saint Mary of the Angels and the Carceri to the Franciscans.

Leaving the plains of Umbria to climb up to the house of Saint Benedict is something of a trip, even today, but the splendid natural beauty of the scene makes the traveler forget his fatigue and suggests a whole train of reflections, some of which must have occurred to Francis. One has to go by the ancient roads. Along the way the forest-covered Sabine Mountains rise higher and higher, irresistibly evoking the impression of powerful shoulders trying to stop the heavens from crushing the earth and frail humanity with their magnificence. Few landscapes convey such a strong idea of God's grandeur, and we readily see what drew Francis toward these summits. But if he went and took up residence so high up, wouldn't that mean deserting his flock?

At this point we can get a clearer view of how different Benedictine

and Franciscan schools of spirituality are. And yet, despite that difference, Dante put the two founders together at the very top of his
paradise. Six hundred years before Francis, it took a giant of the stature
of another Umbrian, Benedict of Nursia, to block the tide of invasion
from the East and save Europe, whose patron he became. He himself
was a mountain peak, like the ones he lived near. Rugged, immovable,
he was made to attract to his isolated monasteries the men fleeing the
barbarians, and to preserve civilization. The perfection of his rule is
such that it has come down to us without modification, but it is a harsh
one. And that very harshness was the key to its power to attract
thousands of young men, generation after generation, eager for austerity and obedience. Benedict's faith was matched by brilliant common
sense. Compared with him, Francis looks like a madman, but Providence was behind both the prodigious intelligence of the one and the
irresistible lunacy of the other, which had been unleashed by the
reading of a few verses from the Gospel. The Church needed them
both.

Some biographers pass over Francis's stay at Subiaco, but the Benedictines, ever careful and precise, don't make light of it. They treasure
the memory of the saint and of his presence in the cell he occupied, a
presence especially memorable because it is attested by the most vital
of all the portraits of Francis. But what is Subiaco, and how to describe
it?

A first visit in 1935 made a singular impression on me that was not
dimmed by the passage of time and that I found still strong when I
returned forty-five years later. The second visit may have been even
more of a surprise because I saw just how accurate my memories were.
At Subiaco one goes from a chapel decorated with frescoes into another
whose painted walls recount the life of the founder and his disciples.
The colors, sometimes vivid, sometimes a bit faded, conjure up visions
of a Byzantium that was still quite near. Other chapels follow, each one
descending a little lower into the rock, down to a staircase leading to
oratories no bigger than cells, where we find figures depicted in liturgical vestments, witnesses to an unchanging religion, all radiant with a
silent splendor. Am I in the West or in some mysterious edifice of
faraway Russia? The name of Boris Godunov comes to my lips. One
almost expects to hear the soft, slowly cadenced thunder of an ortho-
dox church bell. I linger in a tiny oratory at the lowest point in the rock
that the monks have hollowed out to lodge their monastery. Its walls

disappear behind the layers of color, pale or energetic, depending upon the date.

Did Francis see these places where religion saturates the air, these altars where the little red flame of a candle animates the mighty personages on the walls? He must have thought about the humble appearance of Saint Mary of the Angels, which was just as beautiful in its own way. Where I am now, he once stood and prayed. His picture on one of the walls looks out at the visitor, smiling, youthful, joyous, with his bright eyes, his thin beard, and his protruding ears. Tradition claims that an unknown monk of genius painted that slender face and those hands not yet wounded by the stigmata. Next to his head an inscription bears his name: Fr. *(Frater)* Franciscus. Nothing more or less; he was still just a brother, a brother passing through, whom they loved. So they wanted to keep this souvenir, this sketch, later transformed by the artist into a great portrait, which has become so familiar to us that it rivals the painfully touching version of Francis by Cimabue. But Cimabue couldn't give us anything except a wholly intuitive image, whereas the Francis of Subiaco finished in 1223 shows him before the trip to Syria, which aged him prematurely.

One leaves that mystical stronghold by crossing a long courtyard where two superb crows, male and female, seem plunged into meditation interrupted by a sudden beating of wings, as if to make us admire the metallic black of their wings. From time to time the male croaks rather unpleasantly. He and his companion are there to remind us of Saint Benedict, who had a fondness for crows. Many of them now fly noisily overhead, vying with the monks in the austerity of their dress. Francis, though, must have put them under a spell and, as at Bevagna, won their homage as they flocked silently before him.

To get back to his stay at Subiaco, it's interesting to note that while his biographers may not mention it, they do pay attention to the portrait left us by that unknown artist. In our day this image is probably the favorite of the saint's admirers, because it mirrors the way they like to think of him: as a young, radiantly happy saint. This is a sort of popular canonization that corresponds to an inner truth; it is based on more than sentimental reasons. Thomas of Celano describes Francis before his conversion as "an exquisite young man," with a wealth of convincing detail. He points out the form of his ears, the long face, the fine lines of his mouth, the merry look. Another painting, more convincing still, is universally ignored. It shows Francis standing behind the bishop of Ostia, as the latter consecrates a chapel (the site of the frescoes). Francis's face is clearly recognizable and reveals one more feature—though this didn't escape Celano's keen attention—the fact that his eyebrows, instead of having the usual arch, were almost perfectly straight.

We know for certain that the portrait was retouched in 1223, but the artist wanted to preserve his model's boyish appearance, and we shall have to take a closer look when we get to that year. There will be some surprises in store for us.

The Damned Soul Snatched from Satan

In the rich anthology of Francis's miracles there is a great deal to choose from. The most moving ones, I find, are those that stress his resemblance to Christ, when he heals the soul by healing the body. The dates are uncertain, but Francis was already living and acting in eternity, where dates no longer matter.

Recall the story of the nasty leper whom he wished to care for. Francis had already had his most celebrated meeting with a leper, the one whom he kissed. That moment signaled the liberation of the young convert and gave him to God forever; but he helped many other lepers, and he had yet to attend to the most cruelly abandoned of those doomstruck creatures. Jacques de Vitry said of them that it took a martyr's courage to endure their stench and lend them a hand. Consider what a very famous Franciscan tertiary says in his *Divine Comedy:* " . . . I have never seen a stable boy / whose master waits for him . . . so ply a horse / with currycomb, as they assailed themselves / with clawing nails—their itching had such force / and fury, . . . / And so their nails kept scraping off the scabs, / just as a knife scrapes off the scales of carp / or of another fish with scales more large. . . ." And Dante has Virgil address one of the lepers in the *Inferno* with this burning phrase: "O you who use your nails to strip yourself . . . may / your nails hold out, eternal, at their work."*

The leper whom Francis saw one day bore a remarkable resemblance to Dante's Griffolino and Capocchio. Beside himself with pain, he beat and insulted anyone who tried to care for him. His speech was a torrent of blasphemy against Christ and the Virgin. Possessed as he was by the devil, he may have been experiencing a foretaste of damnation, or so the Middle Ages thought, when Francis gently approached him and gave him his blessing. "May God give you peace." But the leper, who was plunged into his own personal hell, saw in those words a total failure to understand his situation; and his answer has the accent of bitter despair that Dante has so masterfully captured in his encounters with the lost souls from the other world: "What peace can I have from God, who has taken away my peace and my well-being, and has made me all rotten and stinking?" Francis told him to be patient: If he was suffering in his body, it was for the salvation of his soul. Exasperated, the leper replied that he couldn't patiently endure uninterrupted suffering, and he complained about the brothers, who took poor care of him. Francis left him to pray for a moment; then, returning to the sick man, informed him that he would care for him himself. The leper was skeptical.

"What will you do better than the brothers?"

"I shall do whatever you want."

"I want you to wash me all over, because I smell so bad I can't stand myself."

Without hesitation, Francis had hot water brought to him, with sweet-smelling herbs soaking in it, and he began to wash the man with his own hands. The filthy crusts fell away beneath his fingers, and the flesh regained its natural color. And the leper, who saw himself gradually healing, became aware of his wretched spiritual state and shed tears of repentance. His purified soul found joy, for his soul had been more leprous than his body.

Let me interject here that some scholars place this episode, so purely evangelical in style, after Francis's reception of the stigmata. But that seems unlikely to me: He couldn't have washed a leper with his wounded hands, which he took the greatest care to conceal.

---

*Inferno, Canto 29, lines 76–85, 89–90, trans. Allen Mandelbaum (New York: Bantam Books, 1981), 269.

A Feast of Joy

Francis had resolved that twice a year, on Pentecost and September 29, all the brothers who weren't too far from la Portiuncula should gather there. This was called a chapter. Its object was to reawaken the spirit of the brotherhood and to decide where to preach the Gospel.

The choice of Pentecost recalled the day when the Spirit, as promised by Jesus to his disciples, had come down upon them. Perhaps Francis unconsciously remembered Joachim de Floris and his prophecies about the Third Kingdom. There is no way of knowing if he did, but he certainly resolved to establish "provinces," and that was his first effort at organizing the brotherhood. Each of the provinces—Umbria, Tuscany, the Marches of Ancona, Campania, Apulia, Calabria—was placed under the direction of a "minister." Missions would be sent to foreign countries.

Assistance at mass, with fervor and profound attention, was taken for granted. One eloquent but seldom stressed detail is that Francis recommended to his brothers that they fix their eyes on the host at the elevation and adore the Real Presence with all their heart. If this custom had been widespread in Italy, Francis wouldn't have insisted on it but, as we have already indicated in the pages on his travels when he was younger, the practice came from France, a protest against the heresy of Bérenger. This would seem to prove that he had been struck by it during a trip with his father. Francis found the gesture, which evoked the whole mystery of transubstantiation, very beautiful and very moving; and he never forgot it.

We have a number of details on the code governing the chapters, and they are precious because they show us Francis at his sensible best. The rule of the Gospel was the fountainhead of all the rest, which flowed from it by a rigorous logic. The respect due the Church was sacrosanct. Meeting a priest, the brother had to greet him and kiss his hands. There was a formal prohibition against judging the rich, with their fine clothes and their lives given over to luxury and pleasure. They too must be respected. After all, who could say that the great sinners and the people most blessed by fortune might not someday become disciples of Christ? That had happened many times since the founding of the brotherhood. *Gentilezza* was especially recommended as a form of charity. They were never allowed to raise their voices. As for news about the world—and there was some exciting news in those days —it was never to supply topics of conversation among the brothers. Rather they should talk about the lives of the Fathers of the Desert and how better to imitate Christ.

Francis himself, if he had to reprimand a brother, did it gently, without ever wounding the guilty party. Still, a very serious fault would be punished by immediate expulsion.

But for Francis, as for all the brothers, whether they came from near or far, the chapters were for the most part happy reunions, so strong were the bonds of spiritual love linking these messengers of peace. True feasts of joy, they had for Francis the irresistible appeal of the festivities he had hosted in his youth. His essential character, though purified, remained the same. God takes us the way we are.

Once business had been attended to, they celebrated in the woods surrounding the church, with crusts of bread as the chief delicacy. All these beggars, so glad to be gathered together around their brother, had a thousand things to tell one another, but their happiest moments came from hearing Francis speak to them of God. In this state of perfect destitution, he had in his voice a torrent of mystical joy that sprang from a heart permanently detached from this world.

With the passage of time these chapters took on greater importance. Churchmen who were curious about the spread of the brotherhood or even disturbed by it came to observe these gatherings beneath the trees of la Portiuncula. Soon there would be bishops and cardinals there. Though Francis was unaware of it, a sort of competition developed between the successful Franciscans and the official Church. While Sunday preachers failed in their efforts to reach the hearts of the people, the simple Friars Minor, who spoke about God without having studied theology, found themselves with crowds of enthusiastic followers. It was more than a question of the language they used. Vast problems loomed over the future of society. Was it possible that by opening the Gospel one became a revolutionary without realizing it? Then these *Poverelli* were gentle revolutionaries, with no other weapons but love.

Francis's dream was close to coming true. Wasn't this what his visions had foretold: brothers who had come to him from all over and whom he sent off to plant the seed of the Gospel in countries that he didn't know? We would like to think that everything went well, but there were disappointments aplenty. The brothers who left for Germany didn't know a word of the language, or rather they knew only one, *Ja,* which sometimes got satisfactory results but mostly got them into deep trouble. They were asked if they were Catholics. Answer: *Ja.* Then they were well received. But if some mistrustful person asked if they were heretics or Cathars, the same reply landed them in jail and earned them beatings with a stick. Clarifications were needed, but things weren't cleared up without a lot of pain and vexation. The first mission to Germany was a failure.

In the meantime, Francis was fascinated by the East, where he planned on going personally someday to convert the Muslims. To prepare the way he chose Brother Elias, evidently an extremely valuable man. Elias left, bearing the title of Guardian of Syria, for the part of the Mideast where, thanks to Francis, he could contact the Arab world. This was to entrust him with a vital mission, but Elias had an impressive mind. At this point there is no guessing what Francis thought of him, but we may be sure that he liked him a great deal; but sometimes he wondered about him, with reason as we shall see. He sensed that this remarkable man had a taste for power and was attracted by the world. No matter, Elias was the right man in the right place. Francis would have much preferred to go in his stead. He asked his brothers to pray for him so that he might know his mission, and when they returned, he announced to them: "I choose France." How often, having asked for advice, we simply go ahead and do what we were going to do anyway. Francis was in love with France, and so . . .

He set off without delay and traveled to Florence, the first important stop along the way. As propriety demanded, he went and presented himself to the legate of Tuscany, Cardinal Ugolino, who had once been so friendly to him in Rome. Ugolino must have been happy to be able to converse with the great spellbinder; but he himself was a great judge of men, and he felt that Francis's expression, at once gentle and burning, betrayed a certain lack of social experience. All his life Francis would be surrounded by the high and mighty, or people who pretended to be, people who were better informed than he was about the things of this world, and who sometimes helped him and sometimes slightly abused their influence. In any event, Ugolino couldn't see Francis going to France and told him to stay in Italy, where his brothers had need of his vigilance. To clinch his argument, he warned him about the opposition to him in the Curia, which would profit by his absence. It must have been a hard blow, but Francis took it. He was disappointed, yet he appreciated the affability and courtesy of this bishop, who spoke to him as with a friend. Ugolino voiced his regret that so many Franciscans had been sent to the East "to undergo so many trials so far from home and to die of hunger." Francis may have been touched to the quick by the rejection of his mission to France, and he had an eloquent answer ready: "My lord, do you think and believe that the Lord God has sent the brothers only for this province here? God has chosen and sent brothers for the sake of all the men and women in the world. They will be received not only in the lands of the faithful, but also among the infidels. Let them keep their promises to God, and God will give them, both among the faithful and the infidels, everything that they need."

Ugolino admired the nobility of this, and recognized that Francis was right, but he insisted, gently but firmly, on the prohibition against going to France. So Francis wouldn't have the joy of hearing Jacques de Vitry preach the Fifth Crusade at Vézélay and Paris, not to mention the unspeakable happiness of seeing his mother's native land, but he had to obey.

To the end of his life, he would never be allowed to do things entirely his own way. Someone would always be there to block the road, an important person with good reasons. And his brotherhood too would get away from him the dream of a child who remained faithful to his childhood.

The Child, the Night

One Franciscan story with an engaging poetic quality tells about "the very pure and very innocent child" who came looking for Francis and asked to be received into the brotherhood. Too young to be a brother, he might have been politely shown the door, but Christ had said, "Let the children come to me," and so he was accepted. Where and when? The date of 1218 is not unlikely, and the place was a little convent on a hill in Umbria where Francis had come for a visit.

At the hour of compline, Francis went as usual to lie down on the plank that served as his bed. Well before daybreak he would secretly get up to go pray alone in the woods.

Extremely attentive to all the saint's doings and no doubt moved by a hidden desire to imitate him, the young newcomer waited for the right moment. Then he slipped in next to Francis, who was still sleeping, and tied their cinctures together so he would be sure to wake up when Francis left his bed. This little ruse was quickly thwarted. In the dead of night Francis quietly untied the cords and went outside, leaving his overcurious little companion buried in sleep.

But a moment later the child woke up and leapt into the air when he saw that he was all alone. Where to find Francis? An intuition led him toward the woods, which were ordinarily closed by a barrier, but this time it was open. Proud of his cleverness, the boy began to wander among the trees when he heard voices and let them guide his steps. An extraordinary surprise awaited him, as terrifying as it was astonishing: The man he was looking for, Brother Francis, was surrounded and seemingly clothed with light, as he spoke with Christ and the Virgin, who were accompanied by John the Baptist, while numberless angels flew about and sang in the shining night.

The boy fell down on the ground as if dead.

Meanwhile, Francis's ecstasy had ended. He left the woods to return to the convent and was walking under the trees when his foot struck against the boy, who lay there in a faint. Francis was moved; he lifted him up and carried him back in his arms.

When he came to, the guilty lad admitted everything, but Francis didn't scold him. He simply ordered him never to reveal what he had seen and heard in the woods that night. Need we add that the boy, who had entered the brotherhood so early, lived a holy life in it until he died?

Episodes of this sort remind me of those little predella paintings whose freshness I so much admire. One never tires of observing this or that exquisite detail, and the spell cast by the painter ends by compelling one's assent. There is no more room for doubt: Things must have been that way.

The Dead Travel Fast

Far from these places where Francis was lost in contemplation, the world was jousting in the nightmare of war. The Crusade against the Albigensians kept going on and on. Once again the frightful Simon de Montfort had set siege to Toulouse, which was valiantly defended by a young man nineteen years old, the son of Raymond VI, count of Toulouse. The siege dragged on forever; it was now in its six month. Wave upon wave of Crusaders swept up to the city, but in vain.

At another end of Europe, Otto VI, deposed after losing the battle of Bouvines, had locked himself up in his castle in the Harz Mountains. That sly, intelligent man had seen all his allies take flight and now reigned only over his duchy of Brunswick. Remarried to a young princess of Brabant who found him revolting, he fell prey to the schizophrenia that had threatened him for years. Having boarded up all the castle windows and hung black draperies in the rooms, as Charles V would later do at Yuste, he lived by candlelight, shouting out his sins in the hope of winning forgiveness from God and the pope, who had put him under interdict. Because of this the region around the castle was deserted and the churches were closed. At his request the monks from a nearby convent came to whip him as they sang the *Miserere.* He thought he might appease God's anger this way, but he died exhausted and covered with blood on the pavement of his guardroom.

Honorius lifted the interdict, but only long enough to let Otto be buried in the cathedral of Brunswick. Frederick II no longer had any living rivals.

It was May 19, 1218. Less than ten years before, on his way through the duchy of Spoleto to receive the imperial crown from the hands of Innocent III, Otto had passed by Rivo Torto in a show of unheard-of luxury. The reader may recall that, although the population rushed off to see that magnificent cavalcade, Francis allowed only one of his brothers to attend the emperor's progress and remind him that human glory did not last. In 1218, which of the two, the saint or the mad emperor, still thought about that incident? Both, perhaps, having seen for themselves the fragility of glory.

A little more than a month later, on June 25, death struck another spectacular blow, this time beneath the walls of Toulouse. Guy de Montfort, Simon's brother, was struck by an arrow shot from the city; and Simon ran at once to help him pull it out. Then something happened that threw the ranks of the Crusaders into disarray. Some matrons and young women who were defending the city with the intrepidness of their sex accurately aimed a swivel gun and, with that clumsy machine, fired a stone cannonball that changed the course of destiny. Smashing the count of Montfort's steel helmet, it crushed his brains, eyes, teeth, and jaws into a pulp. Simon de Montfort fell dead to the earth, all bloody and black. The siege was lifted.

In those days news traveled faster than we might think. It sped across Europe, which held its breath in anticipation. After Otto's sinister death, word of the the tragic fate of Simon de Montfort must have reached Francis's ears. The Crusade was ending, and the Catharist heresy had been wiped out in the land of Provence, to which the saint's thoughts had so often strayed. So much blood had flowed to insure the triumph of the faith. And then there was the horror of the Inquisition's bonfires. Heresy too had its martyrs. If Tertullian was right, their blood would make an abundant harvest of believers sprout in the coming years. Francis could thank God that in Italy the Church had not had to win such costly victories. Did he realize that his mere presence and the gentleness of Franciscan preaching had sufficed to dispel the strange error that made the human body Satan's creation and denied that Jesus was God? The people followed him, the *Poverello,* as they would have followed Christ. There was no need of armed knights, massacres, and torture. The voice inspired by the pages of the Gospel kept all the simplicity of the original message. Where was the limit to this power, which was stronger than the violence of armies? It seemed possible to believe that Francis would ultimately convert the world. But what use are the dreams of the greatest visionaries when the experts set about putting them in order? Inevitably, transformations came that bore a close resemblance to deformations dictated by common sense. Still a multitude of men flocked to Francis of Assisi. Convents arose, regulations began to weigh down the initial text of the rule, which had been implacably brief. The prospects for growth were enormous. The dream of 1209 now threatened to drown in success.

To the Men in Red

Nevertheless, Francis knew how to take action and defend his ideas. After all, the battle was to be fought for God. They didn't want to let him go to France; very well, Brother Pacifico would go in his place. It was around this time that, by request of the cardinal of Ostia, Francis was invited to preach before the pope and his cardinals. All of them, in fact, showed some curiosity to hear the man famous throughout Italy for his eloquence, which raised him above the most learned preachers of the day. No doubt they also wished, as good theologians, to test the purity of his teaching. They knew he had never studied. But a surprise was awaiting them.

The cardinal of Ostia loved Francis and wanted him to come through this trial honorably, so he himself wrote a sermon for him in solid, well-turned Latin. Francis was advised to learn it by heart, which he did with great docility; but when he appeared before that highly intimidating audience, he couldn't remember a blessed word of the text he had known so well the night before.

Here we see the man of God. Without turning a hair, he collected his thoughts for a moment and prayed to heaven for help. The answer he got still astounds us. Opening the book of Psalms on the altar, he read the verse "All day long my disgrace is before me, and shame has covered my face" (44:15). This theme furnished him with a sermon of unparalleled daring. What were all those prelates but the face of the Church, a face dirtied by their pride, their love of luxury, and the bad example they set for the Christian world? Whereas that face ought to shine with beauty, like the very face of Christ . . . These words—in the vernacular—poured from his mouth in a stream and, far from stirring his listeners to anger, they plunged them into amazement. They stole a look at their rich ornaments, then an even more rapid glance into their consciences. They fell silent before that man in an earth-colored habit, who told them with the vigor and simplicity of a prophet that God wasn't happy with his Church. And the tears flowed.

Joy

How could one get the joy that spilled over from Francis into the hearts of thousands of men and women? Was it enough to live as he did? People ran after him to ask for peace and liberation from the tyranny of the senses. Was it simply a matter of willpower? The mystery was somewhere else. Of all the miracles Francis worked, the most stunning one would always be the great Franciscan adventure, which almost changed the world forever. We can easily see why it was destined to fall short of its goal. Harder to understand is the chance it had of total victory, as its originator conceived it.

Imagine young people sacrificing their youth and rushing into penitence as if to a feast. Seized with madness (in the eyes of the world) they abandoned everything at one fell swoop, the pleasure of the senses and all the promises of happiness from the world. Why? Because in 1204 a young enthusiast read three verses of the Gospel and won a love without limits. By imitating this imitator of Christ, the Franciscans quite expected to get the same results. It was an enormous wager. And if they got nothing in exchange for giving up everything? That possibility wasn't even worth considering. They had been called to God by the voice of the *Poverello*. Francis couldn't be mistaken. Francis was like Christ. The mistake would be to take him for Christ; there was the trap. But God was faithful. With a burst of enthusiasm that the Church hadn't known since the first centuries, the first generation of Franciscans welcomed the kingdom of God like children.

The adults followed, with equal fervor. For them the trial was perhaps still more severe. The young had neither careers nor fortunes nor magnificent houses to sacrifice. Their generosity was blind, while that of grown men calls for reflection. In most cases that sober thought would be set aside the way a young person head over heels in love thrusts aside all objections. Italians are great lovers.

Men came, lived with the brothers as brothers, and left after weeks or years (so long as the brotherhood wasn't an officially constituted order), but their life was changed forever.

Francis and Women

But some questions remain to be dealt with. At the head of the list is the eternal problem of the flesh. There has been much talk about Francis's sweetness. Even today it figures prominently in the portraits drawn of him. With a glance, with a smile, he made people accept the hardest demands of the community. But his rule maintained the austerity of the pages of the Gospel it had sprung from. That accounted for much of its power of attraction. What youth asks from religion is severity, just as adults don't renounce the easy ways of the world only to return to them behind monastery walls. To see how this works out in practice, you need only go to Umbria, for example, and see the faces of the young brothers one passes in the convents. The striking thing about them is their charming high spirits. Among the older ones you find a serenity always ready to smile. Francis, the brother par excellence, has not left them. He detested sadness, and he has bequeathed joy to his numberless children. You can breathe it like the air in the forest after coming from our plague-ridden cities.

For all that, Francis was, we know, terribly rigorous on the subject of the flesh. Nowadays his horror of sexual sins would be considered morbid. In any case it tells us so much about him that we ought to dwell on it. One short anecdote will give an idea of the problem. A brother who didn't know about the prohibition against entering a convent of nuns went on the orders of a minister to the Poor Clares to help them with something or other. His name was Stephen.

One December day while out walking with Francis along the Tiber, he confessed to this violation of the rule. Perhaps he didn't foresee the storm about to come crashing down on his head. Francis tore into him unmercifully, and then bade the overzealous brother dive into the river, which he immediately did. Minutes later he clambered out of the freezing water, shivering with the cold, and in that condition he went back with Francis to the hermitage a mile away. He had learned once and for all that "the company of women is posioned honey," that speaking to them without being contaminated was as easy as walking in fire without burning one's feet. "One would have thought," Celano remarks, "that this was fear or disgust rather than prudence." For Francis, holy as he was, avoided women and never replied to their "babble" except in monosyllables. He rarely gave them even a fleeting glance. He confided to a brother that if he ever happened to look at women, he would only have been able to recognize two of them. Writers have puzzled over who these two might have been. Lady Pica, no doubt, because one doesn't forget the face of one's mother. And the second? Again, there is no hesitation possible: the face of Clare, the lady always on the mind of her faithful knight, the woman who had become for him Lady Poverty, sent by Christ himself.

And since the world is full of curious people, scholars have come up with a third, a singular woman known as "Brother Jacqueline," who will put in an appearance later on.

Francis's terror of fleshly desire made love for him a passion akin to angelism. What he condemned, sometimes quite brutally, in others, he was on the lookout to annihilate in himself through all sorts of mortifications. "Don't canonize me too quickly, I am perfectly capable of fathering a child." Need we remark that this is not the way a male virgin speaks; this is a man of flesh and blood who has known pleasure and speaks from experience.

Meanwhile, Sister Clare often expressed her desire to take a meal with him: a quite innocent wish that created difficulties of which she had no idea. Francis bluntly refused to grant her the favor. What was he afraid of? Of falling in love in the ordinary sense? In any case no one could make head or tail of his attitude toward the holy nun whose beautiful hair he once had cut, and the brothers insisted that he give way, so finally he said yes. The meal took place at la Portiuncula in memory of her reception of the habit. Clare came with a companion. All the brothers were on hand, and the table was set on the ground. The guests had barely sat down when Francis began to speak of God. That was all that was needed to send them off into ecstasy.

The people passing la Portiuncula that day were terrified to see the woods and the chapel in flames. The citizens of Assisi watched from their walls, as the fire raged. They rushed to put out the conflagration, but when they got to the convent they realized that the fire had consumed nothing, that it was a manifestation of the divine presence, setting hearts ablaze.

The Chapter of the Mats

It was called the Chapter of the Mats, but all the chapters ever since the one on the first Pentecost, May 29, 1219, could have been given the same name. A straw mat thrown on the ground served as a bed for the Friar Minor, who sat and rested on it as well. For men like him, inured to a hard life, sleeping out of doors on a mild spring night in Umbria hardly qualified as a mortification. Everything about these chapters was festive. The one held on May 26, 1219, drew brothers from all over Italy, so many, in fact, that the nickname "Chapter of the Five Thousand" seems just right. If Francis had wanted proof that his vocation came from God, that prodigious crowd gave it to him. Unfortunately he wasn't there when that brown-robed multitude first arrived. There was some panic in Assisi over the invasion: where to lodge so many people? How to feed them? In quiet haste a house was put up, a large, rather rudimentary building, but at least it had a roof. In the middle of all this confusion Francis returned, unaware of what was going on. When he saw the house, he didn't believe his eyes. No one who knew him could be surprised at the heights his anger reached. In this case, it climbed up with him onto the roof, where he took it upon himself to knock off the tiles. He knew a thing or two about masonry. A house! What an offense against holy Poverty! The tiles flew through the air like projectiles aimed at the devil's head. Not knowing how to put a stop to this demolition, the brothers were very upset. Some knights, who had come to watch out of curiosity, managed to calm Francis down; and his brother Angelo, the provost of the commune, informed him that the house was rightfully the property of the town of Assisi and not of the brotherhood.

Apart from this bothersome house, the brothers lacked everything —which delighted Francis. God always provided. They would see.

In the surrounding fields shelters rose out of the ground, built with reeds by the resourceful friars. They all had a little of the boy scout spirit in them. Mats stretched out on the earth, and that was all, whence the name of the chapter.

The commissary problem was quickly dealt with. From Assisi, Spoleto, Foligno, and Perugia came all the necessary victuals in generous quantities, enough to feed all the beggars in Italy. This burst of charity spread a spiritual joy that Brother Body had his share in. At all events, it must have made Francis understand, and palpably grasp, the enormous force that was sweeping him forward—and ahead of his age. The movement was deeper than he could have dreamed. His prayers and those of his brothers had unleashed a wave of enthusiasm that had to be directed. Was he capable of it? Too reflective not to wonder about that, he must have thanked God for sending Ugolino his way. The cardinal had taken him under his wing at Florence; and in his humility he had recognized that men like Ugolino, wise and experienced in worldly affairs, could help him to solve practical problems. But what sort of humor was he in at the Chapter of the Mats? A pugnacious one, it seems: His demolition of the roof augured poorly for the rest of the day. Did he regret having been so docile with the cardinal protector?

Ugolino, who would succeed Honorius as pope, was present at that unprecedented chapter. Some prudent individuals had a piece of advice for the future Gregory IX. The size of the gathering struck them as disquieting. Wouldn't it be a good idea for Francis to follow the guidance of learned, experienced religious? Someone might propose to him the rule of Saint Augustine or Saint Benedict or . . . Ugolino agreed and broached the question with Francis. But that day Francis wasn't his usual self. To everyone's surprise, he grasped the cardinal's hand and begged him to come with him to the assembled chapter. There he gave the boldest speech in his life: "My brothers, my brothers," he cried in his warm voice, "God has shown me the way of simplicity. I don't want to hear talk about the rule of Saint Augustine or Saint Benedict or Saint Bernard. The Lord has told me that he wished to make me a new madman [*pazzo*] in the world, and God doesn't want to lead us by any other knowledge than that. As for all your knowledge and wisdom, God will use it to bring you down." There followed the astonishing threat: "God has his policemen to punish you. And I place my trust in him." Silence—and consternation. The brothers trembled, while Ugolino understood that at times like this the *pazzo* was in the grip of inspiration, and he made no reply.

Whatever Ugolino's merits, as I read this account, I can't help thinking of Jacques de Vitry's commentary on the chapters of the early Franciscans: "I believe that it is to shame the prelates, who are like dumb watchdogs, unable to bark, that the Lord has chosen by means of these poor, simple men, to save many souls before the end of the world." Faithful to his vocation, Francis barked valiantly whenever necessary. Ugolino had already warned him at Florence about the maneuvers by the Curia to adapt his ideas to the traditional norms of religious life. For Francis, accepting this was treason. That day there was no muzzling him; his opponents would have to wait.

While their father vented his indignation, the brothers conversed in the woods and meadows around Saint Mary of the Angels. They were seated in groups of fifty or sixty on mats of woven straw; sometimes they all stopped talking and plunged into a deep silence that impressed observers as more eloquent than the most learned sermons. From all sides people came to watch, without saying a thing.

It was more than just curiosity. An instinctive urge led those men and women toward the brothers, who had left everything for the Gospel. The temptation somehow or other to flee the world tugged at countless souls in those days, but that dream dates from the beginning of history. More than once during the chapters postulants would break away from the crowd, go to la Portiuncula, and ask to be clothed in the brothers' habit. Francis received them himself, in his unique way, as persons sent from God. His gift of reading hearts inspired him with words that were not forgotten, that illuminated the new brother's whole life.

Among the many notable people who sometimes came from far away to the chapters was Domingo de Guzmán, who had just founded the Order of Preachers. He admired Francis and wanted nothing more than that the Friars Minor and the Preachers should join together to form a single troop, but the *Poverello* had politely refused. At the chapter of 1219 Domingo was amazed that Brother Francis hadn't arranged any supply system for his enormous spiritual family, trusting instead to the generosity of the people. Where Francis simply counted on God's charity, Domingo saw a radical failure to plan ahead, a serious lack of organizational thinking. On this point the two men, the Spaniard and the Italian, differed, but the provisions continued to flood in.

In the days that followed, however, some of these physically idle religious began to grumble. They were being taken care of, there was no shortage of food, but still they complained. Brother Leo had a vision of Christ lamenting their ingratitude. What did they want? Gathered together by the thousands, the brothers aired their griefs, especially one: The bishops would not let them preach. Francis gave his sons a good chiding. "You don't know God's will, and you don't let me convert *the whole world,* as God wishes. You say the bishops won't let you preach. Then convert those prelates by your obedience . . . and they themselves will ask you to convert the people."

The same brothers, devoted but occasionally quarrelsome, gave Cardinal Ugolino a jolt of compunction when he walked with his entourage of knights and clerics around the site of the chapter, which was drawing to a close. The brothers' camp looked like a resting place for animals. In the face of that sign of perfect poverty, Ugolino couldn't hide his emotion. He shed tears and cried out, "See where the brothers sleep! What fate will come upon us, we who live in comfort?" We can imagine the luxury he wanted to be forgiven for. Knights and clerics at once burst into tears, as if rivaling one another, at this humble admission by a prince of the Church. And their consciences felt more at ease.

The decision was made to try to apportion the domain of poverty, that is, to settle the boundaries of the provinces to which each brother would go under orders from his superior. A mass said by the cardinal rounded out the work of that memorable gathering.

This Chapter of the Mats is extremely important for anyone seeking to understand what sort of man the *Poverello* was. It shows him resolved, whatever the cost, to struggle to defend his ideal against the powers of this world. Immediately afterward he had a brainstorm and determined to go to the East.

The Orient

Perhaps they were taken by surprise, perhaps not; still none of Francis's superiors lifted a finger to stop him. But old Pope Honorius was strongly interested in the success of the Fifth Crusade, where the presence of religious might have a salutary effect. And Ugolino's attitude toward Francis was changing. Earlier he had urged his spiritual son to remain in Italy to watch over his brothers, rather than go to France. But since then it was becoming apparent that the man was unconsciously causing problems. Not that Ugolino loved him any the less, or was provoked by his unexpected tirades: He was too high-minded to resent the pious upbraiding Francis, in his inspired moments, made him endure. You didn't criticize a prophet when he was swept by the divine afflatus; you bowed your head and bemoaned your sins. He had done all that, but there remained the problem of providing the whole order with a logical organization; but so long as the founder was around, with his unattainable dream and his touching stubbornness, there could be no progress.

Francis saw things differently. How could he have mistrusted Ugolino? That same prelate had once warned him about the Curia of which, as cardinal-bishop of Ostia, he had been a member. But the *Poverello* was beyond such considerations. It was hard to leave the children whom heaven had given into his care. Wasn't that desertion? It could be justified only by the folly of the cross—together with the folly of the Crusades. The cross he had long ago sketched in chalk on his gardener's smock had engraved itself in his heart. He couldn't fight, and he had no wish to. His goal was to convert the infidels, beginning with the sultan. It was his deepest desire.

Before embarking at Ancona, he entrusted his authority to two brothers, Matthew of Narni, who was put in charge of receiving the newcomers at la Portiuncula, and Gregory of Naples, a learned man—maybe too learned—who would visit the provinces. As might be expected, the brothers were stirred by his departure and didn't hesitate to follow him in a crowd. But at Ancona a very awkward situation arose: It was impossible to take everyone along. At this heartbreaking juncture we see Francis's whole character summed up in his delicate charity: "The people in command of the boat refuse to take all of us, and I don't have the courage to choose among you—you might think that I don't love you all equally. We are going to try to discover God's will." A child happened to be standing there, and Francis asked him to point his finger at those who were to get on board, which he did, taking it as a game. Thus the finger of a child became the finger of God. No one was hurt, even those on the verge of tears. Twelve brothers were chosen, counting Francis.

On June 24, the feast of Saint John the Baptist, Francis's patron, the ship lifted anchor and sailed for Syria, stopping at Cyprus. About a month later the travelers reached Saint John of Acre, where they were welcomed by the Guardian of Syria, Brother Elias of Assisi.

Destiny plays surprising tricks. Francis left behind in Italy one destroyer of dreams, Ugolino, only to meet another, whom the future would reveal to be even more formidable. As we have seen, Francis's feelings toward Elias spanned a strange gamut, from affection to aversion, then giving way once more to the impulses of his heart. He sensed the presence of something, without knowing what it was. Francis was victimized by clever people, since he sometimes made his way through the world by blind instinct.

Elias, who had exceptional intelligence and willpower to fuel his limitless ambition, had always loved and admired Francis, and Francis lavished his affection on Elias, with a shadow of reserve, as if he were in the presence of a mystery. The fact is that Elias was bafflingly complex. In the years to come there would be clashes, occasionally violent ones, between these two men.

For the moment we are in Acre, that Syrian town in the Frankish kingdom, where Brother Elias had every reason to be happy. With its gardens, its terraces, its refreshing fountains, the place resembled Granada as we know it today, in all the splendor of its Moorish beauty, the Granada of the Generalife palace and the Albaicin. The pitiless sun made Francis blink, but the cypress-lined walks would protect him till he rested in Elias's mansion, where shade was guarded like a treasure, for the Guardian of Syria had been seduced by the charm of the Orient, and someone looking for austerity would have to leave his exquisite rooms. The odds are that Francis kept his own counsel.

It would be a mistake to write off Elias as a voluptuary. He understood the Muslim population and even won a few vocations from among them, which sounds like a miracle, but then he was a good speaker. A man of a thousand talents, he especially shone in the art of persuasion. He had once been a consul in Assisi, then in Ancona, and he knew all about organization. His desire to use his influence was very strong.

One man in his entourage could bear witness to that, Cesare of Speyer, who, thanks to Elias, had found a direction for his life. In his native city, even before he became a cleric, he had set about preaching, and converted the women, much to their husbands' outrage. Frightened by the threats he received, he fled all the way to Paris, hoping not to be burned as a heretic. From France he had made his way to the East, where Brother Elias restored his peace of mind by welcoming him into the brotherhood. So Francis wasn't entering terra incognita, but rediscovering a bit of his original dream far across the sea.

His stay at Saint John of Acre was brief. Along with several brothers, including Peter of Catania and Brother Illuminato, he boldly sailed for Damietta in the Nile delta to visit the sultan and convert him. His plan had an audacious and entirely Franciscan simplicity to it.

The man whom the chroniclers call the sultan of Babylon resided in Damietta, but the Crusaders had the city surrounded and were preparing their assault. The capture of Damietta would cut Egypt off from Palestine and deal a severe blow to the Arab supply lines by attacking the Egyptian wheat fields. The holy places, deprived of the sultan's military support, would then fall into the hands of the Frankish army from the kingdom of Antioch. And if those armies failed, the keys to Egypt, Damietta and Alexandria, would make an excellent trade-off for the return of Jerusalem.

Francis's first concern was to pay a visit with his brothers to the Crusader camp. When he saw the motley swarm of humanity that bore the name of the Christian army, he must have been momentarily stupefied. *That* was the Crusade—the magic word that had haunted the years of his youth? As he would soon discover, there was a little of everything in that crowd: Mixed together with the soldiers in hopeless disorder was a menagerie of suspect creatures, thieving, criminal tramps, the low rascals male and female, who followed the troops, right behind the commissariat. Illuminati and seers moved amidst that bizarre assemblage, echoing with all the languages of Europe. There were Frenchmen, Germans, Italians, Englishmen, believers who wanted to fight for Christ alongside atheists with blasphemy in their mouths and profit on their minds.

One look was enough to show Francis that he had to begin by converting the Christians. The Saracens would come later. This camp was his battleground in his war against the devil; God had brought him from Italy to station him here, in this pandemonium, to win souls. In the heat of August dozens of multicolored tents provided shelter for the leaders, the haughty, wrangling barons. There were chapels where one mass was celebrated after another, dormitories for the soldiers, not far from the Muslim fortifications of the city, with its hundred red ocher towers, and the muddy waters of the Nile. Dominating the tumult, the clear, passionate voice that had won over Italy rang out, and the irresistible current of love that ran through his preaching touched the hardest hearts. People underwent sudden conversions in this place ridden with boredom and despair. Francis's companions rejoiced, but he still felt disturbed. He thought the assault to be launched against Damietta and the sand-colored tents of the sultan was doomed to defeat. But he hesitated to say it.

Brother Illuminato, direct as an arrow, strongly urged him to speak out: Heaven's warning must be heard. Francis obeyed. There were complaints, then shouted insults: "Coward!" Francis persisted unfalteringly in his prophecy, but his warnings interested none of the leaders, because the camp was full of exalted visionaries announcing disasters sent from God.

The attack took place on August 29. The Crusaders rushed out against Damietta and fell into a trap. The sultan pretended to flee toward the desert, and the Franks chased him all the way into the dunes where the bulk of the Muslim army lay hidden. The Christians were taken by surprise and massacred. Nearly six thousand fell. From the camp where he had remained to pray, Francis sent Brother Illuminato to scan the horizon, but it was clear that no fighting was going on before Damietta. A cloud of dust brought the news of disaster. Francis was staggered to see his prophecy come so painfully true. He had but one idea: to bring peace by any means possible. Upon reflection the only way was to go straight to the sultan. The plan was crazy, but Francis's mind worked simply.

After a few days, while the Crusaders buried their dead in the sands of the Nile and skirmishes continued to keep the war alive, Francis, having reached his decision, went to inform the man who was running the camp, though not its military leader: Cardinal Pelagius, the pope's legate. A fanatical Spaniard, fiercely impressed with his own rank and importance, he wasn't satisfied with his red robe, which covered him from head to toe, but rode a horse covered with a scarlet saddlecloth and reins to match. Case-hardened in his pride, he had his own catastrophic theories on how to run the war, demanding that the sultan give up both Egypt and Jerusalem. Francis had dealt with cardinals before, but this one was a tough nut to crack.

When he was presented to this prince of the Church, Francis told him of his intention and awaited an answer. It was firmly negative. Converting the sultan? An absurd dream. What was this "little monk" getting mixed up with? Let him go back to his prayers. And the man in the red robe showed the man in the ragged brown habit to the door. Francis respectfully took his leave. So much for politeness; he was now going to obey his heaven-sent inspiration.

Francis's initiative took place not, as some writers mistakenly assume, during a truce, but at a time when hostilities were going full blast, when the Crusaders, exasperated by their recent defeat, were harassing the sultan's outposts every day. Along with Brother Illuminato, Francis left the camp and headed for Damietta. Brother Illuminato, solid, brave, strapping fellow though he was, trembled with fear. It was a long way down the road beneath a burning sun that devoured the earth, but Francis marched on with his usual resolute step. The terrible reverberation of the sunlight must have made him suffer because of his sensitive eyes. At the edge of the city two soldiers arrested them and threated to decapitate them then and there, since the head of a Christian was literally worth its weight in gold. Francis cried out, "Sultan! Sultan!" and the men, taking them for emissaries from the defeated Christian camp, led them to the sultan's palace.

Face to Face with the Sultan

What could Francis expect? Could he succeed in making the sultan, commander of the Muslim faithful, a true Christian or, on the contrary, might he become the victim of a glorious martyrdom? The latter possibility was not without its appeal, and it may have been what he really had in mind to begin with. But there was a surprise in store for him.

Saladin's nephew, Malik al-Kamil of Egypt, who was the same age as Francis, had nothing of the bloody tyrant about him. He was one of the most refined men of his day, passionately fond of religious poetry, curious about every sort of intellectual activity, a former student of medicine, and on very good terms with Venice, whose merchants he protected. He had had enough of war, which he judged useless, and he feared a new offensive by the West against the plains of Egypt, where famine was raging. He surrounded himself with learned men, astronomers or doctors, disciples of Averroes, and with Sufis, to whom he liked to submit all sorts of questions about the immortality of the soul. One of the finest ornaments of his court, Sheikh Alam el-Din Tasif, toyed with complex problems in geometry; and the sultan himself knew by heart all the poems of Attar, whom he had met as a child.

When he saw the two poor brothers, he at first took them for deserters coming to surrender and embrace the faith of Islam. Such cases weren't rare, but Francis informed him that he would never turn Muslim and that, on the contrary, he had come from God to save Malik al-Kamil's soul.

Far from losing his temper, Saladin's nephew found the situation highly interesting. A philosophical conversation of some promise seemed to be in the offing, because Francis's expression radiated intelligence, and an immediate sympathy sprang up between the two men. The sultan decided to keep his unexpected visitor for a few days at the palace, where he would be treated with courtesy.

Nonetheless, he wanted to test the Christian faith of this ardent "missionary." Tradition, zealously carried on by painters, claims that he invited Francis to walk across burning coals. Malik al-Kamil was too liberal for such excesses, and it should be recalled that the Church forbade such ordeals, which were in effect a way of tempting God. But Christians and Muslims also had a tradition of setting great store on triumphs won over the other side in this trial by fire. I am inclined to believe that the sultan merely forced Francis to undergo the inoffensive, but morally distressing, trial of treading on the cross: A splendid carpet with crosses embroidered all over it was stretched out before him. The sultan observed his guest: With no hesitation whatever, Francis marched boldly over the crosses, and then simply said, "As you see, I have walked on these crosses. They are the crosses of the bad thief. You can keep them if you wish. We keep our own, which is the true cross." The deftness of that response totally disarmed the sultan, and Francis took this opportunity to make a presentation of the Christian faith. The sultan listened with attention and good will. Then, by way of ending the interview, Malik al-Kamil remarked, "I would convert to your religion, which is a beautiful one, but I cannot: Both of us would be massacred."

The encounter had been a battle of wits. Francis's great dream of martyrdom was rapidly winging away. We can be sure that good manners were in evidence on both sides, and that Francis showed courage, along with his charm, which never failed. Saladin's nephew was very much taken with him and called him Brother Francis. Not wanting him to leave empty-handed, he offered him, in keeping with the laws of Oriental hospitality, precious gifts—that were politely refused. Some writers go so far as to maintain that he persuaded Francis to accompany him to a mosque. The saint supposedly agreed, while specifying that he would pray to his God there, later adding a phrase that leaps across eight centuries and brings him still closer to us today: "God is everywhere."

He accepted a safe-conduct for the holy places and promised to pray for the sultan, as the latter had requested. Then he was honorably escorted as far as the path leading to the Crusader camp.

This apparently unsuccessful visit would not bear fruit until long afterward. There seems to be no doubt that Malik al-Kamil was unforgettably impressed by Francis, and that Francis himself discovered a new humanity in the person of his host. The notion he had of Islam had to be modified: The essence of faith—belief in God—could be found outside Christianity, and that belief deserved respect. This broad view of the problem of religion had an enormous, almost revolutionary, force. The only way to win over souls is by gentleness and honest example. If so, what sense did the Crusades make? That question, if it occurred to him, would eventually be answered.

Ten years later, without striking a blow, won over, perhaps, to the *Poverello*'s ideas, Malik al-Kamil handed over Jerusalem to Frederick II. Both men may have had certain political considerations in mind, but their accord at least cost no human lives.

The Franciscans had permission to preach their religion, if they didn't provoke the Muslim faithful. But Francis was not destined to see this victory of wisdom and tolerance. Quite the contrary, in 1219 he would witness a great deal of cruelty.

In the Crusader camp fronting Damietta, Cardinal Pelagius was growing agitated as he called for an offensive that Jean de Brienne, king of Jerusalem, advised against. But the pope, likewise meddling in military affairs, ordered the Frankish army to obey his legate, and they stormed Damietta, which fell in the assault launched on November 5. The sultan had left his fortress to take refuge on the Nile delta, at an impregnable site between two branches of the river. The city he built there would be called Mansourah, that is, the victorious, and would become the theater of many battles down through the ages.

In Damietta the Christians ran wild and indulged in an orgy of slaughter. There were so many corpses that plague soon broke out, and the official entrance was put off until February. During almost three months Damietta wasn't simply a dead city, but a city of the dead; and Jean de Brienne withdrew from the Crusade, leaving the bloodstained cardinal to savor his victory.

All this must have been a violent shock for Francis. He had seen the carnage at Collestrada up close, but that was a war between two communes—an act of fratricide, but alas, nothing out of the ordinary. Here in Damietta men were killing in the name of Christ. The cross was triumphing over the crescent amidst butchery and rape—and they called that a Crusade. In his disgust Francis decided to join the entourage of Jean de Brienne. In March a ship brought this group to Saint John of Acre, where Francis, having shed his illusions about chivalry, rejoined Elias and Cesare of Speyer. He may have gone with them to visit the holy places.

At this point the curtain falls: From March to July 1220 we can only guess about Francis's comings and goings, but judging from what we know about him, he probably didn't stay put. We have no proof that he went on pilgrimage to Palestine, but there is no lack of solid reasons for presuming he did. As of 1217 the pope had excommunicated Christians who traveled to Jerusalem, because they were obliged by the Muslims to pay tribute to get in. It seemed intolerable to do anything to enrich the infidels. But, since he was armed with the safe-conduct given him by the sultan, Francis could enter with his brothers for free, and the papal objection no longer applied.

Jerusalem, however, was by now only a phantom city. El Muazzan, the sultan of Damascus, had destroyed it during a raid. The celebrated walls were no more than ravines. The fortifications were gone, along with all the great monuments, with the sole—and crucial—exception of the Holy Sepulcher and, of course, the two great mosques. We can imagine the *Poverello*'s feelings at the tomb of Jesus—but that's all we can do. Nothing has come down to us of what he said, or might have said, to his brothers. He left no trace of this voyage in his writings, where the least allusion to it would have been precious.

One episode that never fails to touch us is Jean de Brienne's friendship with Francis on board the ship taking them to Syria. The king of Jerusalem would become a Friar Minor after the death of the saint, and wished to be buried in the upper church of the Assisi basilica in 1237. Thus Francis, who wanted so badly to follow the valiant Gautier de Brienne and could not, added to his flock another Brienne, this one the king of Christ's city.

Back in Acre, he continued to preach; perhaps he wanted to prolong his stay indefinitely to evangelize the infidels, in the land "beyond the sea."

His words, as usual, had an inexplicable power. A large part of this power came from his physical presence, as if his soul were visibly manifest in his person. Converts would come out of the blue and join his brotherhood: One dignitary, the prior of Saint Michael, left his post and became a Friar Minor. Jacques de Vitry, the bishop of Acre, cites this example and gives others, not without a touch of humor. Francis took one of his clerics, the Englishman Colin, and two of his companions, one of whom, Dom Matthew, was in charge of a parish. Nothing helped; the man deserted to follow the *Poverello.* His attraction was irresistible. The precentor too wanted to leave, and the bishop had to use all his influence to hold him, but there were others who got away, including a whole garrison of Hospitalers. The bishop's explanation is noteworthy, because the Francsican ideal was always in danger of dropping out of sight. "The order of the Friars Minor," he writes, "is making immense progress in the universe, and the reason is that it expressly follows the way of life of the primitive Church and of the Apostles." Abolish time, go back to the dawn of the Christian experience, and the world was saved. What did the official Church think of that? Too many heresies spoke that language, but Francis clung to the Church with all his might.

At the end of spring he heard a piece of news that sent shivers through him: Five of his brothers had undergone martyrdom in Morocco, in January. Francis's heart was filled with joy. For the first time Franciscan blood had been shed among the infidels, as Christian blood had flowed in pagan Rome. There was no cause to mourn them; this

was a time for rejoicing and thanking the Savior. A victory had been
won. The Gospel was moving ahead, now they were in the Acts of the
apostles. The names of the five witnesses to Christ were recalled with
enthusiasm. They had labored hard to gain their palm. In Seville they
preached against the Koran, for which they were subjected to the
bastinado. But that was only the beginning. They climbed atop a tower
and shouted that Muhammad was a fraud, even while he was being
celebrated below. They were thrown into prison, then released. Expelled from Seville, they went to try their luck in Morocco. There, in
the presence of the Miramolin (Amir al-mu'minim: the commander of
the faithful), they insulted the Muslim faith. They were tortured, then
driven out of the country. They returned to Marrakech and slipped into
the mosques, where they repeated their abuse. To get rid of these
troublesome characters, the Miramolin offered them gifts, which were
immediately and derisively rejected. He tried to change their attitude
with torture, but they responded with intense efforts to convert their
tormentors. Finally, granting them what they wanted all along, the
Muslims decapitated them. Gentleness was not the strong suit of these
Franciscans or part of their style, but they had taken heaven by storm,
in the manner of the first Christians. The beloved brother could be
proud of his children, who had died in his place. That thought must
have pierced his heart. Could it be that he had missed the chance for
his own martyrdom in the palace of the sultan of Egypt? Francis's
power to captivate was part of the drama of his life: He couldn't help
exercising it, and so he had charmed Malik al-Kamil. But one day his
blood would flow, and his cross was still awaiting him, a high and wide
one.

Come Back, Brother, Come Back

In July of 1220, while Francis was making plans for the future,
Brother Stephen arrived from Italy with some disturbing news. At the
May chapter, in Francis's absence, Matthew of Narni and Gregory of
Naples, the two vicars in charge of overseeing the brotherhood, had

taken it upon themselves to introduce changes, which had created a rift among the brothers. Among the many alterations, one of the most important concerned the rules for fasting, which were to be brought into conformity with those of existing orders. This was a step toward transforming the brotherhood into an order. Another report announced that John della Capella, one of the first brothers, had founded an order of lepers, and Philip the Tall had petitioned Ugolino and the Curia and obtained privileges for the Poor Clares that the nuns wanted no part of. There was a rumor going around that Francis was dead. Brother Jordan of Giano relates that Francis learned of these things while he was dining with Peter of Catania, a former jurist, whom he calmly asked what ought to be done.

"You are the master; it is for you to decide. I am ready to obey you."

"Well then, Master Peter, let us obey the Gospel, which bids us eat what is set before us."

Francis wasn't the sort of man to lose his head in this situation. As soon as it was possible, he embarked for Italy with Elias, Cesare of Speyer, and Peter of Catania. Francis must have understood why nobody had tried to stop him when he decided to go to Syria. From Saint John of Acre to Venice, if the winds were favorable, it would take three weeks, plenty of time for reflection. And where better to think things over than on the high sea? Francis turned over in his head the vexing news that Brother Stephen had brought him. And, needless to say, he prayed. He had occasionally been told that he lacked a sense of organization. Perhaps Domingo de Guzmán had suggested as much when he attended the Chapter of the Mats. And, in fact, the brotherhood was badly organized; it was coming apart. Elias, who was traveling with him and who loved him, wanted to be of help to him, but it's very hard to say what Elias thought. He never let his guard down, and this time he saw his chance for glory.

Francis was no dreamer when his brotherhood was at stake. His absence, he now saw clearly, had put it in danger. If he wished to save it, he would have to create a parallel brotherhood. There was already one for men, the Friars Minor, and one for women, the Poor Clares. They would make another group for everyone, men and women, who could live according to the Franciscan rule without leaving the world. And since people wanted to establish orders everywhere, this would be the Third Order. He wasn't losing sight of the fact that the whole world had to be saved, which was still his ultimate dream. Meanwhile, all the evidence indicates that he kept his serenity, because when he got to Venice, he took time out to make a retreat on an island in the lagoon, Desert Island. There he must have gotten a silence unbroken except by the birds that uttered cries of joy at the sight of him. Then he wrote to his Sister Clare, as if he had a premonition of the preparations being made to deprive her of her poverty. The letter is too fine not to cite it in its entirety: "I, little Brother Francis, wish to follow the life and the poverty of our most high Lord Jesus Christ and his most Holy Mother, and to persevere in it until death. And I beg you and advise you to live always in this most holy life and in poverty. Beware of departing in any way from it because of the advice or teaching of anyone whatsoever."

Francis's fears were justified. Honorius III was urging Clare to accept the right to own property, but she remained faithful and refused to cheat. At Orvieto, in Francis's presence, no one raised the question of privileges or of modifying the life of the Poor Clares—the papal bulls of 1219 and 1220, *Cum dilecti, Sacrosancta romana,* and *Pro dilectis,* were purely and simply annulled—but in 1228, after Francis's death, Ugolino, who was now the pope, was at it again. He got this magnificent answer from Clare: "Lord Pope, absolve me of my sins, but let me follow the way of Jesus Christ." And the pope bowed to her wishes.

Six centuries later, in 1893, when the body of Saint Clare was exhumed and transferred to a crystal reliquary, the rule of the Poor Clares was found in the folds of her dress. One of the articles, the sixteenth, was Francis's letter.

Old Honorius, driven from Rome by the dog days, had installed himself and his court at Orvieto. This city, under papal obedience, was one of the places where the popes liked to flee from the bloody insurrections of the Roman proletariat. It was a city of phantoms too, for the Etruscans had dug wells and raised ramparts there, and their disquieting presence could always be felt in the ruins that even now excavators are continually bringing to light at the base of the rocky wall.

Leaving Venice, Francis took the road to Orvieto and passed through Verona. At Bologna he stopped to visit the brothers' house founded by Bernard of Quintavalle, but instead of a modest convent he was surprised to find a magnificent residence where his Franciscans had settled in. Furious at this affront to Lady Poverty, he threw everyone out, including Brother Leo, who happened to be there (he had taken sick), and ordered them to find lodging elsewhere. His authority was still intact, but his action had required an extra burst of energy, and he was, in fact, at the end of his strength.

While journeying to Orvieto, he had a dream that showed him what he must do from now on: A black hen was trying, in vain, to gather its chicks together. The meaning seemed clear—he was the black hen, incapable of reuniting his scattered children. When the appointed day came, he presented himself to the pope and asked him to have the Church take the brotherhood under its wing. A cardinal equipped with all the necessary powers would become the protector of the Friars Minor. Francis proposed a man in whom he had total confidence: Ugolino. Honorius agreed without hesitation to this request, which was perfectly in line with Rome's views, and it became part of the Church's common law. Francis's move may seem surprising, but we must keep in mind that his health was bad, and this made him fear that he might not be able to continue leading his brothers. His liver and stomach had suffered from the climate of the Middle East; and, more painful still, his eyes had been damaged by the sun in Syria and Egypt. They were seriously affected by a progressive disease incurable in his time, granulous conjunctivitis.

Honorius was glad to see Francis displaying such an exemplary attitude of obedience to the Holy See, and he readily approved the creation of the Third Order, which extended the Church's power. The founder was also granted permission to compose its rule. Striking while the iron was hot, the pope decided, on the advice of Ugolino, that Franciscan postulants would do a one-year novitiate. Francis agreed. Once the principle of total obedience had been admitted, everything else would follow naturally, along with the convents that would have to be built. The era of sweet evangelical anarchy was over and done with. The bull *Cum secundum* was promulgated on September 22, 1220. Francis worked over his rule on the spot at Orvieto. Friendly advice rained down on him from all over the Curia, which was anxious to safeguard monastic traditions. Ugolino especially showed his expertise at framing ingenious formulas. Francis listened and then did everything his own way, or tried to.

Physically, the Francis who returned to la Portiuncula was no longer the same man, but the radiance of his soul seemed only that much more powerful. The news of his return flashed across the country and brought joy back to the thousands of brothers who had been disoriented by his absence. Once again he was in their midst, and all at once what Saint Benedict calls the mortification of common life faded away. No more arguments, no more quarrels. Like a magician, this man, who had to keep wiping the tears from his sore eyes, brought with him peace, the ineffable peace of the heart that the world never manages to give. Meeting him, you couldn't help thinking of Christ.

Francis's first concern was to learn about everything that had happened at la Portiuncula and elsewhere. What did he have in mind? Mastering the disorder, taking things in hand, was an enormous task when there were six thousand people involved. With God's help he would succeed, but his strength was declining. Perhaps the dream of the black hen flitted through his memory like a bad omen. Absurd, but sinister, rumors were spreading. People claimed that while Francis was gone Catharism had infiltrated the brotherhood.

Finally, September 29 arrived, the feast of Saint Michael, the date of the chapter when all the Friars Minor throughout the land would gather together. Their spirits were particularly high because they were coming to celebrate the return of the man whom God had given them as their guide and whom they loved with an almost fanatical love. They thought they had lost him, and once again they were going to see him and hear him. But their joy would be dealt a violent blow. In the middle of the chapter, with many problems still awaiting a solution. Francis made this alarming declaration: "From now on I am dead as far as you are concerned, but I present to you my brother, Peter of Catania, whom we shall all obey, you and I." And with the feeling he had for the dramatic gesture, he prostrated himself at the feet of Peter of Catania and did him obeisance. It sounds like a scene out of *The Brothers Karamazov.* And he added this magnificent prayer: "Lord, I place in your hands the family which up until now you have given to me for safekeeping. Now that I am no longer capable of caring for it, most sweet Lord, because of the infirmities that you know, I pass it on to the ministers. They will have to render an account before you on the day of judgment if their negligence, their bad example, or their excessive severity brings any brothers to perdition."

Francis was abdicating, though he still kept the right to draw up his rule. His choice of a successor was a good one. Peter of Catania had followed him from the very beginning, on that morning of April 12, 1208, when Francis went to San Nicolò with Bernard of Quintavalle. Peter had spontaneously joined with Francis for good. Wise and very

shrewd in handling all legal problems, he would make an ideal administrator till the day he died, which, unfortunately, came quite soon.
Before six months had passed he was laid in his grave on March 10,
1221.

His death plunged Francis into a state of confusion, but not for long.
With Ugolino's backing, someone was there, more than ready to fill the
empty place—Elias. With the tireless patience born of ambition, he
would be able to carry out his grandiose plans for the brotherhood.

A Sublime and Embarrassing Story

If Francis sometimes put a brother to the test, he never spared
himself when it came to killing "the old Adam," who died hard.
Thoughts of his youth wandered like phantoms through his memory;
thoughts, for example, of his prodigality, which had scandalized Assisi
in a time of want. That was why he poured out his curses on money,
which had become a phobia to him, but there was something else, a
subtler temptation: the aching desire he had felt since adolescence to
enter the ranks of the nobility. His father hadn't discouraged him, not
at all. Becoming a knight meant becoming a nobleman. To do that,
armor—among other things—was indispensable, and many suits of
armor had glowed in Francis's dreams when he was young: halls full
of them, with cuirasses blanketing the walls. It was as if the devil
himself were contriving to make them glitter in those slightly childish
visions. But behind all this lay something more serious. His mother, the
gentle Pica, was supposedly a distant relative of the most glorious of
all the knights, Gautier de Brienne, who had galloped from one end of
Italy to the other and through the dreams of the young Italian. Unfortunately, one might say, there was the clothier; the clothier ruined
everything, and the clothier was his father.

In his hours of solitude at la Portiuncula, and in his bouts of insomnia, pitiless memory set to work, and Francis thought he would die of
shame. Was he sure that in the darkest depths of himself he still didn't
have a trace of that nostalgia for high rank and blue blood? Brother

Bernard was noble, but with a perfectly evangelical humility. Francis
would not have forgotten that years before he had sent him to Bologna,
exposing him to an ignominious welcome. He knew all the details of
this, because Bernard had been obliged to report them, and the *Poverello*
's questioning was close. What to do? He must expiate, but how?

By dint of having wept over all his sins, Francis was going blind.
No saint ever shed more tears. One day he went looking for Bernard,
who had retired to the Carceri, on Mount Subasio, and he told him:
"Come talk to this blind man."

But Bernard was lost in contemplation and didn't hear him. Francis
called him again, twice, three times, with no success. Now Bernard was
a saint, and Francis knew it, and so he venerated him in his heart. Still
he was saddened by this silence; and in a fit of scrupulosity, he threw
himself face down against the earth and asked God why Bernard hadn't
answered him. The reply was clear and instantaneous: "O poor little
wretch, what are you fretting about? Must man leave God for his
creature? When you called Brother Bernard, he was at one with me. He
never heard what you were saying."

Francis was deeply embarrassed, but there was a positive side to the
situation: He had been looking for something to accuse himself of to
Bernard, and he had been given it, by the Lord himself. He had his sin
now and, full of remorse, he cast himself at the feet of Bernard, who
had finished praying. What to call his sin? A burst of impatience? No
matter, he confessed it and asked Bernard in the name of holy obedience to do what he would bid him. Here begins a disturbingly brutal
tale. Bernard listened and found himself constrained to obey: "I command you . . . that, to punish my presumption and the insolence of my
heart, as soon as I lie down on my back, you shall put one foot on my
throat and the other on my mouth, and that you shall walk on top of
me three times this way, while shaming and reviling me, and in particular say, 'Stay there, flat on your back, you lout, son of Pietro Bernardone, where did you get so much pride, you who are the vilest of
creatures?'"

So it was done. The trial must have been excruciating for both men,
more perhaps for Bernard, who was revolted by it, than for Francis
who, as he swallowed that cup of gall in long draughts, savored the
defeat of pride.

Living on Dreams

The Pentecost chapter of 1221 announced major changes for the sons of Francis of Assisi. Three thousand brothers were present amid the same background of foliage as the year before, but this was the aftermath of a defeat, and the new era inspired a vague sense of disquiet. Still the natural good humor of the brotherhood got the upper hand.

If the previous chapter stirred the feelings of the spectators, the one held in May 1221 must have made an almost equally painful impression. Elias presided. His whole personality is wrapped up in that single word. His natural nobility, the force of his intelligence, his character, his grand manner, all shone forth in his dominating presence. At his feet a brother shrunken by illness had humbly taken his place: Francis of Assisi. And when he wanted to get the minister general's attention, he gently tugged the edge of his habit. Power had changed hands, and those hands were itching to act.

The problem of the missions to Germany was discussed. We know about the hostile reception given the brothers who had earlier traveled to those regions, which were, to put it mildly, still primitive. There had been bloodshed. The palm of martyrdom they so ardently desired awaited those brave souls longing to preach the faith and die for it. Ninety brothers stood up at once, as if volunteering for war. Cesare of Speyer and Thomas of Celano were among those who went. One man was taken by mistake, Jordan of Giano. He would come through safe and sound and leave behind a passionate, if biased, account of that expedition and of the beginnings of the order.

Then Francis intervened. After tugging on the hem of Elias's robe to get permission to speak, he arose and read out his rule. In his whole life we scarcely find a sadder or more poignant moment. Francis believed with all his heart that he had received this rule from God. Men judged otherwise. It was provisionally set aside as too long and too packed with quotations from Scripture. Francis was advised to write a more succinct version.

It may in fact seem long, but it remains full of beauty, and it provides us with a first-class psychological document. Francis the man is there in his entirety, as he always was, both before and after his conversion, with the enthusiasm that came naturally to him and the youthfulness of spirit that overcame every trial. Saint and sinner, he had the same qualities, and his rule was the work of a man eternally capable of love. That was what gave him his strength and his magnetic power over young people. The rule banishes sadness, which he always suspected, as contrary to hope, and ends with a song that resounds with joy, like a psalm of victory.

References to himself are not lacking in it. Some of them remind us of the extravagant young man who dressed with all the refinement of a dandy, but now he was talking about coarse fabric patched with bags.

He commands the rejection of money with the vehemence of a man who has wasted a fortune on pleasure. Money is ordure.

Chastity, without which the love of God is only fantasizing, glows like an irreplaceable treasure. Penance is forgotten in the joy of liberation from the slavery of bodily passions.

To the nonprejudiced reader all this contains a mixture of common sense and metaphysical delirium. It is the disorder of crazy love that begins with practical recommendations of exemplary lucidity and ends with a fit of divine intoxication. Unless you become like a little child, Christ said, you will not enter the kingdom of heaven. We must remember that this rule was composed with the help of Cesare of Speyer, who in large measure shared Francis's exaltation, so we can almost hear the groans from old Honorius when he read these pages with their total otherworldliness. This mass of sublimity had to be cut down to size; the beautiful, tremulous bird had to have its wings clipped.

On the seventh and last day of the chapter, the brothers' farewells were marked by a melancholy they had never felt before. Usually they bade one another a solemn adieu, for these pilgrims of the absolute were haunted by their hope of martyrdom, but this time leaving the man who had so long been their guide must have cost them more effort. He remained the brother part excellence, but he had ceased to be their leader. There was no great outpouring of love from the new minister general. Elias knew how to govern, that was all.

And Francis, staff in hand, once again became God's vagabond.

Brother Jacqueline

As close to his heart as Brother Leo and the very first disciples, Jacqueline di Settesoli had a special place in Francis's life. Cardinal John of Saint Paul, bishop of Ostia, introduced her to Francis when he came to Rome to see Innocent III in 1212. A widow at the age of twenty and mother of two boys, she was descended from one of the most illustrious families of ancient Rome, the Frangipani. The name in itself had something like the accent of the Gospel in classical antiquity: Flavius Anicius, the ancestral founder, had saved the people of Rome by distributing bread to them, whence the name *frangere panem*. She was, needless to say, extremely rich; It is not known whether she was beautiful. In any case she gave unstintingly of her wealth and thought of becoming a nun.

When she saw Francis, the two of them were bowled over, spiritually speaking. Certain souls move toward one another as if they had already met. At the first opportunity she entrusted herself to him and took him as her advisor. What Francis admired about her was that she lived in the world as if she weren't there. Unbeknownst to herself she already embodied the ideal of the Third Order. Her example may have ignited in Francis's mind the magnificent vision of a universal brotherhood and sisterhood of lay people. Her brave fidelity to the teachings of Christ awoke the saint's admiration.

Given Francis's views on the danger of familiarity with women, he raised between Jacqueline and the brotherhood a sort of psychological barrier that rendered her harmless. Nevertheless her personality remains something of a mystery because of the silence about her physical appearance. This raises a delicate problem: Perhaps she simply wasn't feminine enough to pose a danger to the brothers. I see her throwing herself at Francis's feet, begging him to free her from herself. Countless men and women have taken refuge in convents not so much to flee the world as to flee themselves. With his habitual delicacy Francis invented the name "Brother Jacqueline." He called her that thanks to the odd propensity men have for giving male names to women whose energy they approve of.

Each time he stayed in Rome, Francis was the guest of Brother Jacqueline. She baked him a little cake that he accepted, as if this tiny concession to human weakness amounted to a breach in his everyday ascetical regimen. It was an almond cream cake, à la Frangipani.

The Big Bad Wolf

The wolf of Gubbio is so well-known that he needs no introduction. This was the least miraculous of Francis's miracles. The real miracle would have been if the wolf had eaten Francis, since there is no record of any animal ever harming him. The entire animal kingdom respected him for reasons that are still a secret. The simple fact is that beasts loved him. Did they see in him an aura of love that our eyes can't discern—perhaps in the form of the halo we see only in the portraits of saints, something that worked on them and made them happy? Such instances are not rare. One of the most celebrated is that of Saint Sergius, who was accompanied through the woods by a bear with whom he shared his bread. And I'm not forgetting Saint Jerome's lion, who patiently allowed him to pull a thorn out of his paw, thereby beginning a long friendship between two rather difficult characters.

Gubbio is a very old little town whose fortifications zigzag down the slopes of Mount Igino. Less pleasant than Assisi, it seems even a bit severe, but the immense Piazza della Signoria in the heart of the town gives it the majesty of open spaces. Houses form the border on one side; opposite them a terrace overlooks the lower town with its dark red roofs. And at each end of the great rectangular piazza two palaces face one another. This would be the backdrop for the final scene.

In Francis's day Gubbio lived in terror because of an exceptionally large wolf that haunted the countryside. The inhabitants had to lock the gates of the town and went outside—if it was absolutely necessary to go—only when they were armed with pitchforks and pikes. But the infernal creature feared nothing and no one and, emerging from the woods, took its tool of victims like the Minotaur.

Francis decided to straighten all this out and went to Gubbio, where the townspeople begged him to remain. But he didn't listen and, leaving the town by the Roman gate, went with his companion down the path to the forest, the lair of the master murderer. First he had to cross a deserted stretch, a place of horror where bones strewn here and there spoke for themselves. From atop the ramparts the townsfolk cried to him to come back. Francis had no thought of fear, while his companion's every limb was quivering. Suddenly in the nearby woods there echoed the drawn out howl that everyone knew.

Petrified with horror, his companion stood riveted to the spot, but Francis went on his way. Almost immediately, with long, loping strides, the most famous of all wolves was seen running toward him.

Francis marched straight up to the predator, made a broad sign of the cross over him, and cried out: "Brother Wolf, come here. In the name of Christ I command you not harm anyone any more. And you will not eat Brother Ass" (as he called his body). The wolf stopped, his pendulous tongue disappeared in his gaping mouth, which he closed. He approached Francis, who gravely lectured him. "You are very bad. You wound and eat God's creatures without his permission, and not only animals, but men made in God's image. That is why you deserve to feel the pitchforks like a robber and murderer. Everyone cries out and murmurs against you. But I wish to make peace between you and the people of Gubbio." The wolf wagged his tail and twitched his ears, then bowed his head to signify his agreement. But that wasn't enough. He had to promise to renounce evil, which he did by placing his paw in the hand that Francis stretched out to him. Francis commanded the new convert to follow him back to the Piazza della Signoria. All the people were gathered to witness the marvel: Francis with a miraculously tamed public enemy number one right behind him. Unwilling to let slip such a fine opportunity to proclaim the word of the Gospel, he revealed to his listeners that the sins of each one of them had brought this scourge upon them, and that the fires of hell were more to be feared than the red maw of a ferocious beast. Repent, repent, and without delay.

Afterward, it was decided that since Brother Wolf had amended his ways, the inhabitants of Gubbio would furnish him with food every day, a wolf's hunger being proverbial. By this means he would stay peaceable. Brother Wolf was invited to affirm his good intentions, which he did by moving his tail and ears once more. Did he promise? The wolf lifted his right paw and put it in Francis's hand.

A new life began for both Gubbio and the wolf, who became the pet of all the townspeople, entering their houses and making himself at home. Alas, he enjoyed this delightful existence for only two years. He was heartily mourned, and buried in a chapel dedicated to Saint Francis. In 1873 workers raising a flagstone uncovered his skull, which testified in its own way to the prodigy and glorified his first human friend.

Part Four

GOD ALONE

Francis, Friar Minor

The papal and episcopal decisions affecting the brotherhood had reduced its founder to the most humble rank possible. He himself had expressed a desire for this. He was now simply a Friar Minor, a little brother among thousands of others, but his inner radiance stayed the same. All his humility was powerless to hide it. He was no longer in command, but he remained the brother to whom the others looked up with love. It was no use shrinking down; his incandescent spirit gave him away.

One charming story shows us the side of him that made him so necessary to everyone. A brother was tormented by the desire to have his own Psalter and admitted this to Brother Francis. The superior wasn't against it, but the young brother wanted permission from Francis himself. He was knocking on the wrong door. Francis didn't like the idea of the brothers being contaminated by the love of books—leave that to the scholars, to the clergy, to the orders that had libraries, like the Benedictines. A true Friar Minor had no business owning a book. The community's text of the four Gospels, which was read aloud at specified times, was enough. But the young brother kept at it. One evening when he was seated with Francis next to the fire, he ventured his request again. "First a Psalter," Francis grumbled, "then you'll need a breviary, and after that you'll sit in a big chair and say: "Brother, fetch me my breviary!" And with one of those unexpected gestures he sometimes made, he seized a fistful of cold ashes, rubbed the top of the young brother's head, and burst out laughing: "A breviary! A breviary! Here's your breviary!" And the lad withdrew, covered with shame.

But the story doesn't end there. Several months later Francis met the young bibliophile out on the road. Incredibly, the brother once more raised the issue of his Psalter and of the minister's permission. This time Francis sent him packing: "Go and do what your minister tells you." The brother went off and left Francis standing alone in the road, a perplexed Francis who suddenly cried out, "Wait, brother, wait!" Having caught up with him, he asked him to return with him to the scene of their first discussion. When they arrived there, Francis got down on his knees before the brother and asked his pardon. *"Mea culpa,"* he said—but added that a brother wasn't allowed to possess anything except his tunic, his cord, his underpants and, when needed in case of illness, a pair of shoes. The refusal stood, but the tone was different. From then on there was no more talk about the blessed Psalter.

The further we press into Francis's life, the more he tends to elude us. His very simplicity baffles our desire to understand him. We think of those hollows in the rock where he sometimes went seeking refuge at dizzying heights. His reactions disconcert us; to the very end he would be a man of contrasts. One follows him as best one can.

The installation of a Franciscan library in Bologna sent him into a rage. Not that he hated learning, far from it. He admired it in others, but he wanted none of it in his house. He realized that he was "unlettered," but he instinctively knew that this (quite relative) ignorance preserved in him and his brothers something more precious than human knowledge; that is, the message of the Gospel in all its purity, the state of spiritual childhood that is the key to the kingdom of heaven. Like Saint Paul, he wanted to know only Christ, who is above all human knowledge.

This love of unknowing is all the more remarkable in that it appeared while Europe was undergoing a pronounced intellectual evolution. The University of Bologna was the oldest and the most renowned back in 1222, but others were just emerging. Frederick II founded the University of Naples and the School of Medicine at Salerno. He had translations made of Avicenna, Averroes, and other Arabic texts on astronomy, anatomy, and medicine. This marked the first serious attempt at relations between the Christian world and Islam. An analogous effort was made to foster understanding with the Jews of Cordova and Seville. Italy saw the establishment of a university in Padua, following that of Naples. Institutions of learning were cropping up all over. Anything might come of this. Theological debates once held in the public square or in the street would now take place within their walls. It wasn't long before Francis sensed the dangers of scholasticism.

Amid the vast intellectual ground swells rolling through society, he stood apart, faithful to his vocation of charity, alone. What was he, properly speaking? They looked at him and listened with astonishment. Why did his voice bring joy to the most troubled hearts? His smile was the very smile of love. The most ordinary phrases from his lips reawakened faith and reconciled the individual with himself, even the men and women lost in the crowd, as if the crowd were made up of human beings and were no longer what it usually is—a headless monster. We are tempted to say of him, as was said of Christ, that no one ever spoke as he did. He had the peculiar quality that, among the infinitely diverse mass of people who watched him, he represented man as God wished him to be. Nothing could be less complicated than that, and nothing more beautiful. There was no end to the miracles wrought by Brother Francis, almost all of them healings, of both body and soul, similar to those in the Gospel and manifest signs of holiness.

It was in 1222—or earlier, perhaps, but we don't know for sure—that he agreed to become a deacon, which conferred on him the right to read the Gospel at mass and, something else he treasured, the privilege of carrying the ciborium at certain liturgical functions, holding it in his hands, swathed in the humeral veil. He felt he was holding God against his heart.

Sermon at Bologna

In the middle of this welter of conflicting opinions and doctrines, would the brotherhood of the Friars Minor shift its position—and what did Francis think about it all? He never hesitated. For him the cross remained the fixed point on a revolving earth, and yet in 1222 he could find no peace. He would have to search for that peace at Fonte Colombo, in one of the hermitages in the Rieti Valley, hidden high up within the dense forest. There he could reflect. Too many things were going on in the world for the echoes not to reach him. The brotherhood was changing. Francis's friends, Elias and Ugolino, had gotten it into shape by making an order out of it. The conspiracy had been woven in masterly fashion, ever so quietly. His great dream of humanity marching all together toward salvation had vanished in the face of the practical measures taken to save his initial "idea," and it made Francis suffer. "Who has torn up my rule?" he would cry out in pain one day.

And yet no one ever had a more beautiful dream than Francis, and more than twenty generations would feed on the memory of that dream. There is no killing an idea.

Accompanied no doubt by Brother Leo, he went from hermitage to hermitage, visiting the first brothers: Bernard, Rufino, Giles, Masseo, Juniper—and Sylvester, the most inaccessible, one might say the shiest, of all. No one who really knew Francis could suppose that he was content with taking a nostalgic tour and speaking to his brothers about the good old days at la Portiuncula and Rivo Torto. More likely, he presented his problems and listened to these wholehearted friends as they gave their advice. In the tranquil, calming beauty of the dark green hills, the schemes of the people in Rome must have seemed a petty affair to those anchorites oriented to God alone.

But Francis couldn't delay. He wanted to act; he had his rule to defend. The first one had been rejected; he was working out a second in his mind, in response to Christ's unforgettable call.

Once more he left his brothers to go elsewhere. What else had he done for the past thirteen years? Did his irresistible fascination with the open road make him forget that the Lord had shown him the exact spot on Alverno—the hollow of a rock over the abyss—where he was to devote his time to prayer? He didn't go to La Verna very often, but if he bore the whole Gospel in his heart, he had something of Saint Paul in his peripatetic legs.

An inspiration led him to Bologna. He had gloomy memories of that city, so proud of its architectural beauty. He hadn't forgotten the meanness of its inhabitants who, for two whole days, had insulted and ridiculed a man as holy as Bernard of Quintavalle when he came there to found a very modest convent of Friars Minor. Ten years later, while passing through the city, Francis had found his brothers comfortably lodged there in a rich residence and wrapped up in study rather than living outdoors and preaching in the countryside and the villages. Francis had no regrets over the violent sensation he had caused by throwing the brothers out onto the street. They had betrayed holy Poverty and succumbed to a kind of intellectual pride. He had spoken out loud and clear and poured forth curses like an Old Testament prophet, but Ugolino, who was on hand, had intervened. Everything could be arranged as he saw fit because the walls of the new convent belonged to him, and the brothers returned to their fine house. Ugolino was always around to manage things his way. Francis must have been thinking all this over on that feast of the Assumption, 1223.

Standing on the steps of the old Romanesque church in the middle of a huge piazza that could hold the entire city's population, he was in sight of two sumptuous palaces—one the podestà's, the other the commune's—with aggressive battlements, rows of magnificent arcades; and as if that were not enough, above the roofs he saw the towers of the aristocratic mansions, each one a little higher than its neighbors, all aiming to outdo each other, some of them slightly askew from the effort to affirm their superiority. Here, like everywhere else, arrogant men were fighting it out beneath the burning sky of summer.

Still more imposing in its glory was the presence of the university founded in the fifth century by Theodosius, the oldest in the world, the most learned, the first. Francis couldn't see it from where he was, but it was nonetheless in his mind's eye. What did he think of it? We know very well that he recognized the value of knowledge, but not without serious reservations. Others might profit from it, not he or his brothers. It nourished pride and damned more souls than it saved. Mother of a vast and vain body of learning, the university sent forth from its walls men full of self-satisfaction, easy prey for the eternal adversary. "A single demon," he would later write, "knows more than all men put together."

Meanwhile the Piazza del Commune was full. It seemed as if the whole town had gathered down on the pavement, up at the windows, and even on the roofs. Common people, noblemen, doctors of law and theology, philosophers, physicians, all were curious to see how the little man in brown would carry it off, because though his reputation was enormous, he was in Bologna. And Bologna knew everything, whereas he had made a profession of voluntary ignorance. Was he intimidated? Not very likely, because he wasn't counting on himself but on his Lord. He had made cardinals weep without knowing a word of what he was going to say. Here he found himself in a great disputatious city, divided by bloody hatreds passed down from father to son. Francis wouldn't stick to giving the proud city a dressing down. He had the intuition that among this multitude that he was supposed not to provoke there were many people hungry, not for studied eloquence, but for pure and simple religion. As for him, his prophetic fury was ready to be unleashed. "Angels, demons, men." That was the subject he had chosen, humanity caught between the powers on high and those below. What an opportunity to make his audience tremble . . .

But now he had scarcely opened his mouth when the Lord made words of love and peace come out of it as if he were simply taking his place. Francis expressed himself in such a familiar style that he seemed to be conversing with the crowd, but his language was so clear and his words hit home so squarely that no one, whether cleric or layman, could help listening to him with avid attention. The academics looked at one another with astonishment: This was no ignoramus talking. His quotations from sacred Scripture were applied with an aptness that would have done honor to a theologian; and yet there was nothing of the preacher about him. As he grew more animated, his phrases were like the beats of a loving heart; it was love speaking out, and each of his listeners imagined he was the only one being addressed. How did he do it? And how did his every least syllable reach the farthest corner of that immense piazza? We don't know, any more than we know why, when he prayed, enemies shook hands in the joy of reconciliation. The emotion was so strong that in one of those somewhat frightening swirls of enthusiasm people rushed toward him en masse and tried to rip his tunic to shreds to make relics out of it. The man who had spoken was a saint; an Italian crowd knew the real item when it saw it.

Thomas of Spalato, who witnessed the sermon, has left us an account of the scene.

The Lost Rule

Leaving Bologna, he decided to go to Rieti, because since his return from the Holy Land his eyes, which had been damaged by the Oriental sun, had never stopped hurting. And Rieti happened to be the place where people had always gone to have their ophthalmias cared for. The renown of the doctors there gave Francis some hope of bettering his health, if not of getting completely cured. He had to travel in short stages, longer excursions being out of the question. All the ardor of his youth had taken refuge in his soul, which remained indefatigable while his body grew weaker. Along the way he sought a little rest in the many hermitages where the Friars Minor dwelled. At La Verna, Farneto, Buonriposo, in the upper valley of the Tiber, these cool sanctuaries lost in the wooded hills sheltered him from the light he had always loved so much and whose agonizing brilliance he now fled. There he was well set up for praying and reflecting on his rule, which he wanted to hone to an unassailable precision.

For Francis the very name of Rieti still had a magical quality. During his mission in the autumn of 1208, with his first seven brothers, he had come to Terni and discovered the Rieti Valley. His wonder-struck memories of the place never ceased to beckon happily to him. He saw himself once again on the road that passed by the famous delle Marmore cascades, where the water, despite its thunderous roar, resembled white veins in the green marble of the forest. He had been tempted to stop there and found a hermitage, but he had to move on and convert the people so blessed by the pleasantness of the country that they were backsliding into paganism. Traveling along Lake Piediluco, narrowly squeezed between the Reatine and Sabine Mountains, he had reached a new earthly paradise.

In the last week of December 1222 he went to the little convent of Fonte Colombo. Hidden away in a wood of green oak, it was an ideal spot for the plan he had in mind. At this point let me evoke a personal memory. Having arrived at Fonte Colombo one sunny morning, I pushed open a door and entered a large room where the word *VISITARE* was written on a sign. *Visitare* was just what I wanted to do, and a number of rather modestly dressed persons already there evidently had the same idea. They were waiting on a bench, so I sat down beside them. They looked like a group of pilgrims rather than tourists; and we were patiently waiting when a groan of pain was heard from behind a door, then a loud, reassuring voice saying something like, "Come on, it's not that awful, you'll see, it's nothing." There followed another groan, whereupon I asked one of my neighbors if the visit of the convent would be starting soon. His answer came at once: "It's the doctor. You have to wait your turn." We were waiting for the brother who attended the sick. Thus the old Franciscan tradition of caring for the poor was kept up, the charity of the *Poverello* truly spanned the centuries.

Leaving that miniscule hospital, I went down by a narrow path to a twelfth-century chapel, hardly bigger than an oratory, but with walls that still bore the fragments of ancient frescoes that Francis must have seen in their primitive freshness. I could still make out a Byzantine Christ holding a book. In the embrasure of a window that was scarcely larger than a loophole, Francis's delicate hand had painted the letter *tau,* perfectly visible in a fine orange-red, a letter that served as his signature and that he must have seen for the first time in Rome in a chapel dedicated to Saint Anthony, the first hermit. We have good reason to believe that Jesus was crucified on a T-shaped cross. It was in that tiny chapel that Francis heard mass, and his presence is more moving there than in the splendor of the basilica built in his memory by Elias.

Lower down on the side of the mountain beneath the all-white grotto that he used as a cell, a crack in the rock draws one's gaze into the abyss below with the fascination of dizzying heights that Francis must have felt, for we find them in all the refuges where he hid from the world. With the intrepid nimbleness of a mountain goat, he climbed up to a site where nowadays a guardrail is indispensable. One can dream in that cell. It was here that Francis spent forty days fasting, a tremendous effort he had to make in order to work out the rule in his mind. His two companions, Brothers Leo and Bonizo of Bologna, hadn't been chosen at random. Leo was his irreplaceable confidant and Bonizo a jurist from Bologna. Then, as if to help him to get a clear view of his task, he had a crucial vision in a dream. He was gathering crumbs of bread from the ground to give them to the thousands of brothers around him. The crumbs were so small that he didn't know how to do it. A voice told him, "Francis, make a host with all those crumbs, and you'll be able to give it to all those who desire it." He did, and the ones who received it without this desire were stricken with leprosy. The meaning of the dream eluded Francis, but that evening while he was praying, the voice explained it to him: "Francis, the crumbs are the words of the Gospel, the host is the rule, and leprosy is sin."

When he had ended his fast, Francis called Leo and told him to bring something to write with. The two of them installed themselves in front of the grotto at the foot of a tree, where Francis dictated his rule under divine inspiration. It seemed as if all of nature was reinforcing the inner assurance he felt in his whole being. The valley lay open before him with its wooded precipices, and in the distance the shadowy summit of the mountains gleamed on the horizon. The continual murmur of nearby springs, far from troubling the immensity of the silence, blended with and was lost in it.

All this notwithstanding, the text of the rule was submitted to Brother Bonizo, who could give helpful advice on the legal sense of terms used so as to thwart the cleverness of pettifogging ministers.

Meanwhile at la Portiuncula the brothers were beginning to wonder about Francis's absence. There was no news. They knew where he was, but no more, and with winter drawing to a close Elias and several of the ministers decided to go visit Francis. What worried them more than anything was the rule they were awaiting from him as a replacement for the first rule, which had been set aside. Why did he need so many days for the job? The more time passed, the longer they imagined the rule getting, and they wanted it short and reasonable. So they went to Rieti, and from there on horseback to Fonte Colombo. Francis wasn't happy to see them. Alone with Elias he might have opened his heart, because he never lost his old affection for that protean character who was undoubtedly his best friend from his youthful days, but the presence of the six or seven ministers could only irritate him because of their smugness. He didn't know that at Rieti, fearing that his rule would be too hard, they had insisted on Elias's going to find Francis and tell him they wanted no part of it, that he could keep his rule for himself. Elias had flatly refused. Under no circumstances did he want to expose himself to the *Poverello*'s reproaches, but they wouldn't take no for an answer. Finally Elias gave in, and the troubled little group set out for the hermitage.

"What do these brothers want?" asked Francis when he saw them. Elias, no doubt reluctantly, transmitted the message. Reports differ about the scene that followed. It is sad to have to write that in all probability the ministers won the day. Elias took the rule, promising to examine it at Rieti and to let Francis know his feelings about it as soon as they had all discussed it. The *Poverello* must have suffered cruelly. In a phrase full of pain he remarked to Christ, "Lord, didn't I tell you that they wouldn't trust you?"

Days went by without an answer. In a fit of impatience where Francesco di Bernardone showed his old self, he went down to the town and—surprise, Brother Elias informed him that the rule had been misplaced. They had searched everywhere for it, in vain; it was impossible to lay a hand on it. Just one of those things . . .

Once again they had gotten around Francis. Then he did something that nobody could have foreseen. His rule had been lost, so he decided to rewrite it. I believe that this rule was identical to the one that had been "lost." On the advice of Brother Bonizo, concessions had been made in matters of language and legal form, without which there was a serious risk that the rule might not get through. But, as always happens in such cases, you can't touch the form without altering the essence. Here lies part of Francis's drama. Like Baudelaire's albatross, "his giant wings prevent him from walking." He didn't have his feet on the ground. Between the Gospel as he read it and the world's interpretation of the Gospel there lay an enormous gap, the one where we struggle today, because quite obviously the triumph of the Gospel in our world, in the waning twentieth century, is infinitely far from an accomplished fact. To save Francis's evangelical ideal the Church found itself constrained to make some inevitable adjustments, lest humanity suffer shipwreck and the world return to paganism. If we wish to see where we stand in relation to that ideal, we need only read Christ's prophecies about the events that will precede his second coming on earth. Alongside this the mad predictions of Nostradamus are mere trifles. Christ announces a catastrophe such as the world hasn't experienced since creation. Only the presence of the elect will cut short the overwhelming destruction. It goes without saying that an innocent world would not be blasted by such a tremendous chastisement. Men's hearts will dry up from fear. The stars will fall from heaven. Saint Peter adds that the elements will melt in flames. After that will come a new heaven and a new earth. One reads these things and turns the page, thinking, "All that won't be here tomorrow." But there will come a day among days, with no tomorrow.

Francis made his dream of saving humanity through the Gospel an impractical one on account of his literal and, it must be said, excessive attachment to every verse of that Gospel. Given the state of the world in 1220, the only way the Church could save the evangelical ideal was by fitting it as closely as possible to the people of that day. Francis surrendered to such thinking, and he was obliged to reshape the rule of 1221. Would the new rule be acceptable? Yes and no. One couldn't ask human beings to do the impossible. Once again the Franciscan ideal had to be retailored to fit the wearer. That was sensible enough, it was necessary—and sad. Francis hadn't gotten the cross of martyrdom he had coveted. Christ sent him another that bore a striking resemblance to the one borne by Simon of Cyrene, and he slumped beneath its weight.

He didn't want to trim the Gospel, to be "reasonable." He was one of those uncompromising people whom the world sooner or later breaks, so long as they're on earth, but who win the victory on the other side of the tomb. Saint Francis of Assisi was never more alive than he is today, whereas the great personalities of his age have faded away. He wanted to save the world; in the end he saved hope.

The Curse of Perugia

While Francis was staying at Greccio in his favorite hermitage he was, a Perugian chronicler tells us, "blessed with a vision." His being "blessed" may surprise us, for the vision could only be a somber one. It was about Perugia, whose pride, violence, and vices gave it a detestable reputation at a time when such things were perfectly commonplace. It must be added that Francis had not forgotten the slaughter of Collestrada nor the year he had spent in the cellar of a papal jail. Did he still feel rancor about it? That would be going too far, but it seems a safe bet that Francis judged Perugia in need of a serious warning. It must also be recognized that cursing came easy to this great saint. His patron was Saint John the Baptist, who for his part could curse with all the furor of the Hebrew prophets. Francis's baptismal name, we know, was John (Giovanni), for John the Baptist, in keeping with his mother's wishes. This was the saint whom he must have invoked in evening prayers and whose influence would make itself felt throughout his life. Thus in many Italian Renaissance paintings, all the way until the baroque, Francis is shown in the company of his patron, who is wearing a camel skin.

Still, the Franciscan greeting remained the same, *"Pace e bene!"* and Francis surely was pondering this as he took the road to Perugia. To reform the guilty city and bring it joy and peace by preaching the word of God and repentance—that was his intention when he arrived in the great piazza, where over the immense space bordered by palaces whose crenelated walls dovetailed together, the pink and gray cathedral spread an aura of magnificence.

Curious to hear the most celebrated preacher in the country, the crowd flocked from all sides, without a trace of hostility, because the thirst for God was as strong here as anywhere else in Italy. Only the knights displayed their contempt for all this lower-class emotion, and making a loud racket with their swords and bucklers, they set about jousting and caracoling in place to poke fun at the moralizing "monk." It was impossible to hear anything amid the diabolical fracas of iron-work and mail. And then Francis felt God's great indignation against his people swelling within him. Turning toward the crowd, he poured out his disturbing message: "Pay careful attention to what the Lord announces to you," he said. "Don't say: 'Bah, it's a man from Assisi!' The Lord has elevated and glorified you, which is why you must humble yourselves before God and before your neighbors. . . . Your heart is puffed up with arrogance. . . . You pillage your neighbors and kill many of them. And so I tell you, if you do not convert very soon, the Lord is preparing a terrible vengeance against you; he will raise up some of you against the others; civil war will break out and will cause you unending evils."

Such was Francis's authority that, far from arousing the anger of the people, this sermon moved and shamed them, and many were converted. Despite that, disorders broke out a little later. There was an uprising of the popular party against the knights, and civil war unleashed its ravages. The farmhouses burned, the fields were devastated, the vines were crushed beneath the horses' hooves. Rome sent help to the commune, and the castles were torn down. Class hatred exploded and made so much blood flow that the knights, overcome by the masses, were forced to flee and beg for asylum in Assisi, only yesterday the object of their scorn. And so the *Poverello*'s prophecies came true amidst disaster and confusion.

Heartbroken by what he foresaw, Francis departed from Perugia and took the road to Assisi, leaving his words of fire behind him.

The Rule of the Friars Minor

The Pentecost chapter at la Portiuncula took place on June 11, 1223, and Francis went to it with his carefully reconstructed second rule. Obedient but resolute, he was ready for a confrontation to defend it. If he was expecting resistance, he found it even sharper than anticipated, not only on the part of the ministers, but also of the brothers who had come from all over the peninsula and foreign countries, each one with specific problems. They all agreed that Francis's rule erred by its excessive severity and failed to take into account such realities as differences in climate and audience. It was one thing to preach to Spaniards in the sun, another to face a sometimes recalcitrant crowd in the mud of Pomerania. Extravagant mortifications were undermining their strength, and this could only weaken their zeal. Without damaging the Franciscan ideal, they had to consider, if not mitigations, at least a more humane version of certain articles.

Francis understood these objections, some of which he thought fair. He himself had ordered the burning of piles of instruments of penitence that might chastise the body without reaching the soul. And he insisted on an adequate diet. He willingly gave in on points made by common sense, but he fought hard against the carnal man, and his demands bore down on the need to reform and sanctify the inner life. First of all, one's vision had to be mortified. "Death has climbed in through our windows," says Scripture, which Francis knew well. To look at a woman lustfully was as serious as the act of fornication. Mortify the tongue. Another Saint Francis, a Frenchman and bishop of Geneva, would say that slander was dipping your tongue in your neighbor's blood. Francis would have liked that metaphor. He declared war on everything that could kill love in the human heart. On that point he would never give an inch. But he demanded indulgence for sinners who acknowledged their faults, and he wanted that forgiveness as broad as the kind Christ gave, because it was Christ and Christ alone whom one always had to follow. He spoke with warmth and authority, although he was only a Friar Minor like the others; but if he was no longer the leader of the brotherhood, he was still its soul, and the Francis of the early days could be found intact in such expressions as, "I counsel . . . my brothers . . . I warn . . . I recommend. . . ." And always "my brothers . . ."

Whenever he faced an insurmountable obstacle, he gave way, not out of weakness, but to safeguard the ideal. No doubt he would have to compromise. He no longer forbade traveling on horseback when necessary, just as he dropped his prohibition against taking anything along on journeys. The energy of the first rule was slightly diminished. The second, less rigorous, also seemed less vigorous, but it would remain faithful to the essence of the first and in the end would be accepted.

Francis had one obligation left: the redoubtable trial of presenting the rule to the pope. He left la Portiuncula neither victor nor vanquished but a little more disillusioned than before. The opposition from the brothers had wounded him. "The rule is too hard!" He never thought he would hear that cry. His first companions had never uttered it. It was like a protest against the demands of the Gospel, and the Gospel was losing ground. Had it ever stopped losing ground since Christ ceased to walk the earth? The dream of the young convert back in 1206 was going to pieces.

The Hermitage

Francis needed a refuge to find himself and complain to God: "Lord, didn't I tell you?" Poggio Bustone in the Reatine Mountains offered him a peaceful, refreshing solitude, far from the world and its quarreling voices.

The village is on the side of the mountain at an elevation of more than twenty-three hundred feet; the very modest convent some three hundred feet higher up consisted in Francis's time of three or four caves arranged as a hermitage. Francis had founded it in 1208, but he wasn't planning to head there. Another six hundred feet higher in a combe at the foot of high chalk cliffs he had discovered a still more secret cavern where he went to hide, like a wounded bird.

When he came back down to the hermitage to speak with his brothers or take a meal with them, he could see, in the setting sun, the Rieti Valley with its meadows all rose colored in the dusty haze of summer light, and in the heart of that immense botanical garden a long lake shining like a steel blade. All of nature seemed, in the silence, to be prompting him with the words of the song of praise that were unconsciously coming together within him, overcoming his sadness.

Francis's Face

The problem of the portraits of Francis will never be solved, because so many of them were made in the years following his death, and they don't agree. The finest one, by Cimabue, was done about fifty years afterward. Its merit, apart from its pictorial beauty, lies in the painter's intuitive genius. It shows us the Francis of the later years, a Francis who is sick, worn out by suffering, sad, but nonetheless radiant with love.

If we are interested in Francis as his contemporaries saw him at the peak of his mystical adventure, then we have to look for him elsewhere, in the Benedictine abbey of Subiaco, where we find two pieces of evidence that strike me as conclusive.

At the hermitage of Poggio Bustone, Francis spent ten days or so, then went on foot to Subiaco where, as we know, he remained for July and August. He wanted to assist at the dedication of the chapel of Saint Gregory that Ugolino would preside over on September 3, since the cardinal of Ostia was the lord of Jenna whose lands were enfeoffed to the monastery of Subiaco. Begun by Innocent III in honor of Saint Benedict, the sanctuary, which was built around the grotto where Benedict of Nursia had long ago composed his rule and founded his order, was now close to completion.

Francis was attached to the Benedictines, and they returned his love. They welcomed him with joy, and there was always a cell available for him. But this time, along with his need to put a little distance between himself and his brotherhood which, as he saw it, was changing too rapidly, he also felt the desire to do honor to the patriarch of Western monks at this splendid consecration. He arrived alone at the monastery because, out of obedience and humility, he had just given up having himself accompanied, as usual, by one of the brothers most dear to him.

I am convinced that the dedication of the chapel of Saint Gregory could have occurred only in 1223, and not in 1222 or 1224, as some writers maintain. But before getting to the portrait of Francis begun in 1216 during his first visit, I would like to draw attention to a second portrait (on another wall of the same chapel, to the left of the window), which represents the dedication ceremony. It shows three standing figures: Cardinal Ugolino, the officiant; behind him a tall young man in an alb, Rainaldo di Jenna, one of the cardinal's nephews, who would later become pope under the name of Alexander IV; and between them a man wearing a bluish gray, triangular hood that we have already seen in another portrait of Francis; and next to him, a processional cross heavily encrusted with gems. Unlike the other frescoes, this one shows sign of retouching; the artist was that mysterious master of Saint Gregory, also called the master of Saint Francis of Assisi, whom certain specialists believe was a painter of the Cosma family. He was in any case an excellent frescoist of the Roman school.

Without getting into sterile arguments that only muddle the evidence, and keeping in mind what Berenson said about inner reality, I maintain that these two portraits are the only authentic faces of Francis, not forgetting, however, the one of the *Poverello* wiping his eyes, a naive work that we shall see once more at Greccio. Reading the inscriptions beneath the fresco only confirms my notion that here at last we have Francis as he was, his true self.

The first inscription simply explains that it was Pope Gregory IX, then bishop of Ostia, who consecrated the church. The second, in larger characters against a faded red background, says: "This house was painted in the second year of the reign of the Sovereign Pontiff. Before receiving the greatest honor, this man stayed here and led a perfect life, for the two months of July and burning August. He mortified the flesh in holy exercises like Saint Paul, who was ravished and carried away to the third heaven. It was no longer he who lived, but Christ in him. That is why one should say a prayer here."

Ugolino was elected pope on March 19, 1227, so this fresco was painted in 1228. Why two inscriptions? Because the second, the big one, evidently refers to Francis. (He was canonized in 1228.) Our attention is drawn to the importance of the cross next to his face. The Latin words are in the past tense and bear witness to the holiness of the model. They could hardly have been written during the lifetime of Gregory IX or of the future Alexander IV. Because of the precise reference to the months of July and August, the year can't have been 1222, since Francis was in the Romagna, to be specific, in Bologna, on August 15, 1222. And it can't have been 1224, because in August of that year the saint was at La Verna. Hence I believe that this inscription clearly indicates that Francis lived in the Sacro Speco at Subiaco and led a monastic life there in 1223 during two summer months. He already bore within him the image of Christ that would later be reflected in the stigmata. And because he was a saint, the visitor could pray before this image, which would be unusual for an image of a noncanonized pope.

A number of resemblances can be pointed out in the details of the two portraits: the contour of the cheeks, the shape of the ears, the drawing of the mouth and chin, the cut of the beard and hair, the fineness of the nose, and above all the barely arched eyebrows mentioned by Celano. The look, however, is different in each case: In the dedication fresco the eyes are sunken, and the expression on the face seems turned inward. It distances itself more and more from worldly events. There is, unquestionably, a kind of self-scrutiny after Poggio Bustone, and the desire to give up struggling for his ideal except by example.

In the other portrait, Francis holds in his hand a scroll that reads, "Peace to this dwelling." This is Brother Francis. His hand is youthful, the face is smiling, the uniform of poverty is well cut and not without a certain elegance. Even the feet tally with Celano's description: They are small and almost feminine. The neck is slender. This is the Francis of 1216, with his enthusiasm and his illusions about men. Joy flashes in his look; his whole body seems young, even if we recall that parts of the fresco, notably the folds in the habit, were restored in the middle of the nineteenth century. Francis is alive. This is the most perfect image ever made of him, and the world knew him when it saw him. But let's look more closely—a careful examination of this face will reveal more than first seems apparent. Francis's first stay at Subiaco most likely dates from 1216, the second from 1223. Between those two dates destiny stepped in, and the man changed a great deal. A transformation took place in him that the artist shows in his own way and with exceptional discretion and skill. It's as if he wanted to hide what he had to say. The distracted observer will miss the whole point here.

In my opinion, the artist who did this fresco lived in the monastery. If we cover the left side of the face, what do we see on the right? The eye is large, bright, joyous, the eye of a man casting a dazzled glance on creation, as if all of nature's beauty had entered and possessed him. Here is the young Francis, with the passions that he fought against and all his dreams about the good will of others. There are distinct traces of a smile, lifting the corner of the mouth and nostril.

The left side of the face has an entirely different message. The eye has a peculiarly enlarged iris that touches the edge of the eyelid. Yet the eye is smaller, and the joy has gone out of it. We can't say that this eye is diseased, but it's different from the right eye. It has been affected by something, its expression is serious, almost severe. No smile turns up the corner of the mouth or nostril. This side of the face is immobile and sad. This is the Francis of the summer of 1223, and this part of his face may have served as a model for the other fresco. Between 1216 and 1223, there was the journey to the Holy Land and the struggle to defend the first rule, the persistent ophthalmia, and cruelly felt disappointments. Above all, those two years bracketed the man who was still young and buoyed up by love and the man who had overcome his instincts but for whom the apparently smashing success of his ideal was only a defeat disguised as victory. "The rout of an army is nothing compared with the rout of an idea," wrote Sabatier in 1898.

Thus the painter did that portrait in two stages. We may suppose that he first sketched Francis in all the glory of an untested vocation. Seven years later, having seen Francis in his maturity, he retouched the left side of the face to show the profound changes that life had wrought there. All that nothwithstanding, this magnificent portrait gives a very strong impression of supernatural joy. The shadows are fading; the beloved child of God has not been abandoned. If trials have altered his face, the depths of his heart are still the same, full of the tenderness that brings him close to us. It seems as if he were asking only to live with us and come help us in difficult times. He wasn't a doctor of the Church; he knew only what Christ taught him, but he knew it well. Through him the Gospel is offered to us for a second time.

We find the milk of human kindness all through his writings, but nowhere more so, perhaps, than in the few lines he addressed during this stay to Brother Leo, who had voiced the desire to see him. Here they are: "Brother Leo, greetings and peace from your brother, Francis. I tell you this, my son, like a mother, that all the words we have spoken out on the road together, I sum them up for you in this saying and counsel, and even if afterward you have to come to me for another piece of advice, here it is: Whatever way seems best to you for pleasing the Lord God and following his footsteps and his poverty, do that with the blessing of the Lord God and my permission. And if it is necessary for your soul or for another consolation, and if you simply want, Leo, to come see me, then come." How much love there is in that final word. Writing has never been so close to life, one can almost hear Francis's voice.

Christmas

In the middle of September, Ugolino, who had gone back to Ostia, was awaiting Francis and his rule to present it for papal approval. From Subiaco to Rome is a short distance, but the trip must have seemed very long to Francis, who thought no good would come of it. His relations with the great men of this world had so often left him disappointed. He may have been comforted by the presence of his friend Ugolino, who was waiting for him in the Eternal City. And in fact he was warmly received by that prince of the Church. They had had quite a career together. After Francis's death Ugolino would claim, in his bull *Quo elongati,* that he had actively participated in drawing up the rule of the Friars Minor. But it seems that his contributions were primarily negative. He had a number of articles modified, particularly regarding the absolute obedience owed superiors, except for serious cases of conscience, as in the other orders. This was the first formal step toward the regularization of the brotherhood. Francis gave in out of obedience.

On this occasion he pronounced some words that arose from his inner depths, words that remind us of the Desert Fathers and that Ignatius Loyola would one day recall: "Take a body that the soul has departed from and place it anywhere. It will not object to being handled, will not complain of the position you leave it in. Put it in on a throne, it will not look up but down; dress it in purple, it will only appear twice as pale. Here we have the perfectly obedient man. . . ." Even if this sounds contrary to Francis's love of life, it presents us with a matchless image of his spirit of obedience.

In November Honorius III had in his hands the modified text of the rule, and for his part the pope paternally imposed a radical addition: The term *order* now made its appearance, obscuring the vast and generous word *brotherhood,* which has, however, remained in the language and the heart of Franciscans.

Finally the pope approved the rule on November 29 in the bull *Solet annuere.* To insure against troubles with the Friars Minor who were attached to the spirit of the first days, the ones called *zelanti,* the pope soon promulgated a second bull, *Fratrum minorum,* threatening with excommunication those who failed to observe the new rule.

Francis's disillusionment was complete. He now feared that the reformers of the rule would manage to drive the most faithful brothers into the solitude of the forests. And that would actually happen when the ministers general, one of whom was Bonaventure, persecuted the Spirituals. Thus Cesare of Speyer, thrown into prison during Elias's administration, was beaten to death with a staff by a brother jailor, under the pretext that he was trying to escape. Bernard would have to hide in ruined hermitages, and the famous scrolls on which Leo recounted the whole history of Francis and his own memories were so well hidden that they were never recovered.

Before leaving Rome, Francis obtained from the pope, by way of compensation, the right to celebrate Christmas with special splendor and in keeping with his personal ideas. He chose Greccio because because the lord of the place, Giovanni di Velita, "who valued nobility of blood less than nobility of soul," had made a gift to Francis of the wooded mountain that overlooked the rocky spur of his village and the Rieti Valley all the way to the blue-tinged summits stretching to the horizon.

Francis had founded a little hermitage on a sheer wall of rock, using, as he habitually did, one of the caves supplied by nature, and transforming it into a chapel. On his request a manger was installed and generously provided with straw. An ox and an ass followed, the witnesses demanded by tradition.

In the middle of the night the torches were lit, and the people from all around the region walked up through the trees, torches in hand, making the mountain paths surge like streams of light. A priest came to say the mass, which was celebrated over the manger, now become a crib, the *presepio* Italians are so fond of, and Francis, wearing the dalmatic of a deacon, read the Nativity Gospel. The crowd was amazed at this rediscovery of the great mystery, and they closely followed the least details of the ceremony. Many believed they saw Francis holding in his arms the Child swathed in light. Medieval faith, which was nearer to childhood than ours, instinctively translated into visions the religious truths that spoke most strongly to its heart.

That night had an exceptional sweetness, which was never forgotten. The brothers went singing out into the woods, and the torches glowed almost everywhere, as if to join in that explosion of unexpected good cheer and to respond to the limpid darkness of the sky. That was the first midnight mass, full of the poetry that only a Francis of Assisi could have discovered. A year of dubious battle ended for him on a note of ecstatic joy.

Letter to Brother Anthony

After Christmas, or at the very beginning of 1224, Francis wrote a four-line letter to Brother Anthony, in reply to a letter he had gotten from him:

"To Brother Anthony, my bishop, Brother Francis, greetings. It pleases me that you are teaching sacred theology to the brothers, provided that in this study you don't extinguish the spirit of prayer and devotion, as prescribed in the rule."

Without being curt, the letter is wary; it seems to be giving permission because the times were changing, as one might entrust a dangerous medication to an inexperienced young person. The phrase *my bishop* shouldn't mislead us. It is not a matter of friendly chaffing, but the title given to a preacher, whether a prelate or not. In any case, in this brief message it might appear that Francis had a muted distrust of theology, a fear that it might endanger the spirit of prayer and devotion. But why this warning, and what reason for concern had his correspondent given him?

Born at Lisbon around 1195 of a high-ranking family and "beautiful as a flower," the man who was first known as Fernando rejected the allurements of the world and entered the order of the Canons Regular of Saint Augustine, where he acquired immense learning. He was a canon at Holy Cross in Coimbra when, in 1220, the Franciscan martyrs of Morocco were buried in his church. Without a moment's hesitation he decided on the spot to become a Friar Minor. The Augustinians tried to keep him in the fold, but to no avail. Taking the name of Anthony, he entered the Franciscans in Portugal, then went to Italy and took part in the chapter of May 30, 1221, at la Portiuncula. The young brother was sent to a hermitage in the Romagna, where he swept the floor, tended the garden, and lived in a cave.

Called to assist at an ordination in Forlí, he was ordered to address the group when the religious belonging to the various orders on hand refused for lack of preparation. He obeyed, and his improvised sermon transported the audience, all the more so because until then he had told no one about his gifts and the extent of his learning. He was in demand everywhere as a preacher, and his reputation grew in inverse proportion to his modesty. Bologna did him the immense honor of offering a chair to this twenty-eight-year-old friar, and other cities too clamored for his services. The ministers of the brotherhood encouraged him to pursue this career, but he wanted permission from Francis himself. For all his misgivings Francis couldn't have asked for a better response to his letter. Anthony put all his learning to work for the Franciscan spirit, and he became as famous in France as he was in Italy. He was invited to lecture at the new University of Pisa in 1229, after having taught at Bologna. Francis of Assisi had an ideal brother, Brother Anthony of Padua.

The Last Chapter

Francis spent the end of the winter at Greccio, lost in the depths of Christmastide, a feast he wished would never end, a celebration of love, when he wanted the poor to be treated royally by the rich, and not only men but animals, oxen and asses, not to mention the birds. "If I were to see the emperor," he cried out like a child, "I would beg him to command that grain be scattered on the roads at Christmas to regale the birds, especially our sisters the larks." The larks were particularly dear to him because they were dressed like nuns, their heads capped by a miniature brown hood.

With time and hard trials his inner deprivation was nearly complete; he was about to achieve total simplicity. It seemed as if the reality of the world was fading from his sight. He had never understood more clearly the emptiness of all frenetic human endeavors. The old Crusader was laying down his arms, somewhat as Angelo Tancrede had laid down his to become Brother Angelo.

A painting from this period shows Francis in a painful light. It's a naive and slightly awkward work, but we shouldn't ignore it. It depicts a little man dressed as a poor monk wiping his eyes with a handkerchief, a detail that seems right. One gets the impression he is shedding a torrent of tears. The condition of Francis's eyes was worsening from month to month with no hope of a cure. With an improbable gesture, he is raising his right hand, opened wide and thereby revealing the stigmata that he was always careful to hide. This must have been added after his death.

Francis prolonged his stay in the Rieti Valley until the month of June, then he went to la Portiuncula to assist one more time—the last, in fact—at the Pentecost chapter.

A short while before he left Greccio, there occurred a very minor incident that might be omitted. But that would be a shame, because it shows us all the tenderness of the Francis we love. The *Poverello* isn't always an easy man to grasp. He could be gruff and then unexpectedly warm. Here are the facts.

Two brothers had come from far off to see him and ask for his blessing. It was Lent, and Francis had withdrawn to his grotto to pray. At such times no one was allowed to disturb him. He didn't have a fixed schedule, and nobody could say when he would return to the convent. And so the two disappointed brothers went sadly away. Seeing their distress, Francis's companions tried to console them on their way back to the outskirts of the village, but the frustrated visitors were convinced that their sins had brought about this mishap. They had already gotten to the bottom of the hill on which the convent lay when they heard someone calling them. Thanks to a sudden inspiration Francis had come out of his cave, and at a glance he understood what had happened. He called a brother and sent him to tell the unlucky visitors to turn toward him, which they immediately did. Then from his natural balcony on the cliff overlooking the highway Francis made a generous, sweeping sign of the cross. The brothers felt that the whole mountain was engulfing them with its blessing and, full of a marvelous joy, they went back to their province.

At la Portiuncula Francis found a shrunken chapter. The brothers had come in much smaller numbers than usual, because provincial chapters had been established now. Nothing could have been less festive than this meager gathering. Especially conspicuous by its absence was the joy of the first days, the gaiety of reunion, and their happy chatter. Something had changed. Someone wasn't there. Actually he *was* still there, but missing, lost in the crowd, a little brother like others, silent.

What was going on in his mind? Decisions had been made: Nine brothers would be dispatched to England. The term *order* was coming into use as a substitute for *brotherhood,* which must have caused Francis pain. *Order* sounded like military language; in *brotherhood* there was love. What connection could there be between the two? Nobody talked about love any more. Had he been mistaken? Had he misunderstood what the Lord was asking of him? No, that wasn't possible; Christ had told him in his heart that his rule was good. Men had torn it up. Someone who . . .

Grandeur and Wretchedness of Brother Elias

A few days later Elias was at the Foligno convent with Francis and wanted to speak with him, but Francis turned his head away. Surprised, the minister crossed over to Francis's other side, only to be rewarded by another turnabout. Part of the day was taken up with this kind of evasion—every time they ran into each other—until Elias, seeing Francis off by himself, touched his sleeve and begged him to tell him what his grievance was.

The situation was a little strange and slightly comical, but not for long. It was curious to see the minister general of the Franciscan order humbly requesting the favor of an answer. But we mustn't forget that Elias loved Francis with all his heart, and that this friendship bordered on veneration. An odd man, this Elias of Cortona, as he would be called, the head of a veritable army that kept growing and growing. What could such a prominent figure be afraid of? Francis knew, but he wasn't saying.

Elias was uneasy and insisted on being told the truth. Francis's silence had become terrifying. Elias asked one last time. For Francis the limits of charity had been reached. He bluntly announced, "Elias, you're heading for damnation."

These grim words had a terrible effect on the minister general. Were his sins really so enormous? He was a sinner—like everyone else. Where was God's pity? Nonetheless, Francis held firm. God had shown him alarming things about elias's future. History spells out the details.

The mad desire for power would dominate his career, but how could he not succumb to it when he had become the confidant of a pope and an emperor—and they took his advice? Already a counselor to Ugolino, he would be one to Frederick II, and two times over the absolute master of the order of Friars Minor. An architect of some talent and a great builder, he would spend his life in beautiful residences like the one he had laid out for himself at Cortona in the highest part of town, now in a distressing state of abandonment. With his renowned, first-class chef, Brother Bartholomew of Padua, he would set a table that was famous for its exquisite fare. Young and rather too-elegant pages assigned to his house, golden trappings on his horses . . . He wanted all that pomp not for himself but for what he represented. He was aware of the importance of his role and rank in society. One day in Cortona, when he was the pope's ambassador to Frederick II, he wouldn't even take the trouble to stand up for the podestà of Parma and remained sunk in his armchair by the fireside.

Out of fantasy, an innocent one this time, he would take to wearing an Armenian cap, like Rousseau five centuries later. But as devoted as he was to his brothers, he increasingly felt the pull of politics. Scandal lay in the offing. He had no more time to govern his brothers; his missions to the pope and then to the emperor monopolized his agenda. A layman himself, he promoted laymen over clerics for the leadership posts in the provinces, and the clerics resented it. In years to come they would blacken his memory, treating some of his human weaknesses, for example, for over-refined cuisine, as shameful vices. He had a foolish fascination with chemistry, because he was curious about all the sciences, which his adversaries transmuted into a quest for the philosopher's stone.

The day would come when he would be driven from his position of minister general on account of the ever more important role he was playing in the life of the emperor and his open hostility to the pope. Like Frederick II, Elias was ahead of his time, and he championed the separation of the temporal from the spiritual power, hoping to be the bridge between them. Gregory IX, who was imbued with a sense of the power of the two swords, couldn't tolerate such clear thinking. The imperial correspondence should be closely examined; no doubt it contains documents destroyed at the Roman end by Elias's enemies. Politics poisons everything. Nevertheless, under his generalship the order, now magnificently organized, spread out in all directions; and the Friars Minor in the professorial chairs of Bologna, Paris, England, and Spain opened up a new perspective in theology.

Excommunicated by two popes, Gregory IX and Innocent IV, Elias wrote a letter justifying himself to the first, but it was intercepted by his foes; and the former bishop of Ostia would never know what his friend had deep inside his heart. In it Elias probably explained the commission that Francis had entrusted to him before his death: Reconcile the pope and the emperor, whatever the cost. A weight consideration here is that Sister Clare loved and trusted Elias till her dying day.

That day at Foligno he threw himself down at Francis's knees, and said, "Pray for me." How could Francis not have been moved by the pleas of a man he had always loved? He forgave Elias everything: his abuses of power, his arrangements with the Curia, and from the bottom of his heart he prayed God that Elias would be snatched from perdition. Years later, just before he died, Elias was reconciled with the Church and saw his excommunication lifted, owing to a Friar Minor who went in Francis's name to plead with the pope. When all was said and done, Brother Elias had deserved well of the order.

On August 4 of that same year and still at Foligno, Elias had a vision that must have wrung his heart. In the middle of the night he dreamed that a majestic priest dressed in white came and ordered him to go find Francis and announce that within two years death would carry him off to the Lord.

Francis could only welcome this news with joy. "Thanks be to God," he told his doctor one day. "I am not a coward who fears death." It would come as a liberation and, to give it a proper reception, he resolved from the first to go to La Verna, to the very spot where God had bidden him several years before to pray and strip off every last vestige of himself.

The Stigmata

La Verna. One couldn't imagine a more wildly beautiful place. An Old Testament prophet couldn't have chosen a better refuge with a grandeur more dramatic or more favorable for dialogue with the Eternal.

I went up there once during a September storm that seemed to

shake the mountain. A thick curtain of white mist veiled the landscape, soon to be torn apart by a torrential rain. Near the summit
enormous rocks appeared to have been flung in a ditch at the bottom
of which a breathtaking precipice could be seen through a hole. Francis had hidden himself in a corner of this opening. These rocks,
which had been shattered in immemorial cataclysms, symbolized in
his eyes the wounds of Christ. Did he need vertigo to lose himself in
God? This man who was already between two worlds bore an abyss
within himself.

Just below here a cave opens up where one can take a few steps
inside. Flat on top of the rock an iron grille stretched at my feet: the
place where he lay down. Tall, slender trees bent over the rocks and
softened the horror of this solitude. Two silvery birches shone against
the black background of the firs. Farther ahead, as the rain suddenly
stopped, I discovered the boundless landscape that must have drawn
the hermit with the delicacy and immense variety of its shades: the
tender green of the meadows, the forests touched by the first cold
nights of autumn that made them burst into flame in the rays of the
setting sun.

One feels a certain hesitation in approaching the most mystery-
filled moment in Francis of Assisi's entire life. Some people would call
it the hardest to believe, but by an inexplicable contradiction I am
perfectly disposed to accept it *because* it's so hard to believe. Rejecting
it would mean denying too many personal testimonies. I realize that the
Middle Ages was a fertile source of hallucinations, individual and
collective, but they have their limits; they don't explain everything.
They don't explain *anything,* as soon as one makes the effort of looking
beyond them. More important to me is the value and, I dare say, the
usefulness of certain mystical phenomena. Saint Paul may have had the
stigmata. His remarks on this point are hurried and not very clear, as
if his message needed no support from such an experience. In the same
way, would Francis have been less of a saint in our eyes if he hadn't
borne the stigmata? I doubt it, but I believe he had them. There were
many saints who never received these marks of the love of Christ, and
just as many Christians who did receive them and weren't declared
saints for all that. Why such a peculiar distribution of graces? That's
God's secret.

In front of the cave where Francis slept a crevice opens up, bristling with tall birches that seem to be growing there to conceal the horror of the precipice. A wooden bridge spanning the void makes it possible to cross over that cleft, where it's best not to look down if you get dizzy easily. The bridge is two planks laid across the chasm. On the other side a path leads to a rocky platform that Francis chose for setting up a little rudimentary hermitage. His three companions, Leo, Angelo, and Rufino, took care of all these modest operations.

Here he was so far away from the place where his brothers stayed that even if he cried out no one would hear him. Leo watched over him as best he could, giving him all the attention a mother gives her child; but he had no more right than the others to disturb the solitary without his express permission. In the morning he brought Francis bread and a jug of water. At midnight he went a little way down the path to the hermitage and recited the first verse of matins, and if Francis intoned the next one, then Brother Leo would come. Otherwise the silence told him to go away.

The rest of the time was devoted to meditation on the sufferings of Christ. The hermitage became another Golgotha, because Francis wanted to share with Christ all the tortures of his passion, to feel them with the same intensity, to identify himself with him as far as was humanly possible. Was this the "transforming union" or nothing like it? So many mystics have begged for love and for the pain that accompanies it, because the two were mingled together on the cross.

What went on in the cave where Francis experienced the unheard of grace of union with the crucified Savior? We would have no idea if Brother Leo hadn't disobeyed Francis's strict prohibition and seen many things. He also heard words that were destined to remain secret. Readers in love with the marvelous will find all this described in some detail in Saint Bonaventure and in the *Considerations on the Stigmata*, which are dazzling but occasionally garbled.

The essence of the commonly accepted version can be reduced to this: On September 14, the feast of the Exaltation of the Holy Cross, during the night, a seraph with wings of fire—straight out of Isaiah (6:2)—bearing the image of the Crucified, swooped down from heaven on Francis as he was contemplating outside his cave and imprinted on his flesh the marks of the nails as well as the lance wound in the right side. One fact that seems beyond doubting is that the whole population of the region round about saw the summit of La Verna enveloped with light, as if the sun had already risen.

As for Brother Leo, he too saw a ball of fire falling from the heights down on to Francis's face, then rising up to heaven. Brother Leo couldn't lie, and so great is the power of his sincerity that I'm persuaded he's recounting the truth when I read his version of these extraordinary facts. But once the page is turned, the magic evaporates, and I fall back into the certainty that Francis's secret will forever remain with God.

The problem is not the authenticity of the stigmata, but what the witnesses make of them. They have plunged into them to draw up a treasury of prodigious images; they have pillaged them the way the Crusaders pillaged Byzantium to carry off piles of relics.

It would be excessive to say that the thirteenth century presented the spectacle of a world full of visionaries, but we must never forget that visions were common currency then. Everyone had his or her own visions; they were always useful in time of need and generally accepted. And what did they call visions? Weren't they in most cases premonitory dreams? Even today we sometimes have such dreams, but reason and Doctor Freud have gone over this ground, and we make nothing of them. The Bible is full of them, from Genesis to the Gospels, and this sacred imagery once meant a great deal to humanity. The visions of the prophets were something else again and didn't necessarily belong to the world of dreams. The vision of the six-winged seraphim that appeared to Isaiah must have left a lasting impression on Francis. Oneiric memories of Scripture must have stayed with him from his conversion to his death. All during the Middle Ages the inner life tended to externalize itself in the form of images.

Brother Leo, the most serious of the witnesses—one could almost say, the only one—is the source of everything that we know about the stigmata, and he saw with the eyes of love. For his part, Francis didn't want people to talk about them and jealously hid them from sight, because the wounds were like mouths that said too much.

The Return

In the last days of September, Francis regretfully decided to leave La Verna. He had no doubt in his mind about Elias's prediction: He was going to die. He wanted to use the time remaining to him by saying farewell to his beloved earth and, above all, by preaching the Gospel one more time to the towns and villages. The melancholy of departure, however, gave way before the memory of graces received and the hope for his salvation. But while he rejoiced, he had an intuition one evening that Brother Leo was facing a cruel temptation that he didn't dare admit, not a fleshly temptation, but—quite the contrary to what Francis felt—the terror of not being saved. Francis took a pen, and in his large, clumsy handwriting traced these words on a sheet that has come down to us: "May the Lord bless you and keep you! May the Lord show you his face and take pity on you! May the Lord turn his countenance toward you and give you peace! May God bless you, Brother Leo!" It was signed with the famous *tau* and even adorned with a little sketch supposedly representing Brother Leo, something like a passport to paradise. Mad with joy, Brother Leo took it and kept it next to his heart until he died. It is preserved today at Assisi, in the Chapel of Relics in the lower church.

On the last day of September, Francis, greatly weakened by his physical sufferings, mounted an ass, with his feet swathed in bandages and his hands hidden beneath his long sleeves. On the way to Assisi, he stopped first at Chiusi to say good-bye to Count Orlando and to thank him for the ass he had given him for his journey; then on to Borgo San Sepolcro, Monte Casale, and Città di Castello. It was the longest route, but the short stages were necessary. It took a month to take a trip that ordinarily would have taken three days.

The people came out in droves before him, and he only let them kiss his fingertips, so as to keep the secret of the stigmata; but he couldn't prevent the wound of the lance from leaking blood beneath his habit. Brother Leo never left his side and dressed his wounds as well as he could. The crowd's emotion was great when they saw their *Poverello* all emaciated. Leo, Angelo, and Rufino were hard put to prevent them from cutting his robe to make relics.

Each time, Francis stopped to look at the landscapes that had counted for so much in his life. Looking out through his sore eyes, he lost himself in admiration of the earth, because his soul never tired of the beauty of the visible world. At Ponte San Giovanni, the last halting place, his heart must have been rent at the memory of the many men from Assisi who fell there fighting against Perugia in his youth.

Finally in November he reached la Portiuncula, where he rested a bit, but the next month he got back on the ass to make a final round of preaching in Umbria and the Marches. Such energy in a body so fragile is still a cause for wonder today, but his fidelity to love knew no letting up. He saw Gubbio again, but not his friend the wolf, who had died two years before. He revisited Ancona, where he had twice embarked for the lands beyond the sea. He came back by way of Jesi, Macerata, and Spoleto, where the Lord spoke to him in a dream and where his life had changed. Montefalco received him, and Bevagna, where the birds had listened to him; then Rivo Torto, where the brothers had thought they were in paradise because their joy was so great. In the harshest time of winter, with what strength he had left, but almost more dead than alive, and white as a corpse—not surprisingly many people confused Francis with the idea they had of the Crucified, calling him another Christ—he preached the Gospel throughout the country he had traversed so often in the enthusiastic days of his youth. It was not until March that he got back to la Portiuncula, exhausted. There he found Elias, who wanted to have him treated immediately by a doctor from Assisi. Francis obeyed, but all efforts were of no use. Very concerned over Francis's health, Elias informed the pope, who ordered the sick man to Rieti to be cared for by his personal physician, an Arab. As usual, Francis promised to obey, but first he wanted to bid farewell to his Lady Poverty, Sister Clare.

He had scarcely arrived at San Damiano when his health began to worsen. He had to be installed in lodgings outside the cloister. The cold was so intense, even now in April, that there could be no question of bringing him to la Portiuncula, on account of the dampness from the nearby marshes where the brothers went to cut their reeds. Almost blind and suffering atrociously, he was put in a room where a sort of camera obscura had been built out of mats to protect him from the light that had become his enemy after being the object of his fervent wonder.

For fifty days he remained enclosed in absolute darkness. Clare and her nuns took care of him, along with two brothers who were assigned to the monastery of the Poor Clares (without having the right to enter it) and who came every day from la Portiuncula. Francis's pain was indescribable: As well the burning sensation of the ophthalmia, he had violent headaches that are nowadays thought to have come from an acute and (back then) untreatable sinusitis. As if that weren't enough, Francis was tormented by an invasion of mice that scurried all over and jumped on his body when he ate his bread. They troubled his sleep, which had already become very unsettled because of sickness; but he patiently bore his trial, which his companions didn't hesitate to blame on the devil.

Hymn to Joy

In the excess of his pain, when despair may have been lying in wait for him, Francis called to God for help and got the most comforting of all possible graces: the assurance of his eternal salvation. "Rejoice," he was told by the inner voice that never deceived him. "Rejoice, as if you already shared my kingdom." This came to him as the most overwhelming proof of love that God could give him this side of the grave. From now on the world and the devil would be wasting their time to rage against him; and from the heart of this agonized man there sprang a cry of joy of which he has left us an imperishable record.

A good deal has been written about "The Canticle of the Sun." It remains the first great Italian poem in the vernacular, which was barely out of its Latin swaddling clothes. In it we find, as in the great biblical texts, a balanced periodic structure that has been compared to the alternate beating of two powerful wings.

Is it all from Francis's hand? Yes, in its air of improvisation, its energy welling up from his entire soul, a soul already singing in glory.

But the form was provided by Scripture, in the third chapter of Daniel as masterfully translated by Saint Jerome (the text is not found in the Hebrew Bible). This is the Song of the Three Young Men, the Jews thrown into Nebuchadnezzar's furnace who raise their voices amidst the flames, uninjured, as they invite all creation to praise the Lord. The resemblances to Francis's poem are evident, but in the brazier of physical suffering his faith and his genius inspired him to make a change that marks the work as peculiarly his: He calls each of God's creatures brother and sister, and asks them to intone this hymn of joy that is worthy to be in Scripture.

The text in Daniel contains no fewer than thirty-four verses. With the instinct of a true poet, Francis makes a striking choice of eight creatures, the most familiar and close to us, confers on them an almost human personality, and greets them with courtesy and tenderness. He calls none of them *"Messire"* except the sun, the great lord among all the creatures, but the wind is the only Brother Wind and the fire Brother Fire, like simple Friars Minor.

Here is an attempt at translating that text, which has its obscurities, the most important being the word *per*. This is usually rendered as *for*, and I have kept *for*, even though *by* would be more in line with the meaning of the original, particularly in the strophe about the sun. But *by* sounds formal, almost official, whereas *for* is a cry of thankfulness.

THE CANTICLE OF BROTHER SUN

> Most high, omnipotent, good Lord
> To you alone belong praise and glory
> Honor, and blessing.
> No man is worthy to breathe your name.
> Be praised, my Lord, for all your creatures.
> In the first place for the blessed Brother Sun
> who gives us the day and enlightens us through you.
> He is beautiful and radiant with his great splendor,
> Giving witness of you, most Omnipotent One.
> Be praised, my Lord, for Sister Moon and the stars
> Formed by you so bright, precious, and beautiful.
> Be praised, my Lord, for Brother Wind
> And the airy skies, so cloudy and serene;
> For every weather, be praised, for it is life-giving.
> Be praised, my Lord, for Sister Water

So necessary yet so humble, precious, and chaste.
Be praised, my Lord, for Brother Fire,
Who lights up the night,
He is beautiful and carefree, robust and fierce.
Be praised, my Lord, for our sister, Mother Earth,
who nourishes and watches us
While bringing forth abundant fruits with colored flowers
And herbs.
Praise and bless the Lord.
Render him thanks.
Serve him with great humility. Amen.*

When his work was finished, Francis showed no false modesty: He was enchanted with his poem. He called his brothers and Sister Clare to read it to them, better still to sing it to them to a melody of his own devising—what wouldn't we give to have it today? One wonders if he got back his old sweet voice. In any case he decided that the brothers were to sing it every day, and so did he, morning and evening, tipsy with the knowledge that he had given the world a masterpiece. He asked the Friars Minor to see that his song of ecstatic admiration for God's world was heard everywhere.

In our day the most beautiful commentary on this canticle of joy is a piece, still too little known, by the young Stockhausen. In his fluid, sweet music we hear from time to time the clear, joyous voices of young boys saying only one or two words—*rain, fire, snow*—as in a game. They seem to be walking past refreshing waterfalls and smiling in happiness. Occasionally a rather long time goes by, and tunes that go nowhere, but delicately harmonized, trickle down, impalpable as the wind; then suddenly one makes out the word *sun* or *moon* or *stars* or *flowers,* like cries from the mouths of children. These children, who have been taken down into a hell, struggle there as in a new paradise lost.

"The body, that's the enemy!" The brothers sometimes heard this phrase from Francis's lips. To us, at the end of the twentieth century, it seems monstrous; but let us return for a moment to the thirteenth century, to try to understand the *Poverello.* According to him, according to many people in his day, the body was the origin of the sins of the flesh. Shame on the body, then, let's bring it to heel with penance and mortifications, even the most violent. You have to fight it. At this

*Translation (slightly altered) from Lawrence Cunningham, *Saint Francis of Assisi* (San Francisco: Harper & Row, 1981), 37–38.

point, however, Francis drew the line and rejected the barbarous "discipline," which has lasted to our time. In order to calm down that energumen, the body, which is in league with the Evil One and draws man to destruction, Francis recommended a plunge into cold water at whatever time of the year. Fasting, always an effective remedy, would do the rest.

What bothers us about this solution of the problem of sex is that it's more Manichaean than Christian. The kind of curse it lays on the flesh is unpleasant. It separates the body from the soul. Christ said that wicked desires, adultery, fornication, and murder come from the heart, and the heart in Semitic languages often denotes the thinking part of the individual. What good does it do to beat on the shoulders and the rest of the body, when the real culprit is elsewhere? Had Francis breathed in the Catharist heresy as his whole era did?

At San Damiano, in his darkened room, he was suffering so much that the brothers considered giving him sedatives, mostly likely powdered poppies; but he had a scruple: Did he have the right to refuse this pain? He resolved to ask the advice of a brother who had come to take care of him and who was an outspoken man.

"What do you think of the attentions I'm giving my body? Am I not too indulgent because it's sick?"

This brother, who came right out of the twentieth century, felt free to shake Francis and give him some straight talk: "Father, hasn't your body obeyed you faithfully?"

Francis admitted that his body had always displayed an exemplary obedience. "I must grant that it has."

"Then where, father, are your courtesy, your kindliness, and your discretion? Is this how you treat a faithful friend? How would you have served Christ if your body hadn't helped you?"

Francis yielded once more: The brother was right.

"It exposed itself to death for you," the unstoppable dialectican went on, "and now you're going to abandon it when it needs you. Father, don't commit that sin!"

At once Francis blessed his perspicacious advisor and, joyously addressing his body, he told it: "Rejoice, Brother Body, I am now ready to let you have everything you want."

Thus peace was made between them—a little late, for death wasn't far off, but it was good that he acknowledged his error just when the cross was implanted in the depths of his soul.

A month later, in June, Francis added a stanza to his canticle. War was threatening to break out between Assisi and Perugia. Francis's predictions had come true. The commune set up in Perugia had driven the nobles out of the town; and by an irony of fate they had found asylum with their rivals, just as the aristocratic families of Assisi had taken refuge in Perugia at the time of Collestrada. The new podestà of Assisi, Oportulo di Bernardo, saw in this an opportunity to increase his town's prestige, but Bishop Guido struggled against what seemed to him an antipapal gesture, since Perugia, however good or bad its government, remained under obedience to Rome. The bishop excommunicated the podestà; the podestà cast a civil interdict on all the bishop's actions. Was Assisi going to have a new war in the streets?

Without wasting time, Francis sent a brother to the bishop and the podestà, asking them to gather the leading citizens in the inner court of the episcopal palace. There two brothers, Angelo and Leo, sang "The Canticle of the Sun" with its new stanza:

> Be praised, my Lord, for those who pardon through your love
> And bear witness and trial.
> Blessed are those who endure in peace
> For they will be crowned by you, Most High.*

Then the miracle that Francis was waiting for took place. Touched by that song of love, like true Italians, first the podestà cried out, "For the love of Our Lord and blessed Francis, I pardon the lord bishop, and I am ready to give him all the satisfaction he may wish. . . ." To which the bishop, on a similar impulse, replied, "I am naturally given to anger. You must forgive me."

This gesture made a considerable impression at a time when hatred between cities and factions was so bloody and insatiable: Perugia against Assisi, Spoleto against Foligno, Siena or Pisa against Florence, the partisans of the pope against the partisans of the emperor, one district of a town against another. Francis had stopped a war with a song.

One might add that Franciscan inspiration gave the world in that century four poets whose glory has yet to fade: after Francis, the first person to write in the vernacular, Brother Jacopone da Todi, whose *Laudi* are an inexhaustible source of mystical poetry; then Dante, a tertiary who made his Tuscan dialect the language of all Italy. And two

---

*Cunningham, *Saint Francis of Assisi*, 38.

of the most beautiful Latin hymns; perhaps the most powerful, Thomas of Celano's *Dies Irae,* and the most heartrending, the *Stabat Mater* of Brother Jacopone da Todi, come to us from the thirteenth century, as light descends from a mountaintop.

Brother Fire

Just as Francis was rejoicing to see peace reign once more, a letter came to disturb him. It was written by Cardinal Ugolino, who used his authority to order Francis to be treated by the pope's ophthalmologist. An ordeal was on the way.

Always alert to Francis's situation, Elias knew very well that for all his courage, Francis feared an operation. It would undoubtedly be torture. So Elias promised to stay close to the patient while they operated on him. Francis was resigned, but he didn't want to leave Assisi without saying good-bye to Clare and consoling her, for she would suffer too.

Once again Rome was in the hands of rioters, and the papal court settled into Rieti; so the *Poverello* was sent there with his inseparable companions. What would he do without them? Did he suspect that for months Brother Leo had been keeping a sort of journal of his life? Francis dictated all sorts of things to him, and Leo had sharp eyes.

At Rieti, despite his condition, Francis was persecuted by his admirers, who insisted on coming near him at all cost. Many of the common people, but noblemen too and even members of the Curia, were there. Discretion and simple humanity were a foreign language to these curious onlookers. In their opinion Francis was the latest celebrity, and he *had* to be seen.

He sought refuge at Fonte Colombo. There at least he would be left in peace; he would have nothing to do but wait in a darkened room, with all the patience he could muster. That patience would be tested by the absence of Elias who, though he wasn't happy doing it, twice got the operation put off. Would they never get it over with?

As rough as the winter was, the heat of the summer of 1225 was equally overwhelming, even in the hermitage in the heart of the forest. When would that famous doctor come, this time in earnest? Francis was afraid; he didn't try to pretend otherwise. They were going to cauterize the upper part of his cheeks, and nature in him rebelled at the idea; but he had to steel himself to it. Finally the doctor announced that he couldn't delay the operation by so much as a day. Where was Elias? He was thought to be away, but he arrived just in time and Francis thanked heaven for it.

When the doctor appeared, armed with the cautery that he would heat in the fire till it glowed, Francis began to tremble with terror. He knew perfectly well what they were planning to make him endure so as to get rid of his ophthalmia—they hoped. The incandescent iron was to burn both temples from the top of the ear to the arches of the eyebrows. Unable to bear this spectacle, his faithful companions, Leo, Rufino, Angelo, and Masseo walked off. Only Elias remained; he heard Francis address the fire with a prayer of childlike faith: "My Brother Fire, the Most High has given you a splendor that all creatures envy. Show yourself now to be kind and courteous to me. . . . I pray the Magnificent Lord to temper his fiery heat so that I may have the strength to bear his burning caress."

Elias clasped the sick man's hand: Francis was trembling no more; he knew that the prayer he had said in faith was as good as answered. The heated iron, scattering sparks, was plunged into his flesh, but Francis felt no pain. The doctor was astounded. Elias wasn't: The hand he was holding belonged to a saint, and he knew it.

The frightened companions returned, a bit shamefaced, and Francis welcomed them in high style: "Cowards! Poltroons! Listen, I didn't feel a thing!" And the Francis of the old days, the man who made people laugh, turned to the doctor and said, "If it's not cooked enough, you may begin again."

As for the operation itself, it proved a total failure. They had to come up with something else.

The Last Winter

From that day on, his life was no more than stages in one long agony. In September he left Fonte Colombo for San Fabiano, nowadays believed to be at La Foresta, near Rieti, a hill standing amidst vines and olive trees. There in the priest's house a new kind of punishment awaited him. Two doctors decided that to cure his eyes they had to pierce his ears. What they meant by that isn't clear, but it must have been awful and, of course, completely useless.

With his open wounds, his stabbing neuralgia, and eyelids on fire, Francis went off to hide in the cave that served the priest as a wine cellar, to escape the light. He spent a month there, never leaving his refuge until day's end, the blue hour of twilight.

We can imagine him in that cave, the prey of horrible pains that nothing could assuage, reduced to total inactivity. Let me bring up a personal memory here. As a young man, I once knew a religious who was tortured by an incurable disease. When he was asked, "Do you get bored in your solitude?" he answered that absurd question by saying, "I don't get bored because I'm suffering." What, in fact, could be a more absorbing occupation? In Francis's case it is not too much to speak of Calvary. After the garden of delights of his first ecstasies, he was now tasting the bitterness of the garden of olives. Did he experience the horror of the dark night of the soul? Perhaps, but beyond the physical darkness and the loneliness created by bodily pain, he was with God.

At the end of autumn, he went back to Fonte Colombo. His trials seemed to mitigate a little—the medical torture, for one thing, came to a stop. His companions never left him. When the pope or Cardinal Ugolino expressed a desire to see him at Rieti, Francis was brought to the convent the brothers had in town. With winter approaching, he decided to divide his time between the two hermitages. The grim doctors came to visit their illustrious victim, spinning new and always useless treatments out of their rich imaginations.

Francis's courage and good humor were much admired. At Fonte Colombo one day he got the whimsical notion of inviting the pope's doctor to lunch, after their consultation. He eagerly accepted, to the consternation of the brothers, who knew what the menu would be: a few vegetables, bread, and cool water. Still, in the name of holy obedience, they set the table to do honor to their guest. They had hardly sat down when there was a knock on the door, and a peasant woman nobody knew appeared with a hamper, sent by the lady of a nearby manor. It contained fish, grapes, honey cakes, and a crayfish pâté. Crayfish pâté happened to be one of the dishes that Francis was most fond of his youth. And he hadn't lost his taste for it, because he didn't hesitate to eat it with evident relish. They asked him about the unknown lady and her generous gifts, but he said nothing. He simply fêted their guest, as if there had been no hasty improvisation.

The winter of 1225–26 passed without bringing any improvement to Francis's condition. Quite the contrary, he paid dearly for all the mortifications with which he had once crushed his body.

Apart from the tuberculosis that was wasting him away, both his stomach and liver were in a bad way. Death was coming. He had known that for sure ever since Brother Elias made his prediction at Foligno, but what did he have to fear? The heavens were spread wide for him, he knew that too. Nevertheless, when he glanced back at his life after his conversion, he saw a combination of victory and defeat. He had wanted to save the world, and the world was still rushing to its doom. What could his little Franciscan family, his brotherhood, do about it? These temptations to doubt were subtler than fleshly temptations, but they were crueler too. The devil never lays down his arms. He tried to poison Francis's assurance of salvation. Centuries later the same thing would happen to Theresa of Lisieux.

In April an order came from the cardinal protector and the minister general to send Francis to Siena to be cared for by physicians of repute. As if he hadn't had enough of highly reputed physicians. Still he obeyed as a Friar Minor must. His companions prepared two tunics and two cloaks for him, continually changed to conceal the occasional flow of blood from the stigmata, which he was very anxious to keep hidden from the eyes of the world. Did his companions really understand the origin of those wounds? One day a brother who was tightening the bandages around his feet pushed his indiscretion to the point of asking what those holes were. The answer came back sharply, "Mind your own business."

He had six months left to live, and the doctors stubbornly continued

trying their "infallible" methods on him, which failed one after the
other with a sort of professional fidelity, but this time they were caught
unprepared. One evening Francis began to vomit blood in such abundance that they thought he was done for. The brothers in Siena took
fright and sent a messenger to Elias. Meanwhile Francis summoned
Brother Benedict, the superior of the convent, and dictated to him a
little testament. Here it is—a cry from the heart: Write that I bless all
my brothers, those who are now in our order and those who will come
to it until the end of time. . . . Because of my weakness and my
sufferings, I am unable to speak; briefly I shall make known my will
in three words:

May they always love one another in memory of my blessing and
of this testament;

May they always love our Lady, holy Poverty;

May they always prove faithful and submissive to the prelates and
clergy of our holy mother Church.

Elias rushed over. For once, the sick man was feeling better. Elias
took him immediately to Cortona, where he set him up in one of the
hermitages called *celle* that he had built in the middle of the woods.
There, at all events, he could watch over Francis. He loved him; he had
always loved him; and he suffered because Francis had never really
understood him. He would do all he could to relieve his final agony.
Christ himself had trembled in the face of death, as we all do. Francis
maintained that he wasn't afraid, but it was no use. He was counting
the days, he knew the date of his confrontation with what has been
called the queen of terrors. Poor Brother Ass had no grasp of theology,
which explained that he was going to disappear and disintegrate, but
that the soul was imperishable. He didn't want to go.

Francis had dropsy. His legs were swollen, and so was his belly, in
painful contrast to his emaciated face. Inside his cell, where he could
suffer in peace, he dictated his great testament. It is a wholly beautiful
text that reveals his soul and the greatness of his mind. There is something of a confession and spiritual biography in it, but Francis also
recalled the elements of a rule for the ideal brotherhood that he wanted
to give the world. From the very first lines we are gripped by his
overwhelming sincerity: "The Lord God gave me, Francis, this way of
doing penance—I was a sinner and found it hard to look at lepers, and
the Lord God led me among them, and I was merciful to them. As I left

them, what had previously seemed bitter turned to sweetness of body and soul. And then, soon after, I left the world."*

How feeble literary artifice appears next to these words, which seem to come straight from the desert. Fine phrases are ridiculous compared with the brutal language of a soul without illusions speaking the truth.

As for his reminders of the rule, they are precise, with no ifs ands, or buts. Francis speaks as if he were still the head of the order: "I command . . . I firmly wish . . . I forbid. . . . As the Lord God had me, a simple person, simply and clearly put down the Rule and these words, so in a similar way you are to observe these words. . . . And may each one of you who does so be filled in Heaven with blessings from the Most High Father. . . . I, brother Francis, your little one and servant, in every way and as much as it is possible for me, confirm you, within and without, in this most holy blessing. Amen."*

Having finished his task, he announced his wish to return to Assisi, but they hesitated to make him travel.

Farewell, Earth

In the middle of June, Francis once again asked Elias to take him to la Portiuncula. He wanted to end his life there, where his dreams had been launched from after his conversion; and Elias was ready as always to obey him as far as he could. The journey was undertaken beneath a burning summer sun, a new stage in Francis's *via dolorosa*, which he accepted with the resignation he had learned from Christ.

Now he was back in la Portiuncula, but could he even see it with his eyes, which were like wounds? Despite everything he felt the presence of the little church placed under Mary's protection, but his strength kept failing. He couldn't stand the overpowering humid heat. After a fortnight, he had to leave, to tear himself away from this place where he had received so many novices, where he had cut the locks of

*From *The Little Flowers of St. Francis*, trans. Serge Hughes, 218.
* *The Little Flowers of St. Francis*, 219–20

Sister Clare. There is no defense against the assaults of memory. Francis prayed as only he could, but he remembered.

When Elias told him that he was going to take him to the hills, where he could breathe, Francis accepted. The citizens of Assisi, gathered along the roads around the church, wanted to see him. Elias judged that he had to spare the sick man that extra trial. He decided to bring Francis to Bagnara, about eighteen miles to the east. To get there they would have to go through Assisi.

Seeing his native town for one last time ought to have been a joy for the *Poverello,* but how much of it could he see when he got there? At most he recognized the familiar noises of the streets he had walked in his youth, the sound of voices, the accent of the region. They already knew he was there, that the saint of Assisi had returned; the news flew from door to door. His companions protected him as best they could from the crowd. Was he even capable of moving, of lifting his hand to bless them?

Bagnara is a little spa town famous since Roman times for its springs. At an altitude of something more than sixteen hundred feet, its air is light and cooler than in la Portiuncula. A hermitage built there by the brothers was waiting there for Francis, who once again could take refuge in the dark to alleviate his pain a little. The waters did him no good. Little by little he went completely blind and could no longer make out shadows. In addition, the swelling of his legs and belly got worse, he hardly ate a thing, and his stomach constantly tortured him.

July, then August, passed by at Bagnara. Assisi was uneasy over the news that was coming in and wanted to get its saint back. It feared that the people of Perugia, Foligno, Spoleto, or Arezzo might steal its living relic. How to distinguish superstition from love in this outburst of zeal? The brothers were ready to return the saint to Assisi, provided that he was lodged within the walls; because la Portiuncula wasn't safe from a sudden attack. They chose the palace of the bishop, who was on a pilgrimage to Mount Gargano at the time.

As for Francis, all he asked was to go home. Knights were sent from Assisi, accompanied by soldiers, to look for him and block any attempt by the neighboring towns to carry him off.

The return proceeded slowly. Francis, who could no longer even ride on the back of an ass, was carried in turns by the mounted knights, who held him in their arms as they rode from village to village. Could he have imagined this strange scene when, as an adolescent, he dreamed of nothing but armor and Crusades? And now the knights bore him in their arms like a child. They returned by a narrow road across the mountain, the shortest way to go.

At Assisi they transported him to the bishop's palace. He was suffering cruelly in his flesh. The martyrdom he had once asked for had not been given him in the way he had foreseen, but the torment he was enduring was a fair substitute. Leo, Angelo, Rufino, Masseo, and Elias were near him. A doctor came to see him, not one of those executioners ready to put him on the rack in the name of medical science, but a friend from Arezzo, Bongiovanni (Good John), whom Francis called Brother John, because he never gave anyone the epithet "good," since the Lord said, "No one is good except God alone."

Francis asked him, "What do you think of my dropsy?"

"All will go well, with God's grace."

"Brother, tell me the truth. I am not a coward who fears death."

"Father, according to our medical knowledge, your disease is incurable; and you will die at the end of September or by the fourth day of October."

Then Francis found the strength to stretch out his arms and to lift his arms, full of joy, as he cried out, "Welcome, Sister Death."

Nobody knows what death is. Like a person, it has its own particular characteristics. Its strangest feature is that in many cases it doesn't come unless it's permitted to. A man sometimes dies only if he wants to die. He can make the importunate lady wait at the door. Religious in danger of death are asked to offer their life as a sacrifice. That seems a sinister irony when the situation is desperate. We might say that this custom attributes to death the respect for human freedom that God himself has—and death is his servant.

Sister Death

Francis accepted death with the heartfelt joy that had never totally abandoned him, even in the most somber days. When he heard the doctor's verdict, he had his brothers Angelo and Leo called, and asked them to sing "The Canticle of the Sun."

They obeyed. With voices ready to break down and sob, they intoned one of the most beautiful songs of joy that ever arose from human lips. Did they realize that they were filling the cell with the whole cosmos? Fire and water, earth and air, the four elements, joined with the stars, the moon, the sun, flowers, and grass, not to mention the perpetual and magnificent change of scenery brought on by the clouds, all of this in a grand assembly of all the beauty in the universe. And as death approached, he added a courteous welcome to the messenger from heaven:

> Be praised, my Lord, for our sister, bodily death,
> Whom no living man can escape
> Woe to those who die in sin.
> Blessed are those who discover thy holy will.
> The second death will do them no harm.*

If Francis had borrowed somewhat from Daniel and Genesis in composing his hymn of joy, the chivalric salute to Sister Death was entirely his own.

Yet he didn't want to die in the episcopal palace but, as he had said many times, at la Portiuncula. They brought him there, taking a thousand precautions, because he was so frail, and each movement stung him with pain. This time he must have been borne in the arms of his brothers. First the knights and now the poor were carrying him like a little one, as he referred to himself. When Assisi came into view, he asked them to stop. They laid him down on a stretcher and pointed out its different quarters; he made a sign of the cross over the city so dear to him, which he could no longer see: "May God bless you, holy city,

*Cunningham, *Saint Francis of Assisi,* 37–38.

for through you many souls will be saved, in you many servants of God will dwell, and from you many will be chosen for the kingdom of eternal life." He felt so bad that they installed him, first, in the infirmary; but then he demanded the cell where he usually stayed, a few yards from the chapel, beneath the trees.

There, as he took thought for his very last moments, he reflected on what he would wear in death. It's interesting that the young Francis should revive just at the moment when he was leaving the world for good. He asked for ink and paper. He knew now the day he would die on, and he thought of Brother Jacqueline, who would be inconsolable if she couldn't say good-bye. He dictated the following letter, according to the legend of Perugia: "To my Lady Jacqueline, God's servant, Brother Francis, the little poor man of Christ, greetings and the communion of the Holy Spirit in Our Lord. Know, my dearest, that Christ has by his grace revealed to me the end of my life, which will soon take place. And so, if you wish to find me alive, hurry. Bring with you some of that ash-colored monastic cloth, like the kind the Cistercians make in the lands beyond the sea, to wrap my body, and the wax necessary for my burial. And I also beg you to bring me some of that food you used to give me when I was sick in Rome."

By the food that Brother Jacqueline used to give him in Rome, he meant the almond and honey cake. There was no need to spell it out. But there is the extraordinary part. They were going to designate a brother to carry the message, when someone knocked on the door of the convent. It was Brother Jacqueline, who had been awakened by a premonition one night in Rome. A voice in her head had told her, "Go visit Francis, hurry, if you want to find him alive. Bring with you . . ." She had left at once with her two sons and a company of men at arms.

All by herself she entered and went straight to Francis's bed; he received her joyously, and she didn't disguise how happy she was to have come in time. Here was a deathbed out of line with dramatic traditions. Brother Jacqueline unfolded the cloth for his winding sheet and from which the brothers would cut out his last tunic. Then she offered him the almond cake, the *mostacciuolo,* as the Romans call it, which Francis immediately tried to nibble, but he was too weak. All he would have on his tongue was the delicious taste of the marzipan, a last tiny instance of gluttony that makes up a little for ours. Meanwhile there was no checking the tears in this scene, since Brother

Jacqueline di Settesoli was parting forever from Brother Francis, on this earth.

Despite everything, he was so happy with his cake that he wished to share this pleasure with Brother Bernard. Let them go fetch him. Francis reminded his companions that Bernard was the first one to follow him, and that for this reason he preferred him above all the brothers. When he arrived, Bernard tasted the smallest possible piece of the cake, then knelt alongside the bed; Francis put his hand on his forehead and blessed him. "May the brothers love you as if you were me."

A prodigious vitality inhabited that body, which the brothers watched all but vanish before their eyes. The last days seemed to have devoured the dropsy. The skin stuck to the bones, the skeleton stood out, but an inner force was animating that flesh, which was as broken and battered as if by the hand of a torturer. The brothers were there all around him, their ranks stretching back to beneath the trees fronting the cell. He asked for Elias, who was at his left. Francis stretched his right hand across his left arm and placed it on the head of the man he could never help loving despite some passing antagonism. His ample blessing was like those of the Old Testament patriarchs: "I bless you in all that you shall do. . . . May God, the king of the universe, bless you in heaven and on earth."

The others' turn came next, all the others in the convent that he had greatly loved and that was the heart of the brotherhood, as well as the lay brothers, because they represented all the brothers who would come later over the course of the years until the end of time.

There remained his beloved Clare, to whom he sent a letter dictated the day before, because he knew that she was sick and feared to die without seeing him. As she couldn't leave the cloister, he consoled her with words that only he could find, giving her his blessing and absolution for any possible failure in obeying his orders. Still, the most important part of the message was entrusted to the brother who immediately carried this letter to her: "You shall say to Lady Clare to banish the pain and the sorrow she feels at the thought that she will never see me again. Let her know that before her death she and all her sisters will see me and will receive great consolation from me."

"When you see me *in extremis,*" he had said a few days before, "lay me down naked on the naked earth, leave me there at my last breath for as long as it takes to walk a mile with slow steps."

At dusk an exaltation of larks flew down very low and began to whirl about, singing at the top of their voices, over the cell where Francis lay. In human memory no one has heard the song of the lark except in the early hours of morning, rising with the sun. But that evening they left everything behind and came to cry out their love.

While the brothers chanted the psalm *Voce mea,* death came slowly. On the bare earth of his cell, at the beginning of night, Francis breathed his last, faithful till death to Lady Poverty. The brothers laid him out on his bed, dressed in his new tunic, and stood watch till morning. His presence was still so strong among them that their pain was soothed, but there would never be a true, complete, permanent separation. Men and women came from Assisi, they stayed outside, their hands bearing tree branches gilded by autumn. They too wanted to watch over their saint; they were ready to defend him if anyone tried to steal him from them, but the night slipped peacefully by. *"Pace e bene!"*

In the morning, on Sunday, October 4, 1226, Francis's body was placed on the stretcher for the last trip to Assisi. The brothers and all the clergy sang hymns and the psalm *Voce me ad Dominum clamavi,* but they stopped at San Damiano, at the convent of the Poor Clares, who had been forewarned and who were waiting for this moment. The brothers held up the body with their outstretched arms. Clare was standing there with her sisters, and they watched in silence for a very long moment. Francis had kept his word. They couldn't get enough of seeing him and loving him, but he had to go. At last look, the grille was put back in place, and it was over.

Assisi wasn't far now. They brought Francis to Saint George's for burial. What a world of memories he would have about him. The old canon who had taught him religion was dead, but there remained on the walls the story of the knight Saint George that turned the head of the boy Francesco. Who can say if it all didn't start from there: the ideal, the dreams of glory that God had taken and transformed into eternal glory. Now history and the legends began.

A Word from the Author

Having just written the last lines of this book, I am disappointed not to feel the relief I expected. For eighteen months I have worked on these pages, which called for a great deal of research and sometimes long effort to try to discover the truth beneath the variant readings that the chroniclers have imposed on it. And now, having finished the job, I find in my recovered freedom a little of the bitterness of a false joy. I realize that for many days I have lived in the marvelous company of the man I have always admired the most. In a way I have felt him close to me, fraternal and smiling.

Back in my childhood, in the distant days of the rue de Passy where we lived, I sometimes heard his name pronounced, with that tenderness that always accompanies it. My mother especially, Protestant though she was, treated him with an affection that made me think she had known him. He was and still remains the man who transcends our sad theological barriers. He belongs to everyone, like the love that is unceasingly offered to us. You couldn't see him without loving him, they said in his day; and that love has stayed the course.

I have told elsewhere how, upon the death of my mother, which shattered our family's little universe, I looked for the religion that she seemed to have carried off with her. My ties with the Anglican Church fell away of themselves. I came across a book explaining the Catholic faith and read it with passion in a couple of days. Conversion followed in less than a year, and I was received into the church in 1916.

Meanwhile, bookworm that I was, I had discovered the sincere work on Saint Francis by Mme. Arvède Barine and the legend of the Three Companions. I fell madly in love with that marvelous world. I dreamed of becoming like Francis of Assisi, and when the priest in charge of my religious instruction asked me what name I had chosen for my baptism, I shot back, "Saint Francis of Assisi." He wasn't overjoyed by that, and merely remarked in a calm voice, "I would have preferred Saint Francis of Sales, but since it's your choice, it will be honored." I didn't know Saint Francis of Sales; and the Jesuit father, assuredly a holy man, didn't think it opportune to talk to me about Francis of Assisi. But I, though usually silent, babbled away whenever I ventured to eulogize him. I felt driven to add something to the reverend father's fund of information on this great man, whom he seemed not to know very well. He listened to me with a politeness whose ironic flavor completely escaped me. All sorts of insane ideas spun about in my head. How glorious to be like Saint Francis of Assisi! "I want to be Saint Francis," I announced to him one day. His only answer was a long, serious look.

After the baptism I felt more than ready to follow my patron saint, but life saw to it that these blessed intentions were thrust aside, and Francis of Assisi faded away. I kept his medal around my neck, but eventually I took it off, and the years carried me far from my ideal.

And then, abruptly, the saint of Assisi reappeared. Giotto's painting in the Louvre worked powerfully on me like a sort of call. Then I read more or less novelized biographies, reawakening vague nostalgias for a life of perfection that stayed with me all through my youth and maturity. World War II shook my soul the way one shakes somebody by the shoulders. Saint Francis kept coming back. The world at war struck me as one vast atrocity. My mind gradually came to the conclusion that the Gospel was a failure. Christ himself had wondered about the faith he would find on earth at his second coming. The souls he had touched and drawn to him seemed isolated in the storm unleashed by madmen. Almost at the midpoint between the first Christmas and the hell humanity was writhing in, a man had appeared on earth, another Christ, the Francis of my childhood, but he too had failed.

Failed? Apparently . . . He was convinced that salvation would come through the Gospel. The Gospel was eternity, the Gospel had only just begun. What were twenty centuries in the eyes of God?